"This book will both disturb and com[...] ments the multitude of assaults again[...] our world, the reader will most likely t[...] [...] of despair. But as the author reminds us of the unchangeable, ever-enduring, all-sufficient Word of God, which contains the truth that liberates both now and eternally, faith will be strengthened and hope embraced."

Gary E. Gilley
Pastor-teacher, Southern View Chapel, Springfield, Illinois;
Director, Think on These Things Ministries

"The title of David Fiorazo's important new book, *Redefining Truth*, illustrates how modern culture has lost its way. The eternal and essential truths of biblical revelation cannot be redefined, they shine forth as clear beacons for those with eyes to see. Rather, it is secular, postmodern culture that deconstructs truth, shrouding the world in ever-encroaching moral and spiritual darkness. With great lucidity, Fiorazo illuminates the path by which the shadows of materialism and relativism seek to obscure truth, and then reorients the reader back to the unerring light of God's Word. This engaging and well-written book offers something for readers of all ages and faith backgrounds, providing much more than a candle's worth of hope and inspiration for a culture all too eager to embrace the dark."

Dr. Duke Pesta
Academic Director, Freedom Project Academy

"The western world as a whole and the U.S. in particular have lost their moral compass and their Judeo-Christian foundation. As a result, this has produced a very confused and conflicting culture that is getting further away from God's Word and His standard. David Fiorazo has a clear understanding of the issues our nation and churches face. He has addressed these issues in a biblical and thoughtful way that will help the reader make sense of a confusing world. David is a talented writer and this book will be a beneficial resource and a call to action for everyone, especially the Christian."

Elijah Abraham
Founder of Living Oasis Ministries

"Can the truth still make us free? David Fiorazo's compelling new book helps us apply the unchanging foundation of God's Word to our present cultural warfare. Articulate and insightful as always, David has given us yet another powerful resource and apologetic tool. Every Christian needs to read this book!"

Linda Harvey
President, Mission America; Columnist; Author; Radio Host

"While many in the church waver under the pressures of secularism and unbiblical thinking, David Fiorazo is counted among the clear voices enunciating God's truth in these troubling times."

Eric Barger
Take A Stand Ministries; Author

"David Fiorazo, one of the most brilliant authors I know, is notably humble yet intensely bold in raising a standard for biblical truth in a post-modern culture. I am confident that this book, *Redefining Truth*, will play a profound part in helping the reader discern God's truth while defining the foundation of the gospel that saves us!"

Cindy Hartline
Host, Love For The Truth Radio Philadelphia

"Our post-truth culture desperately needs the hope every believer possesses in Jesus Christ. *Redefining Truth* offers convincing facts and arguments pointing us to that hope. With a real understanding of current issues, David Fiorazo provides well thought-out solutions as well as biblical evidence that demands consideration. This book is a must read for every follower of Christ."

Jerry Lewin
Pastor, Crosspoint Church, De Pere, WI

"David Fiorazo's passion for biblical truth is contagious. His genuine concern for the state of the church in these end times is met with a compassion that is disarming, allowing the message to be heard and, more importantly, taken to heart."

Tony Palacio
Good Fight Ministries

"David Fiorazo has an uncompromising, hard-hitting writing style overflowing with compassion for all people, and his perspective is soundly based upon the truth of God's Word. He is one of my most articulate radio guests."

Jan Markell
Founder, Olive Tree Ministries; Author

"David Fiorazo is a rare and refreshing voice for truth in an age of apostasy and deceit."

Joe Schimmel
Author; Pastor, Blessed Hope Chapel, Simi Valley, CA

REDEFINING TRUTH

REDEFINING TRUTH

DELUSIONS OF REPLACING GOD AND CALLING EVIL GOOD

DAVID FIORAZO

ANEKO
PRESS

We love hearing from our readers. Please contact us
at www.anekopress.com/questions-comments with
any questions, comments, or suggestions.

Printed in the United States of America
Aneko Press – *Our Readers Matter*™
www.anekopress.com
Aneko Press, Life Sentence Publishing, and our logos are trademarks of
Life Sentence Publishing, Inc.
203 E. Birch Street
P.O. Box 652
Abbotsford, WI 54405

RELIGION / Christian Life / Social Issues
Paperback ISBN: 978-1-62245-492-1
eBook ISBN: 978-1-62245-493-8
10 9 8 7 6 5 4 3 2 1
Available where books are sold

Contents

Introduction

Truth has never been so assaulted, avoided, denied, downplayed, hated, ignored, reinterpreted, redefined, and suppressed to the point it is today. At the same time, in this fast-paced information age of mass communication, technological advancements, scientific discoveries, and breaking news, people seem less informed, less secure, more distracted, more agitated, and more confused about what is true than ever before. Why?

It starts with rejecting the one true God. Delusion can be defined as the act of deluding, the state of being deluded; deception; something that is falsely believed or propagated; a false belief regarding the self or persons or objects outside of self that persists despite the facts; something accepted as true that is actually false or unreal.

Jesus Christ, the living One who has the keys of death and Hades, and who was dead but is now alive forevermore (Revelation 1:18), stated:

> *"I am the Alpha and the Omega," says the Lord God, "who is and who was and who is to come, the Almighty."* (Revelation 1:8)

Christ, who also stated, *"I am . . . the truth"* (John 14:6), just covered eternity: present, past, and future. According to Webster's 1828 dictionary, the historical meaning of truth is "Conformity to fact or reality; *exact accordance with that which is, or has been, or shall be.* The *truth* of history constitutes its whole value. We rely on the truth of the scriptural prophecies; Veracity; purity from falsehood" (emphasis added).

Truth is the self-expression of God, a transcendent, fundamental reality. If truth is absolute and if God never changes, then this subject really matters and so does the Bible.

Practically everything else changes: people, places, seasons, cultures, countries, the world, and even facts can change. The question is, are there fixed, established standards of right and wrong that apply to everyone in all places at all times in all circumstances? Under what authority and by whose values do you live?

These are pivotal considerations as we dive into the many cultural debates and divides in America today. Your beliefs about truth and the answers to these questions come from your worldview and affect how you live. Christians believe the Bible is *the* source of truth, and we view the world with all its problems and glory through the lens of Scripture. Our faith is established upon the rock of God's infallible Word.

Throughout Scripture, we are warned about being deceived, but countless millions of people have fallen for the Enemy's lies. We've seen it throughout societies in the world, but sadly, we've also seen it within the Christian church. Another definition of delusion is simply the act of tricking or deceiving someone; a false belief or opinion. This is Satan's specialty, and he's been quite effective. There has always been opposition to the truth. The apostle Paul warned the early Christians to watch out and not be deceived by those who would attack truth and the gospel by introducing subtle ideas and false teachings based on worldly philosophy and man's wisdom.

Enemies of God have caused many casualties in the church by getting people to doubt the truth about creation, our origins and gender, and the natural wickedness of mankind which points to the need for a Savior. Some Christians have given in to culture's lies and even deny Jesus's definition of marriage. Once people surrender God's laws, the permanence of marriage, the purpose of procreation, and the importance of family, we're in trouble.

While you navigate through this book, the subject matter will involve Christ, culture, and the church. We will tackle the biggest issues where truth is being redefined.

We have already allowed the Left to redefine the value of life and when it begins, which has led to the increase of abortion and assisted suicide. If we, the church, also wave the white flag of surrender on gender roles, biological sex, and the distinctions between male and female, then objective truth is gone, and we've failed to preserve biblical morality and protect our culture.

New research shows Christians are uncertain about truth and moral absolutes (we will discuss this in detail), so it is safe to say society is even more uncertain as well as deceived. It's not surprising that *Oxford Dictionary*'s word of the year for 2016 was *post-truth*. One might conclude that this generation has grown up putting stock in emotion, experience, and style over substance – but how many of them have read the Bible and evaluated its truth claims?

Oxford's definition and explanation of post-truth is this: "relating to or denoting circumstances in which objective facts are less influential in shaping public opinion than appeals to emotion and personal belief." So apparently, fabrications, fantasy, and feelings are now the driving forces of those in rebellion against their Creator.

One of the biggest lies and delusions we deal with today says gender is not binary; it is "fluid," and people are not necessarily born male or female. Of course, this is in direct opposition to God's Word, and yet even professing believers are falling for it. Secular progressives are advancing through society and so is the LGBTQ (lesbian, gay, bisexual, transgender, and queer [or questioning]) agenda. Things are happening so quickly and people seem to be abandoning truth, common sense, logic, moral absolutes, and reason.

The government education system is partly responsible. A concerned mother recently contacted me and shared a disturbing experience regarding her six-year-old daughter and the gender confusion being promoted in many public schools. Here is what she told me:

> "I've been struggling. After the very first day of school, my daughter comes home from her first-grade class and says, 'There is a girl in my class who is going to be a boy! She is going to take medicine and have a penis put on!' The kids are forced to call the girl by her 'boy' name and she uses the teacher's bathroom.

"Shocked, I needed to take a breath. I told her, 'No matter how much medicine that little girl takes or if she has surgery, she will still be a girl. God does not make mistakes and we are exactly who we are supposed to be.' I'm upset that my child has to be subjected to this. We are moving both our girls to private school next year, and it's going to be worth every red penny! I never thought this could have happened in a small Wisconsin town. What six-year-old wants to be the opposite sex?"

Good question. We need to wake up fast because the language and perverse ideas young children are hearing every day are getting much worse than many of us realize or are willing to admit. And therein lies part of our problem. This mother is right. Some, not all, parents and teachers – under the umbrella of the agenda-driven National Education Association (NEA) – have no fixed moral underpinnings and will go along with what many of us consider insanity and absurdity.

They will encourage their children to be "fluid" and let them decide what gender they want to become, or worse – force them to change into something the parents prefer. In other words, preferences trump truth, health, and reality. We now see a culture in which practically anything goes morally because the idea being promoted is that we can each make up our own truth.

This is the growing wisdom as lawlessness has increased and biblical morality is mocked, while Christians are being targeted and branded as hateful. More corporations jumped on the LGBT bandwagon by not only funding gay causes, but also by abandoning traditional families and producing ads featuring same-sex couples.

The liberal media and technology giants such as Facebook, Google, Twitter, Vimeo, and YouTube ratcheted up their progressive agenda in part by censoring or limiting some conservative and Christian content. Hollywood, academia, and the entire education system constantly prove how far gone they are by despising the biblical Christian worldview while generally supporting liberalism, atheism, evolution, humanism, and Islam, just to name a few.

Violence, crime rates, and drug and gang activity are on the rise in too many inner cities of America, with no apparent solutions. Funded by George Soros and radicals on the left, the Black Lives Matter movement also took off thanks in part to perhaps the most divisive U.S. administration in history which helped set the stage for chaos and civil unrest, including violent protests. We see a dramatic increase in Islamic terrorism, ISIS mayhem, persecution of Christians and Jews worldwide, and in late December 2016, President Barack Obama initiated and supported the anti-Israel UN Security Council's vote against Israel, demanding they return to 1967 borders and allow Jerusalem to become occupied territory.

Obama left a much-divided nation, an anemic economy, and a more corrupt government. But on April 26 of 2016, President Obama actually said, "We are fortunate to be living in the most peaceful, most prosperous, most progressive era in human history."[1]

One month after he said this, on Memorial Day weekend, sixty-three people were shot in Chicago, five of them killed, including a fifteen-year-old girl. In Chicago alone, the murder rate soared in 2016. (Through June of 2017, there have been 1,714 shootings in Chicago!) Why would Obama say something so grandiose? He knew most media fact-checkers would look the other way and people wouldn't care. Believers, watch out that you are not deceived.

> *For you yourselves know full well that the day of the Lord will come just like a thief in the night. While they are saying, "Peace and safety!" then destruction will come upon them suddenly like labor pains upon a woman with child, and they will not escape. But you, brethren, are not in darkness, that the day would overtake you like a thief.*
> (1 Thessalonians 5:2-4)

America witnessed what was perhaps the most heated and vitriolic presidential campaign and election cycle in our history in 2016. People on both sides lost their cool and sometimes their minds, indicating the political divide has never been greater. Democrats may have lost an

---

1   Jessica Chasmar, "Obama: We're living in the most peaceful era in human history," *The Washington Times* 4/26/16, *www.washingtontimes.com/news/2016/apr/26/obama-were-living-in-most-peaceful-era-in-human-hi/*.

election, but they are committed to fighting harder than ever against the Trump administration.

A study conducted by the Media Research Center prior to the 2016 presidential election found 91 percent of the campaign coverage on Donald Trump was negative. Nonpartisan firm Media Tenor analyzed the first month of his presidency and found just 3 percent of the reports on the new president were positive. Three percent. *The Washington Times* noted a study by *Newsbusters* on media coverage of Trump's first 100 days in office: 89 percent negative. (After President Obama's first 100 days, the cheerleading media gave him 82 percent *positive* coverage.)

Most media elites endorse just about any policy or trend that goes against the Bible. For example, did you ever think you'd see a day when people would fight to change laws in order to accommodate a microscopic minority wanting to be referred to by a specific pronoun, and demanding to use any public restroom regardless of their sex at birth?

National Geographic uncharacteristically and irresponsibly came out in favor of child abuse by placing a nine-year-old transgender model on its January 2017 cover. "Child abuse"? you ask. Not my words, but those of a Johns Hopkins University psychiatrist who, along with the American College of Pediatricians have spoken out defending children, science, and biological facts, and they've taken plenty of heat in the process.

Even though many in today's society want to believe they live in a post-truth world, how can they claim "there is no truth" when that in itself is an absolute statement that cannot be proven? I would ask them, why is your starting point "there is no God" or "'there is no ultimate authority"?

Why not begin with the evidence, facts, and history in the Bible as the foundation for truth and work from there? Seriously, try to prove Scripture wrong or even inaccurate. If you have never closely examined the foundations of *both* worldviews, one with God and the other without God, how do you defend your claims?

I recently watched the powerful movie based on the best-selling book *The Case for Christ*. Author Lee Strobel was a former atheist and professional journalist working for the *Chicago Tribune*. Having set out to disprove Christianity, after an exhaustive, two-year investigation, he trusted in Jesus Christ as his savior. In his book *The Case for Christ*, Strobel wrote:

> If you were selected for a jury in a real trial, you would be asked to affirm up front that you haven't formed any preconceptions about the case. You would be required to vow that you would be open-minded and fair, drawing your conclusions based on the weight of the facts and not on your whims and prejudices. You would be urged to thoughtfully consider the credibility of the witnesses, carefully sift the testimony, and rigorously subject the evidence to your common sense and logic.
>
> Ultimately, it's the responsibility of jurors to reach a verdict. That doesn't mean they have one-hundred-percent certainty, because we can't have absolute proof about virtually anything in life. In a trial, jurors are asked to weigh the evidence and come to the best possible conclusion.[2]

How about you? Is your conclusion about truth, the Bible, and Christianity based on evidence or on your preconceived ideas? Please take this quest seriously and pursue the truth with all your heart and an open mind. No decision in this life has such dire future consequences than rejecting Jesus Christ – a decision which will determine where you will spend eternity after you die.

You may remember from history in Scripture when Jesus stood before the Roman prefect Pontius Pilate and said, *"My kingdom is not of this realm."* Wow! What a proclamation.

> *Therefore Pilate said to Him, "So You are a king?" Jesus answered, "You say correctly that I am a king. For this I have been born, and for this I have come into the world, to testify to the truth. Everyone who is of the* [on the side of] *truth hears My voice." Pilate said to Him, "What is truth?"* (John 18:37-38)

This is both fascinating and ironic. Here is a governor – a mere human being – in the position of judging God, the One who is truth itself. As

---

2   Lee Strobel, *The Case For Christ* (Grand Rapids, MI: Zondervan, 1998), 18.

Jesus told Pilate, *You would have no authority over Me, unless it had been given you from above* (John 19:11).

There are seven major areas of society in which truth is being redefined right before our eyes: business/marketplace, education, media, arts and entertainment, culture, government, and even Christian churches. New Barna research (May 2017) shows 23 percent of *Christians* strongly agree that "what is right or wrong depends on what an individual believes."

How is truth being redefined? Society's opinion of what is right and wrong is shifting to the point of calling evil good. The Lord spoke through Isaiah with this warning:

> *Woe to those who call evil good, and good evil; Who substi-*
> *tute darkness for light and light for darkness; Who substi-*
> *tute bitter for sweet and sweet for bitter! Woe to those who*
> *are wise in their own eyes and clever in their own sight!*
> *And take away the rights of the ones who are in the right!*
> *Therefore, as a tongue of fire consumes stubble and dry grass*
> *collapses into the flame, so their root will become like rot*
> *and their blossom blow away as dust; for they have rejected*
> *the law of the* LORD *of hosts and despised the word of the*
> *Holy One of Israel.* (Isaiah 5:20-21, 23b-24)

By rejecting the living God, His Word and commandments, man can then determine his own truth and decide for himself what is right and what is wrong. Severe consequences and repercussions will result from doing this. Another question to ask is, have you ever been wrong and if so, how do you know you are not wrong about there being no absolute truth?

In this book, we will reinforce the fact that truth not only exists, but it is also unchanging and eternal. Truth can be known, and it not only liberates; truth also endures beyond you, beyond me, and beyond this temporary earth. In order to do this in a way that will confirm our biblical foundation and answer skeptics at the same time, it's important that we do a thorough investigation of the facts.

We will also address specific cultural issues as well as what some other religions teach. Since the Christian worldview is based on truth, then every subject in this book is important.

Alexander Hamilton stated, "I have carefully examined the evidences of the Christian religion, and if I were sitting as a juror upon its authenticity I would unhesitatingly give my verdict in its favor."

That's all I am asking as we proceed through each chapter and address some of the most pressing issues of our day. Would you please assess the evidence in the Bible as well as the commentary in these pages? And if you are not a Christian, please do so prior to offering your verdict.

I believe with all my heart that Scripture is strongly supported by archaeology, which shows its amazing accuracy. Secular historians confirm many details in God's Word and offer extrabiblical testimony, and the overwhelming amount of fulfilled prophecy also proves its reliability, demanding consideration at the very least. Let's not forget the hundreds of eyewitnesses of Jesus after His resurrection.

An honest evaluation and pursuit of the truth is absolutely necessary for us to begin this journey together. And if the Christian worldview is the most reasonable, fact-based, captivating, and intriguing, shouldn't we strive to speak and live according to the morality the Bible teaches? We should not only take God at His word but should take our faith seriously as well.

But in America and worldwide, the roots of deception go deep and the rebellion continues at breakneck speed. Absolutes are questioned, history is either forgotten or rewritten, media cannot be trusted, and good people have fallen for lies, broken promises, and identity politics.

This is war! Truth is being redefined, evil is being called good, and God is being replaced by counterfeits. English author and writer of many hymns Elizabeth Rundle Charles stated:

> "It is the truth which is assailed in any age which tests our fidelity. . . . If I profess, with the loudest voice and clearest exposition, every portion of the truth of God except precisely that little point which the world and the devil are at that moment attacking, I am not confessing Christ, however boldly I may be professing Christianity. Where the battle rages the loyalty of the soldier is proved; and to

be steady on all the battle-field besides is mere flight and
disgrace to him if he flinches at that one point."[3]

As soldiers of Christ, are you and I willing to defend His truth about
creation, life, marriage, family, and biblical morality, and call out those
who attack the very foundation of our faith? For the glory of God and
for people to be saved and sanctified, eternal truth is worth the fight.

---

3   Elizabeth Rundle Charles, *Chronicles of the Schonberg-Cotta Family* (New York: M. W.
     Dodd, 1864), 321.

Chapter 1

Truth or Consequences

Make me know Your ways, O LORD; Teach me Your paths.
Lead me in Your truth and teach me, for You are the God of
my salvation; for You I wait all the day. All the paths of the
LORD are lovingkindness and truth to those who keep His
covenant and His testimonies. (Psalm 25:4-5, 10)

"We love the truth when it enlightens us. We hate the truth
when it convicts us." – Augustine

No quest is more important, no question more pressing, and no
venture more critical than pursuing truth. As you approach such
an important topic, there will be distractions, resistance, and temptations because the Enemy knows that by the end of this book your faith
will be strengthened, your biblical worldview reinforced, and your heart
encouraged. You may even change some habits.

Since we are in a spiritual battle, warfare will be part of this process
as with any worthwhile endeavor, so it is best to begin with earnest
prayer. This battle requires of us the utmost diligence to seek truth and
find it, proclaim it, protect it, and persevere to the end because truth is
the foundation of the gospel that saves us.

Decades ago, the respected theologian and author Francis Schaeffer
pointed out the lack of Christian leaders willing to address the most
controversial and pressing issues from a biblical perspective. Today is
no different, and I share his heartache that too many believers have

conformed to this world, while others are deceived by doctrines of devils. Schaeffer stated:

> "Where is the clear voice speaking to the crucial issues of the day with distinctively biblical, Christian answers? With tears, we must say it is not there and that a large segment of the evangelical world has become seduced by the spirit of this present age. And more than this, we can expect the future to be a further disaster if the evangelical world does not take a stand for biblical truth and morality in the full spectrum of life."[4]

At every turn, this book points to Jesus because there can only be one truth, and it all comes down to Him. All others are liars, pretenders, and imposters. Don't believe this? Here's a prayer God will always answer. Ask Him, "Father in heaven, please reveal to me the truth about Your Son, Jesus Christ." We may not know God's will concerning everything in life, but we do know it is His will for all people to be saved. Though not everyone will repent and believe in Jesus, He still wants as many as possible to come to know Him who *desires all men to be saved and to come to the knowledge of the truth. For there is one God, and one mediator also between God and men, the man Christ Jesus, who gave Himself as a ransom for all, the testimony given at the proper time* (1 Timothy 2:4-6).

The distinction to make in this context of God's will is between His eternal, saving purposes, and His desires. The Lord of all creation hates sin, wickedness, and its consequences. And yet, He loves us enough to give us the freedom to obey or deny Him, to accept the sacrifice of Jesus for our sins or to reject His lovingkindness toward us.

Some have argued, "How can a loving God send anyone to hell?" The truth is God allows us to choose. Think about it. How can He send His Son to save us and send us to hell at the same time? God does not *send* anyone to hell, because a person has to refuse the gift and trample over the body and blood of Christ shed for us in order to get to hell.

I'm not sure who said it first, but most everyone wants to go to heaven. They just don't want Jesus to be there when they get there. The

---

4   Francis Schaeffer, *"The Complete Works of Francis A. Schaeffer: A Christian Worldview, Volume Four, A Christian View of the Church"* (Wheaton, IL: Crossway Books, 1982), 401.

Bible has very clear warnings for those who reject God's Word and rebel against Him. Just as there are many blessings for obeying Him and keeping His commandments, there are plenty of curses for disobeying and rejecting the Lord.

It's called justice, and for God to be a good judge, He must punish sin and wickedness.

> *For the grace of God has appeared, bringing salvation to all men, instructing us to deny ungodliness and worldly desires and to live sensibly, righteously and godly in the present age, looking for the blessed hope and the appearing of the glory of our great God and Savior, Christ Jesus, who gave Himself for us to redeem us from every lawless deed, and to purify for Himself a people for His own possession, zealous for good deeds.* (Titus 2:11-14)

Does this sound like God gets a kick out of people going to hell, or does it sound like He has done everything possible to provide a way out?

Since we referred to a jury and trial in the introduction to this book, now think about the judge's role for a moment. Let's say the law was broken, a crime was committed, and the jury heard the evidence and pronounced the defendant guilty of first-degree murder.

What would we say if, rather than pound the gavel and send the guilty criminal to jail, the judge dismissed the case and let the person go without any punishment? Yet this is what some people demand God do regarding sin and the breaking of His commandments. They don't want any accountability or moral restrictions because they only want God to be loving and forgiving, not righteous and just.

But what did God do to solve the problem? Jesus Christ stepped in and not only offered, but also paid our fine and went to the cross on behalf of guilty sinners. The wrath of God was satisfied, the punishment for the crime was paid, and God, the Judge, said to you and me, "You're free to go," that is, if we have enough sense to accept His offer!

Tell me again how you think God wants to send people to hell?

Let's not be duped by those in society who want us to believe lies about God. They don't know Him, but we have His Word. If you really want to get to know an author better, read what he has said or written.

Consequences for rejecting the truth of God and for rebelling against Him are real. Not many people today want to discuss the holiness, judgments, righteousness, and wrath of God. We'd much rather only hear about the love, grace, peace, and kindness of God, which is understandable.

The Bible however, must be read and understood in context and in its entirety from Genesis to Revelation. The apostle Paul referred to *the whole counsel of God* (Acts 20:27 ESV). If God didn't spare His own people from judgment when they rebelled and disobeyed His laws, why do we think Christians in America – or anywhere – should escape the consequences of sin?

You and I and all mankind will live forever – it's just a matter of final destinations. We are spirits, we have souls (a mind, will, and emotions), and we live in a temporary body, an earthly tent we reside in and carry in this life.

Let's agree for a moment that this is all true and God created the heavens and the earth by His great power (Jeremiah 32:17), that there is a perfect deity consisting of three persons – the Father, the Son, and the Holy Spirit, and that there is a literal heaven and hell.

This makes more sense than the theory that we are random accidents of an impersonal "nature" that developed over time starting from a meaningless "bang" that caused something out of nothing which resulted in life leading to molecules-to-man evolution. That takes lots of faith to even consider. Is that a reliable starting point?

Questions are good, and this one is both reasonable and pivotal:

IS THE BIBLE RELIABLE?

Entire books have been written to answer this question, but let's look at a few facts and strong arguments pointing to evidence in Scripture and its history.

In my previous book *The Cost of Our Silence*, the final chapter, "Then the End Will Come," was filled with Bible prophecy and its importance in answering questions about the reliability of Scripture. The central purpose of prophecy is to reveal the one true God and prove there is no other like Him. Who can predict future events in detail other than through divine revelation?

> *For prophecy never had its origin in the human will, but prophets, though human, spoke from God as they were carried along by the Holy Spirit.* (2 Peter 1:21 NIV)

> *Behold, the former things have come to pass, now I declare new things; before they spring forth I proclaim them to you.* (Isaiah 42:9)

The following is an excerpt from that encouraging chapter in *The Cost of Our Silence*:

> According to scholars, 1,845 references point to the return of Jesus Christ in the pages of the Bible. At least one-quarter of the Bible is prophecy (some suggest one-third); Jesus's return is highlighted in seventeen Old Testament books, and within the twenty-seven New Testament books, 321 mentions are made of the second coming. This latter number equates to one out of every thirty verses in which the return of Christ is mentioned.

> Prophecy indicates that believers who are alive when He returns will be ushered into the kingdom of heaven (1 Thessalonians 4:13-18). All of the promises in the Old Testament to Israel will be fulfilled as well as the New Testament promises to believers. Jesus prophesied saying, *Heaven and earth will pass away, but my words will not pass away* (Luke 21:33). Jesus made this statement over 2,000 years ago, and today His words remain indisputable. The Bible is the best-selling book of all time, and hundreds of millions of Bibles and portions of Scriptures are distributed every year worldwide.

> The "God-breathed" sixty-six books in the Bible were written by forty different authors. These messengers of God came from diverse backgrounds, and Scriptures were written in three different languages over a period of 1,500 years

on three different continents! There are no contradictions or inconsistencies in the Word of God, and over 25,000 archaeological finds support the fact that people, places, and events mentioned in the Bible are real and accurate.

What human being could have ever manufactured such an intricate plan – a masterpiece combining thousands of years of historical events, as well as prophecies, in perfect and specific detail? More importantly, what man could have created and insured the carrying out of such an elaborate story in advance, well before many of those written about were born, before nations were formed, and years before events had even taken place?

As for details surrounding the crucifixion and death of Jesus, at least twenty-eight prophecies were fulfilled. Jesus Himself fulfilled more than 300 prophecies from birth to resurrection. For those who have an open mind, evidence produced by an honest investigation of the life and death of Christ should astound even the most intellectual skeptics and mathematicians.[5]

The person genuinely seeking the truth is faced with daunting evidence supporting the reliability of Scripture. It is impossible to explain the prophetic accuracy of the Old and New Testaments apart from divine inspiration and intervention. Sorry, "luck" just doesn't cut it.

Since Jesus Christ gave such extensive testimony and made such bold declarations about Himself, don't you think it's important to at least read what He said and what was written about His life? It is disingenuous, hypocritical, and irresponsible to ignore the Holy Bible if you are sincerely seeking truth.

Did you know that in the world history of detailed, scientific archaeological excavations, not one find has been used to refute a single biblical statement? Thanks in part to archaeological data, thousands of historical and geographical details in Scripture have been confirmed as accurate. If this weren't compelling enough, there are plenty of ideas and statements

---

5   David Fiorazo, *The Cost of Our Silence* (Aneko Press, 2015), 286-287.

in God's Word that line up completely with facts of modern science, even before some of those scientific facts were known and understood.

As we continue our investigation, let us submit the Bible as the only religious Scripture in the world that is inerrant as well as having the greatest moral standards of any book. Consider the genealogy providing a historical record of humankind from the first man, Adam, to the lineage of Christ, to the end of history. In addition, God's Word is living and active, *sharper than any two-edged sword* (Hebrews 4:12). No other written work has the power to convict people of their sin, the ability to change human nature, and the offer of a permanent solution to man's greatest problem.

Consider the uniqueness of the Bible: a record of God's message to His creation, miracles, history, an honest assessment of evil and the heart of man, unique claims, a plan of salvation, and a specific description and vision of the end times.

In a small booklet called *The Facts on Why You Can Believe The Bible* by John Ankerberg and John Weldon, the authors suggest the trustworthiness of the Bible is a critical subject because of its implications. If it truly is God's holy Word, then its importance to every human being is obvious. Truth matters!

> If the Bible is the inerrant Word of God, and if it authoritatively answers the fundamental questions of life, then who can logically be passive and ignore its teachings? If the Bible accurately tells us who God is, who we are, why we are here, and what happens when we die, is there a living soul anywhere who should fail to be impressed? If the Bible gives us reassuring absolutes in a world of menacing relatives, doesn't this introduce profound implications? Who wants to live a life of insecurity and hopelessness when they can actually know the truth with certainty?

> Indeed, isn't the plague of the modern world its own relativism – in ethics, law, politics, sexuality, education, psychotherapy, medicine, religion, business, and so on? If people live only for themselves and do whatever they want

– often disregarding others' welfare – isn't the major reason for this that they feel life is meaningless and that nothing ultimately matters but their own interests? If there is no final authority in anything, and if when you die you are gone forever, why not live any way you want?[6]

Those who prefer to pursue happiness, pleasure, and self-gratification choose to ignore the truth. But the fact is those who argue that the Bible cannot be trusted or is not reliable do not have a foundation to stand on. They speak out of ignorance, and due to their bias, make plenty of assumptions that cannot successfully be supported by facts, evidence, or history.

New Testament documents, for example, are at least 100 percent more reliable than any other piece of ancient literature that the world widely accepts as accurate and authentic. There are thousands of New Testament manuscripts and portions available. The Gospels can be dated within twenty to thirty years of events cited that took place during the lives of hundreds of eyewitnesses.

The Holy Scriptures are more accurately and meticulously preserved than any other text of ancient history. Regarding Old Testament accuracy, manuscripts separated by a thousand years are essentially the same, according to scholars. With so many copies available, reconstructing the original is not the difficult task one might think, and the Bible has not experienced textual corruption as some critics argue.

As you might expect, with thousands of copies of individual books of the Bible preserved, each of the manuscript copies differ, but those differences are generally minor. Here's an example from Dr. Ron Rhodes and an explanation to follow:

Manuscript 1: **Jesus** Christ is the Redeemer of the whole **worl.**
Manuscript 2: **Christ** Jesus is the Redeemer of the whole world.
Manuscript 3: Jesus Christ **s** the Redeemer of the whole world.
Manuscript 4: Jesus Christ is **th** Redeemer of the **whle** world.
Manuscript 5: Jesus Christ is the Redeemer of the whole **wrld.**

---

6   John Ankerberg and John Weldon, *The Facts on Why You Can Believe The Bible* (Eugene, OR: Harvest House Publishers, 2004), 13.

Reconstructing the original in this sample is easy, as it is generally for the entire New Testament – to an original accuracy of more than 99 percent, with the remaining uncertainties being insignificant.

Five thousand three hundred extant Greek manuscripts and portions exist, along with 10,000 Latin Vulgate versions, and 9,300 other versions. The papyri and early uncial manuscripts date much closer to the originals than for any other ancient literature.[7]

With some of the world's best-known classical authors, very few copies of manuscripts are available, and the earliest copies date from 750 to 1,600 years *after* the original manuscript was written! In contrast, massive biblical documentation is available to the tune of over 24,000 portions and versions, with the earliest fragments – including complete copies – dating between 50 to 300 years after originally being written.

We're only scratching the surface here, and yet, I hope it can be determined that the argument for the accuracy of Scripture is incredibly strong and the evidence compelling. It's no wonder the stakes are so high when it comes to redefining truth.

Because it is true, authoritative, and immutable, we can trust and rely on God's Word. After thousands of years of constant attacks, opposition, and intense scrutiny by critics – warfare that no other work has ever seen – the Bible has withstood the onslaught, has gained credibility, and the Christian faith has continued to thrive throughout the world.

Moreover, just because Christianity is not as popular in America as it once was does not mean it is not true. It means we are living in an ever-changing society in which feelings trump facts, relevance trumps repentance, and truth is being molded to fit current trends.

God isn't concerned about fads and changing cultures, nor is He surprised by the growing number of people who hate Him. I believe, however, that God cares deeply about people who are hurting and have never heard the gospel, and His righteous anger is building toward those who claim to be Christian but justify sin, or who do not take their faith seriously.

---

7   Ankerberg and Weldon, *The Facts on Why You Can Believe The Bible*, 21.

James said faith without corresponding actions is worthless, and in Revelation 3:16, Jesus warns a lukewarm people and church that He will spew them out of His mouth because they are neither hot nor cold. Spiritual apathy is destroying America. The opposite of love is not hate; it is indifference. Indifference leads to the reprobate mind, sin, unrestrained evil, and unrighteousness.

LOVE HATES UNRIGHTEOUSNESS

Paul wrote to Christians at Corinth about love being patient and kind, and that it *does not rejoice in unrighteousness, but rejoices with the truth* (1 Corinthians 13:6). Exploring a few key words may be helpful as we continue. *Rejoice*, or in another translation, *delight* means to celebrate, exult, or gloat. *Unrighteousness* or *evil* means sinful, immoral, depraved, corrupt, nefarious, or heinous. The Lord certainly does not rejoice in such things.

It is an interesting dichotomy. *God is love* (1 John 4:8), but He hates unrighteousness.

Looking at our culture and world today, people proudly celebrate sin like never before and, sadly, many in the church say nothing. Even worse, some Christians have given in to public pressure, have abandoned the faith, and joined in the unholy celebration. God is not neutral about this, and He hates sin in part because of what it does to the soul of mankind.

In the powerful and majestic Word-exalting Psalm 119, verse 163 states, *I hate and despise falsehood, but I love Your law.*

In our culture today, people no longer hold the same definition of love and hate as Scripture does. One of the Greek words translated *love* in the New Testament is not an emotional or sentimental love, but a love that seeks God's best for others at any cost. This is *agape* love – John 3:16 kind of love – and is marked by sacrifice rather than selfishness, and giving rather than receiving. God displays this love in the sacrifice of His Son for us and Jesus shows it by volunteering Himself.

If you want answers from a biblical perspective, this will be an encouraging and enjoyable journey for you. But for others, not so much. As the famous line by Jack Nicholson in the movie *A Few Good Men* indicates, truth can be very hard to face and address. American institutions have shaped the beliefs of an entire generation to the point that we are programmed to embrace deception. Sadly, too many people fall into the category to whom we could say, "You can't handle the truth!"

Jesus is the truth, and by the power of the Holy Spirit, the Word that created the world *became flesh* (John 1:14), but the world *did not receive Him* (v. 11) because it *did not know Him* (v. 10). Woven throughout Scripture from Genesis to Revelation are descriptions and prophecies about the person, character, and divinity of Christ, such as:

> *Gird Your sword on Your thigh, O Mighty One, in Your splendor and Your majesty! . . . ride on victoriously, **for the cause of truth and . . . righteousness**; Your throne, O God, is forever and ever; a scepter of uprightness is the scepter of Your kingdom. **You have loved righteousness and hated wickedness**; Therefore God, Your God, has anointed You with the oil of joy above your fellows.* (Psalm 45:3-4, 6-7, emphasis added)

Partly because Christians are often called hateful in our culture today, we back down completely from speaking the truth of God's Word. This doesn't help matters. We know God doesn't hate people, but sinners often use such accusations as an excuse to reject truth. In fact, Paul describes the idolatry of those who *exchanged the truth of God for a lie, and worshipped and served the creature* [created things, people] *rather than the Creator* (Romans 1:25).

This is a good time to examine the meaning of truth from both the Old and New Testaments. It is important to recognize the Bible does not contain the idea of inactive or neutral truth. A few words for "truth" include *actuality, certainty, factuality, reality, rightness, perfection,* and *validity*.

According to *Merriam-Webster's Dictionary*, truth is "1. fidelity, constancy (sincere in action, character, and utterance). 2. The state of being the case: fact, the body of real things, events, and facts; a transcendent fundamental or spiritual reality (a judgment, proposition, or idea that is true or accepted as true). 3. The property of being in accord with fact or reality; fidelity to an original or to a standard."

Though it is being redefined all around us, let's take an extensive look at what is TRUTH, according to *The Eerdmans Bible Dictionary*:

Old Testament – Hebrew *met*, usually translated truth, is related to the verb *aman* "support, sustain, establish," to the noun *muna* "firmness, faithfulness," and to *amen*, "truly," the source of the exclamation *Amen!* God is referred to as "the God of truth" in contrast to false gods, Yahweh is steadfast and unwavering, a God who can be trusted.

This is underscored by the fact that God's "truth" is frequently mentioned with his "faithful covenant love" (*hesed*) emphasizing God's dependability and consistency. God's nature and will remain unchanged by circumstances . . . For this reason, God's commandments are not arbitrary, but firm and unwavering. *Then You came down on Mount Sinai, and spoke with them from heaven; You gave them just ordinances and true laws, good statutes and commandments* (Nehemiah 9:13).

Therefore, the Old Testament standard of justice is not found in abstract sociological or ethical concepts, but in the manner in which God deals with the world and people, which is to be reflected in the world that God created. God desires *truth in the inward being* (Psalm 51:6).

New Testament – In the NT *way of the truth* (2 Peter 2:2) recalls Psalm 119:30 in speaking primarily of the conduct that should characterize those who have been redeemed. The Greek *amen*, the transliteration of Hebrew *amen* and *alethos*, is the Greek translation of the same word most often rendered truly or verily. These are frequently used in the NT, particularly to introduce words of Jesus. This introduction emphasizes that the statement which follows is beyond doubt. The truth in Jesus is God's redemptive work realized in Christ (Ephesians 4:21). Indeed, the truth of the gospel is not only a message, but also a process whereby Christ and the church are making manifest God's redemption to humankind (2 Thessalonians 2:12-13)–God's redeeming plan has become actuality in the coming of Jesus.

For John, Jesus is more than the proclaimer of truth – he is the truth itself. Jesus promises that his work will be continued by the "Spirit of truth." True Christian life is lived by people who have truth in them, in that they admit their wrongdoing – people made free by their knowledge of the truth, who have become *true* (or better *genuine*) worshippers of God (John 4:23).[8]

What you have just read hopefully provides a deeper understanding than the average person has because they do not consider the importance of truth in forming their worldview.

Studies have shown most people develop life rules and make up their minds about what is true early in life and rarely ever reconsider how they came to believe something. One of the main influences in reaching their conclusions isn't whether something is true or not, nor is it their parents; it is the culture.

Children are conditioned to deny truth and dismiss God, the Bible, and eternal/spiritual things, and if their parents are not strong Christians, guess what? Many of those kids will sadly be too far gone by high school because their minds will be pretty much closed to truth and biblical morality. And if they go off to college, forget it.

Once a person's worldview is established, values are set. Those values strongly shape our behavior and choices, which in turn influence those around us. Take politics, for example. Whose values are being promoted for the most part in our government – conservatives' or liberals'? It is clear which side is winning the battle of influence.

It is also crystal clear how the Bible, the eternal word of truth, defines good and evil, love and hate, righteousness and unrighteousness.

Righteous are You, O LORD, and upright are Your judgments. You have commanded Your testimonies in righteousness and exceeding faithfulness. Your righteousness

---

8   *The Eerdmans Bible Dictionary* (Grand Rapids, MI: Wm. B. Eerdmans Publishing Co., 1987), 1,022.

is an everlasting righteousness, and Your law is truth.
(Psalm 119:137-138, 142)

You are near, O LORD, and all Your commandments are
truth. Of old I have known from Your testimonies that You
have founded them forever. Salvation is far from the wicked,
for they do not seek Your statutes. The sum of Your word is
truth, and every one of Your righteous ordinances is ever-
lasting. (Psalm 119:151-152, 155, 160)

If you really want to know the truth, it is revealed through Scripture because God is truth. He is the final authority. As you see people's bad behavior and sin, including open adultery and sexual perversion, being promoted in our culture, remember that they need Christ. They are not necessarily bad people; they're just wrong, and the Lord gives us the freedom to accept the truth or accept the consequences.

If we are lovers of God and followers of Jesus Christ, we should not approve of and love things of this world more than Him. We certainly should not be celebrating what is evil or sinful, and, as we take a stand for what is right, attacks will come.

We must understand the Enemy's tactics and how Satan, the Father of Lies, suppresses the truth, twisting words and meanings using every-day people to advance his agenda. I'd probably do the same thing if I were him. That's next.

Chapter 2

How the Enemy Advances

Be of sober spirit, be on the alert. Your adversary, the devil, prowls around like a roaring lion, seeking someone to devour. But resist him. (1 Peter 5:8-9a)

"I'm not a Christian because it "works" for me. I had a life prior to Christianity that seemed to be working just fine, and my life as a Christian hasn't always been easy. I'm a Christian because it is true. I'm a Christian because I want to live in a way that reflects the truth. I'm a Christian because my high regard for the truth leaves me no alternative." – J. Warner Wallace

Growing up in the 1970s, my dad used to turn on the AM radio every morning in the kitchen as we all sat down to eat breakfast. One of the programs we listened to was Paul Harvey (1918 – 2009). Every week, an estimated 24 million Americans tuned in to hear him on more than 1,350 commercial radio stations, as well as 400 stations of the Armed Forces Network. Elected to the National Association of Broadcasters' Radio Hall of Fame, Harvey was also named Commentator of the Year and American of the Year.

Paul Harvey often pointed to biblical values and morality, and spoke about specific threats to America's Christian heritage. He seemed to understand the spiritual dynamic in play as the satanic assault on God and family gradually infected every aspect of our culture. More prophetic than we realized, the following text is from his 1965 radio broadcast:

> If I were the devil . . . if I were the prince of darkness, I'd want to engulf the whole world in darkness, and I'd have a third of its real estate and four-fifths of its population, but I wouldn't be happy until I had seized the ripest apple on the tree – Thee.

> So I'd set about however necessary to take over the United States. I'd subvert the churches first–I'd begin with a campaign of whispers. With the wisdom of a serpent, I would whisper to you as I whispered to Eve, "Do as you please." To the young, I would whisper, "The Bible is a myth." I would convince them that man created God instead of the other way around. I would confide that what is bad is good, and what is good is "square." And the old, I would teach to pray after me, 'Our Father, which art in Washington.'

> And then I'd get organized. I'd educate authors on how to make lurid literature exciting, so that anything else would appear dull and uninteresting. I'd threaten TV with dirtier movies and vice versa. I'd infiltrate unions and urge more loafing and less work, because idle hands usually work for me. I'd pedal narcotics to whom I could. I'd sell alcohol to ladies and gentlemen of distinction. I'd tranquilize the rest with pills.

> If I were the devil I'd soon have families at war with themselves, churches at war with themselves, and nations at war with themselves; until each in its turn was consumed. And with promises of higher ratings, I'd have mesmerizing media fanning the flames.

> If I were the devil I would encourage schools to refine young intellects, and neglect to discipline emotions – just let those run wild, until before you knew it, you'd have

to have drug sniffing dogs and metal detectors at every schoolhouse door.

Within a decade, I'd have prisons overflowing, I'd have judges promoting pornography – soon I could evict God from the courthouse, and then the schoolhouse, and then from the houses of Congress. And in His own churches I would substitute psychology for religion, and deify science. I would lure priests and pastors into misusing boys and girls, and church money.

If I were the devil, I'd make the symbol of Easter an egg and the symbol of Christmas a bottle.

If I were the devil, I'd take from those who have, and give to those who wanted until I had killed the incentive of the ambitious. What do you bet I could get whole states to promote gambling as the way to get rich? I would question against extremes and hard work, and Patriotism, and moral conduct. I would convince the young that marriage is old-fashioned, that swinging is more fun, that what you see on the TV is the way to be. And thus, I could undress you in public, and I could lure you into bed with diseases for which there is no cure.

In other words, if I were the devil, I'd just keep on doing what he's doing.

Paul Harvey, good day.

Though this 1965 commentary was ahead of its time, it is a vivid description of how Satan works to deceive people. He plots and plans, seeking *to steal and kill and destroy* (John 10:10), and he will use and abuse anyone gullible or wicked enough to do his dirty work. Yes, the Enemy has plans.

Millions of Americans have apparently disregarded the faith they once held dear or have fallen away from the Judeo-Christian values which previously permeated this nation. Many in the church have been duped by the cult of liberalism and the politically correct movement that basically says anything is permissible except biblical Christianity. We have stopped standing against evil and speaking up in defense of the gospel for fear of offending someone, and when Christians are silent, light is squelched and darkness wins. So, what can you and I do to arm ourselves and prepare for daily battles?

THE BELT OF TRUTH

> *Finally, be strong in the Lord and in the strength of his might. Put on the whole armor of God, that you may be able to stand against the schemes of the devil; Stand therefore, having fastened on the belt of truth, and having put on the breastplate of righteousness.* (Ephesians 6:10-11, 14 ESV)

Truth is part of the believer's armor. Truth is both our best defense and our most effective offense. Truth not only defends us, but since Jesus and the sword of the Spirit are the Word of God, truth also gives us an overwhelming advantage over the Enemy. This is key.

I looked up several translations of this passage in Ephesians 6 on the armor of God and particularly on this idea of a belt of truth. We live in a physical world impacted by spiritual activity, and warfare is part of every believer's life whether we knowingly engage in it or not. This passage highlights the spiritual principal of readiness: our need to be prepared for the battle for souls.

Here are some of the translations of Ephesians 6:14:

> New American Standard Bible (NASB) – *Stand firm therefore, having girded your loins with truth, and having put on the breastplate of righteousness.*

> New International Version (NIV) – *Stand firm then, with the belt of truth buckled around your waist, with the breastplate of righteousness in place.*

> New King James Version (NKJV) – *Stand therefore, having girded your waist with truth, having put on the breastplate of righteousness.*

Jubilee Bible (JUB) – *Stand firm, therefore, having your loins girt about with truth and having on the breastplate, of righteousness.*

1599 Geneva Bible – *Stand therefore, and your loins girded about with verity, and having on the breastplate of righteousness.*

During the time the apostle Paul wrote this letter to the church at Ephesus, the gear Roman soldiers wore in battle weighed nearly seventy pounds. Moreover, when we think of a belt, we think of a thin strap we slide through the loops in our pants. However, the belt described in this context was a very wide metal or leather belt, and its purpose wasn't to match your shoes. It was worn around the lower core to hold the armor tightly against your body. It wasn't put on *after* all the armor was in place. The soldier's belt was the central piece of equipment he strapped on *before* the rest of the armor.

A soldier wore a tunic of loose-fitting cloth and when he readied himself for battle, it was cinched up and tucked into the heavy belt. Since most combat was hand to hand, the belt was essential. Otherwise, your clothes became a potential hindrance and danger. The belt also secured the weight of the breastplate holding the rest of the armor in place, including the sword.

The belt of truth pulls in and holds all the loose ends together and is imperative for the soldier's safety and success. Truth is just as crucial for the soldier of Christ today.

According to the Bible, Satan's power over us is already broken, death has been defeated, and the war has been won, thanks to the victory we have in Jesus through His sacrifice, death, and resurrection. The battle and warfare, however, continue – and they will intensify – until the Lord returns.

The cunning schemes of the devil are carried out all around us in this world system over which he has free reign. How does the Enemy work and advance his agenda of lawlessness, chaos, destruction, and unrighteousness? He uses people.

The wicked plots against the righteous and gnashes his teeth at him, but the Lord laughs at the wicked, for he sees that his day is coming. (Psalm 37:12-13 ESV)

From a rainbow-colored White House to Hollywood hype over the latest perversion, from media selling sexual confusion to corporations proudly promoting political correctness, it is difficult to deny the moral and spiritual decline in America. If there's any hope of slowing the decaying culture, truth must be told.

It is virtually impossible to correct and improve the direction of a country if people are not convinced there are problems and that they are way off course. Apathy is another issue killing America, but since we cannot make people care, we need to reach those who may be in the busy, unconvinced, or uninformed categories. This is one reason I keep writing.

But as we try raising awareness in an intolerant culture that is redefining truth, opposition is guaranteed. The Left is shrewd at using words as weapons to silence those who do not agree with them. In fact, according to Dictionary.com, its word of the year for 2016 was *xenophobia*, which can be defined as "fear or hatred of foreigners, people from different cultures, or strangers; fear or dislike of the customs, dress, etc. of people who are culturally different from oneself."

Apparently, the word has been in the English language since the late 1800s. Who knew?

The largest spike in searches for *xenophobia* happened in June 2016, which was the day of Brexit, when the UK voted to leave the European Union. Lookups of the word spiked again when President Obama took his cue later that month and insisted that Donald Trump's rhetoric was a measure of "nativism, xenophobia, or worse." Naturally, Hillary Clinton used the word to falsely accuse Trump during her campaign rallies.

Enemies of Christ will not relax or ease up on their agenda, and one of the greatest battles in the country today is being waged by the LGBTQ movement. Author and teacher Peter Heck stated, "They know the success of their cause depends upon the total abolishment of the Judeo-Christian ethic and the Moral Authority it teaches. That is why any belief that the homosexual lobby is merely a passive group of individuals wanting to peacefully coexist with others who have different beliefs and values is naively absurd."

The Enemy advances when Christians relax. Though Christianity is growing, particularly in underground churches in persecuted nations around the world, who do you think is having more influence on America today?

The marketers of evil claim they are fighting because of discrimination, oppression, injustice, and inequality. They say they fight for love, acceptance, diversity, equal rights, and freedom. We're onto their schemes and the tedious talking points trumpeted by the liberal media, the Left, Hollywood, and many within the government education system.

But it is not just those whose new religion is sex, and it's not just those who claim they just want to "live and let live." It's also those who devalue human life and promote moral relativism. We'll get into this later, but we must remember to clearly define the terms in this and any debate on key issues.

Planned Parenthood and advocates of murder cry out, "freedom," "choice," "it's my body, not yours, not the government's and not God's." The Left is using atheists, communists, socialists, and LGBTQ proponents to blot out God, normalize homosexuality, lie about life in the womb, undermine natural marriage, tear apart the traditional family, create as much chaos as possible, and, well, promote lies instead of truth.

Since we're talking about methods and people Satan uses to do his work, we should also take a sober look at how our perceptions have changed regarding morality and what has become acceptable or permissible. We must recognize the sin in our own camp and call out hypocrisy in the church when necessary.

We must pursue Christ, invest time in the Word, have accountability and fellowship with true believers, be disciplined, and work harder to build others up while we strengthen our faith and especially our marriages. Jesus told His disciples, *If you love Me, you will keep My commandments* (John 14:15). Looking at just two of the Ten Commandments, we must acknowledge the epidemic of idolatry and adultery within Christian circles.

You most likely heard about the Ashley Madison scandal in 2015.

We don't talk often enough about adultery, which is now pretty much accepted by a majority of Americans, including those who claim to be Christians.

> *Marriage is to be held in honor among all, and the marriage bed is to be undefiled; for fornicators and adulterers God will judge.* (Hebrews 13:4)

Years before the Supreme Court gave its tyrannical opinion ruling against God-ordained natural marriage in 2015, the agenda was well underway to remove America's moral anchors. What was most disappointing, however, was to observe the influence secularism was and is having on the American church. Today we can see the undeniable fruit of lacking a solid foundation, with increasing numbers of gay ministers and pastors in several churches and denominations.

The rise of apostasy is a sign of the times as more churches and leadership preach accommodation rather than conviction of sin leading to repentance and salvation. If the church is not much different from the world, we have a problem.

A survey was conducted by ChristianMingle and JDate called "State of Dating in America," and I guess the results shouldn't surprise us. A majority of respondents said they would move in together before getting married, but here's a revealing question that stood out to me: "Would you have sex before marriage?" Eighty-seven percent said yes!

Here's the breakdown:

Yes. 63 percent
Yes, if I was in love. 19 percent
Yes, but only after we're engaged. 5 percent
No. 13 percent

Christian Mingle? Apparently, biblical morality is not as black and white as we thought. In fact, to some folks it's more like *Fifty Shades of Grey*.

You may remember the fallout from the Ashley Madison (adultery/dating site for married people) data breach. Here is a company openly promoting and glorifying fornication by encouraging sin. Their motto is "Life is short. Have an affair."

Apparently, even *after* hackers leaked data on its clients, Avid Life

Media reported "hundreds of thousands of new users signed up to the dating platform, including 87,596 women" in the weeks that followed! Think about the 31 million users whose personal information was released. Many families were left to pick up the broken pieces of shattered relationships.

In Matthew 5:28 Jesus said, *everyone who looks at a woman with lust for her has already committed adultery with her in his heart.*

According to Ed Stetzer of *Christianity Today,* as many as four hundred pastors, deacons, elders, and church staff members were on the list. Not a huge percentage, but a heart problem nonetheless. A few well-known pastors were exposed, leading to resignations, suspensions, and in at least one case, suicide. *But a man who commits adultery has no sense; whoever does so destroys himself* (Proverbs 6:32 NIV).

Now, if you're not a believer and you point to the hypocrisy of a small number of Christians as an excuse *not* to turn from your own sins and trust in Jesus, that won't cut it when you stand before God on judgment day. We are each accountable for ourselves.

The entertainment industry has done much damage influencing children, families, and culture as a whole. For years, sex outside of marriage was depicted as exciting, and, of course, the consequences of unwanted pregnancies rarely if ever came up. Profanity took off in the '70s on prime-time television and radio, as well as in movies, and Hollywood hasn't looked back. They just keep pushing the envelope with very little resistance. This is how the Enemy advances.

But the most blatant immorality being forced on America has been the push to normalize homosexuality. For over four decades now, you can hardly find a scripted show on TV and cable that does not feature at least one friendly, likable, well-adjusted LGBT character. (Soon it will be transgender characters.) Every year, Hollywood honors LGBT-inclusive entertainment with awards from the Grammys, SAG, Golden Globes, and Image Awards nominations. The LGBTQ movement receives plenty of support from corporations, unions, the media, the entertainment industry, and the government.

In 2015, Allstate Insurance produced a video commercial depicting two men reflecting on their "marriage" to each other and their adoption of a baby girl. With his arm around his male partner, one of the men says about the child, "The second we held her, we knew that she was ours. We're her dads."

In 2016, Campbell's Soup also aired an ad featuring two dads. Doritos issued a rainbow-colored bag for gay pride, and Zales featured two lesbians in a wedding ring commercial. We can expect many more to hit the airwaves as more corporations cave to LGBT pressure.

Naturally, this momentum has flowed out into areas of society that we thought were safe for children. One that comes to mind is the Boy Scouts of America. In 1990, they were initially challenged by homosexual James Dale under a "sexual orientation nondiscrimination" law in New Jersey. Ten years later, the case found its way to the U.S. Supreme Court where the Scouts narrowly won their right to avoid having homosexual scoutmasters and members. But several years ago, they caved under corporate pressure, changing their rules to allow open homosexuals.

Forcing humanity to accept sodomy has little to do with homosexual rights. Rather, it is part of a wider campaign to undermine the very fabric of society itself. The Enemy is advancing through our country, culture, and even many of our churches because we have surrendered much ground and have not defended the truth.

Though there is always hope for a revival – and I have no idea what it might take for this to happen – the light is dimming in and on America, and the clock is ticking.

Many have already been deceived as the Enemy has had some success defining the terms of battle, and in many cases, redefining words. The Left has been promoting sin as normal, natural, and healthy, and when Christians speak up, it leads to charges of intolerance. If we do nothing, even more people will call evil good.

> *Let no one deceive you with empty words, for because of these things the wrath of God comes upon the sons of disobedience.* (Ephesians 5:6)

Chapter 3

One-Way Tolerance and the Transgender Agenda

For at one time you were darkness, but now you are light in the Lord. Walk as children of light (for the fruit of light is found in all that is good and right and true), and try to discern what is pleasing to the Lord. Take no part in the unfruitful works of darkness, but instead expose them. For it is shameful even to speak of the things that they do in secret. But when anything is exposed by the light, it becomes visible. (Ephesians 5:8-13 ESV)

"Truth cannot be sacrificed at the altar of pretended tolerance. Real tolerance is deference to all ideas, not indifference to the truth." – Ravi Zacharias

Before we highlight the transgender timeline in this chapter, we will point to the hypocrisy, call out double standards and the intolerance of the Left as we combat moral relativism and open rebellion against God. We must calmly confront the pretenders who fail to demonstrate the very tolerance they espouse. They're trained to label Christians and conservatives as hateful, intolerant, bigoted, racist, homophobic, self-righteous, judgmental, and many other things, but their accusations are baseless and lack evidence.

They declare diversity and insist they are inclusive. They tout tolerance and yet, they often refuse to put up with anyone who thinks differently from them. Rather than have a respectful debate, many of them prefer silencing us so they don't have to hear the truth.

It often starts with silencing the opposition. You may remember the one-way tolerance on display February 1, 2017, at the University of California, Berkeley. Milo Yiannopoulos, an editor for Breitbart News (and also an open homosexual) was scheduled to speak to conservative students. It was cancelled because of radical left-wing students and George Soros-funded groups including Occupy Oakland who staged violent protests, and the result was hateful rhetoric, rioting, vehicles set on fire, and paint and Molotov cocktails hurled at the building the speaker was in.

I'm not a fan of Milo's, but any citizen should be allowed freedom of speech. Cal students along with paid protesters carried signs against conservatives, Republicans, Trump's refugee policies, homophobic attitudes toward gays, and get this: telling an open homosexual and *legal* immigrant (Yiannopoulos) he is not welcome.

Some of the signs read "Kill Trump," "Become Ungovernable," "Shut it down," "Out of Berkeley," "Nazi Scum," "No Fascist USA," "I Love what Trump Hates," and more. In one press release, the rioters claimed Milo was a tool of Trump's fascist government and has no right to speak at Cal *or anywhere else!*

Perhaps you didn't notice the irony. Cal Berkeley is the location where in 1964, anti-war activist Mario Savio helped launch the Free Speech Movement. They fought to lift a ban on political activities on their campus and demanded academic freedom – on the same campus that censored a 2017 speaker whose politics they disagreed with.

Leftists and progressives claim to be beacons of reason, tolerance, and love, but their actions often prove otherwise. The public buys it because the overwhelming majority of Hollywood and the media are on the side of liberal Democrats and as long as the politics are progressive, all is well. They ignore or even defend radical Saul Alinsky tactics implemented by the agitators. What we've seen at Berkeley, in Madison (Wisconsin), New York, Chicago, D.C. and elsewhere is status quo for most hyperprogressive American universities.

On May 22, 2017, Vice President Mike Pence was about to give the commencement speech at Notre Dame, but as Pence began speaking, about 150 people, half students and half faculty members, walked out of the speech. Planned in advance, both students and faculty filed out as Pence spoke. How disrespectful. He said, "Far too many campuses across America have become characterized by speech codes, safe zones, tone policing, administration-sanctioned political correctness – all of which amounts to nothing less than suppression of the freedom of speech." Pence apparently intended to first draw a contrast between Notre Dame and other colleges, but this rude act seemed to solidify today's caustic trends at most Marxist universities. At least they allowed the vice president to finish.

A sad, hostile takeover of morals and values has taken place in our country, including in our education system, from kindergarten to college, and it is practically unsalvageable today. Both of my parents spent their entire careers in education, but over the years, the government has wreaked havoc on the entire system. The NEA has become an arm of the Democrat Party, which no one can deny, based on its activism, political donations, and what children are generally taught.

Christians in America have decisions to make in this divisive environment. How do we respond? Yes, it's true we may be hated for doing or saying the right thing, but when the world hates you, Jesus referred to that as a badge of honor (Matt. 5:11). If we try to address a few of the most controversial movements of our day with love, patience, and sanity, this still triggers people, some of whom end up losing their minds over this stuff. It seems as if so many people are misinformed or uninformed about important issues being discussed today, including who uses what bathroom.

CAROLINA ON MY MIND

Since this chapter is about the redefined modern buzzword "tolerance," let's start by looking at it from the perspective of someone who has been around longer than you and me. Billy Graham will be ninety-nine years old in November. He has used the men's restroom for nearly a century. Why is it now controversial or "intolerant" in America to say that he and those of us born male should use the men's restroom and those born female use the women's restroom?

Aside from the truth of the Bible, which is enough, when did biology, science, and history suddenly change? On February 23, 2016, the Charlotte City Council, perhaps in response to pressure put on by the LGBT lobby, added additional LGBT "protections" to the existing city nondiscrimination ordinance, granting protections in government-run facilities. (Protections?) North Carolina House Speaker Tim Moore called for legislative action specifically clarifying the part of the ordinance having to do with public bathrooms.

Lawmakers called a special session on March 21 to discuss the ordinance and on March 23, the General Assembly passed HB2 (House Bill 2), also known as "the bathroom bill," and sent it to North Carolina Governor Pat McCrory. He signed the bill later that evening. According to the *Charlotte Observer*, the new bill took away some rights and protections for those who are gay or transgender.

Naturally, the American Civil Liberties Union (ACLU) filed a lawsuit against the state of North Carolina challenging the new law, and on March 31 – the "International Transgender Day of Visibility" – DNC Chair Debbie Wasserman Schultz made a statement about fighting "the discriminatory laws" of Republicans when our nation has worked so hard to "distance ourselves from the ugliest chapters in our history" regarding discrimination.

Actor James Woods was one voice of reason putting this in perspective when he tweeted, "The world is fighting Islamic terrorism, starvation, and disease, but Democrats are fighting for men to pee in the ladies' room. #Insanity."

As par for the corrupt corporate course, here are the first prominent corporations who also came out publicly against the new legislation: Apple, Bank of America, PayPal, A&E, FOX, Dow, American Airlines, and Southwest Airlines. (PayPal dropped plans for a facility that would have added four hundred jobs in Charlotte, North Carolina.)

On April 12, Governor Pat McCrory even signed an executive order preventing state employees from being disciplined or fired if they were gay or transgender. For years, North Carolina had laws regulating workplace discrimination, use of public accommodations, minimum wage standards, and other business issues. The new law – known officially as the Public Facilities Privacy and Security Act – makes it illegal for cities to expand upon those state laws, as more than a dozen cities had done, including Charlotte, Raleigh, Chapel Hill, and Durham.

United States Attorney General Loretta Lynch filed a lawsuit against North Carolina, calling the "HB2 restroom restriction impermissibly discriminatory," and the Obama Justice Department asked a judge to suspend HB2 while its lawsuit was being decided, arguing that "damage is done to the LGBT community" every day the law is in place.

Next, the National Basketball Association (NBA) pulled the 2017 All-Star Game out of Charlotte and held it in New Orleans. Many organizations threatened boycotts of North Carolina because of alleged discrimination while these same corporations continue doing business in countries with horrendous human rights records and violations. Some of the most vocal companies – ones that say they stand with LGBT Americans – operate in countries where homosexuality can result in a death sentence.

The Daily Signal provided this list of sixteen corporations that publicly attacked religious liberty measures in at least one of the three states, yet do business in countries that blatantly and sometimes brutally discriminate against LGBT citizens or otherwise have a poor record of defending human rights: Unilever, Microsoft, Intel, Live Nation, The Weinstein Company, AMC Networks, Time Warner, Walt Disney, General Electric, The Coca-Cola Company, Salesforce.com, PayPal, Apple, The NBA, Netflix, and Sony.[9]

Entertainer, political activist, and leftist Bruce Springsteen, along with Pearl Jam, Maroon 5, Ringo Starr, and Bryan Adams cancelled concert performances in North Carolina. Elton John said the bathroom law was dangerous and "traumatic" for transgender people.

Reverend Franklin Graham said men pretending to be women should not use women's restrooms. And I'd go out on a limb and say our grandparents would agree. (They would also wonder why we're having

---

9   Mariana Barillas and Kristiana Mork, "16 'Pro-LGBT' Businesses That Operate in Countries with Poor Human Rights Records," April 25, 2016, *dailysignal.com/2016/04/25/16-pro-lgbt-businesses-that-operate-in-countries-with-poor-human-rights-records/.*

this conversation.) On his Facebook page, Graham stated, "Businesses and organizations shouldn't be forced by law to allow men pretending to be women to use women's restrooms. North Carolina Governor Pat McCrory and legislators were absolutely right to pass HB2 to protect young girls, boys, and women from sexual predators and perverts. Men have no business using women's bathrooms and locker rooms. Period."

According to Nancy Armour at *USA Today*, "North Carolina has chosen to stay on the wrong side of history and decency. It shouldn't be surprised when the NCAA and other major sports organizations refuse to play along." (The NCAA [National Collegiate Athletic Association] pulled seven college championship games from North Carolina and moved them to South Carolina.) Sorry, Nancy. Wanting to protect women and children from predators and from others with evil intent is not indecent. Plus, thousands of years of history suggest it is you and liberals in the media who are on the wrong side.

God has been around for a while, and He created men and women unique and separate, but equal, having distinct differences by design. Biological men and women are both needed to procreate and have a natural, healthy family. So again, with less than 0.5 percent of the population (and this is a very generous estimate) being transgender, who is on the wrong side of history? Even though the transgender population has doubled since President Obama took office in 2009, the estimated number of those identifying as transgender is only about 1.4 million Americans out of a population of over 324 million.

Most polls indicate the majority of citizens are tired of accommodating every fad, trend, demand, right, or perceived offense, injustice, and alleged violation of the (activists) minority. Nevertheless, on November 8, voters narrowly elected Democrat Roy Cooper as governor of North Carolina even though Republicans maintained supermajorities in the General Assembly.

President Obama's political machine, gay rights groups attacking McCrory for months, out-of-state money, mass marketing, and powerful activist groups all contributed to an anti-HB2 political campaign which narrowly defeated him, not to mention corporate extortion and bullying. The infamous bathroom bill was only partially repealed in

March 2017, so the battle continues and the Supreme Court may be called upon at some point.

Opponents of truth demand we overlook facts and common sense as well. There are over twenty-one thousand convicted sex-offenders in the state of North Carolina. Is it bigotry and discriminatory to take an extra precaution to protect women and children from them? In an excellent article by author Dr. Frank Turek, "Six Reasons North Carolina Got It Right," he states:

> Good laws treat all people equally, but not all of their behaviors equally. In fact, the very reason laws exist at all is because all behaviors are not equal and must be treated differently for the benefit of individuals and society. . . . Are we to risk the safety of millions of women and children in public restrooms because an extremely small number of people are experiencing a mismatch between their psychology and their biology?
>
> Who needs the truth when you make so much "progress" by ignoring the truth and engaging in the very bigotry and name-calling you claim to oppose?[10]

We're witnessing the attempted assassination of truth during times in which delusions and emotions rule over sanity and reason. The (biblical) Christian worldview and godless liberalism are polar opposites and cannot coexist. Sound extreme?

Christian business owners in Iowa, Dick and Betty Odgaard were literally minding their own family business, but they now wish laws were on the books protecting Christians from being sued by fascists. After a two-year court battle in which a gay couple cried discrimination, the Odgaards had to pay an excessive fine and were forced to stop hosting weddings. After months of negative publicity, hate mail, death threats, and loss of income, the Gortz Haus Gallery went out of business.

TOTALITARIANISM AND TARGET

Whether you call this intolerance, fascism, or liberal hypocrisy, radio

---

10   Frank Turek, "Six Reasons North Carolina Got it Right," March 30, 2016, *townhall.com/columnists/frankturek/ 2016/03/30/six-reasons-north-carolina-got-it-right-n2141010.*

talk-show host and columnist Dennis Prager describes it this way: "For the Left, tolerance does not mean tolerance. It means first, acceptance. And second, celebration. That is totalitarianism: You not only have to live with what you may differ with, dear citizen, you have to celebrate it or pay a steep price."

Our progressive northern neighbors have had the attitude of minding their own business, and I have heard some respond to these issues by saying, "as long as it doesn't affect me, why not live and let live." Canada's Liberal Party, headed up by new Prime Minister Justin Trudeau, introduced a brand-new bill last year that would punish anyone who disagrees with gender identity or expression, classifying dissent as "hate speech." This could land a *practicing* Christian in jail for two years.

Over a year ago, the New York City Commission on Human Rights declared if business owners fail to call sexually confused individuals by their preferred name or pronoun – even newly invented ones such as *ze* or *hir* – or ask them to use a gender-appropriate bathroom, the business can be fined up to $250,000.

And over on the Target Corporation website, it states, "We're not born with pride. We take pride. Pride in celebrating who we were born to be."

How can we complete this chapter without mentioning Target and their complicit advancement of this dangerous agenda? It did not start with its bathroom policy. According to the *Huffington Post*, a liberal source I will rarely cite, Target featured a gay couple in a same-sex registry ad in 2012, the same year they launched gay greeting cards and an LGBT gay pride t-shirt line.

So, Target, as their own website says, takes pride in "celebrating who we were born to be," but I'm confident they do not mean this in the biblical context of how God created us. They further stated that pride "is a year-round commitment," and added, "We're making our message loud and clear: Target proudly stands with the LGBT community, both as a team member and team player through all that we do – from our volunteer efforts to our long-standing partnerships with groups like [the] . . . Gay, Lesbian & Straight Education Network."[11]

For those who knew of Target's past promotion of homosexual

---

11   Target Corporate website promotion, "#takepride," June 2015, *corporate.target.com/article/2015/06/pride-week*.

lifestyles, it came as no surprise that in April 2016, the corporate office announced, "we welcome transgender team members and guests to use the restroom or fitting room facility that corresponds with their gender identity."

Almost immediately, the backlash began and by the end of that year, about 1.4 million people signed a petition to boycott Target over the policy they claim is "inclusive." If this is simply about the accommodation of a fraction of a fraction of the population deciding to identify themselves differently from how God created them, why demand the rest of society comply?

This all came to a head less than a year after the judicial tyranny carried out by the U.S. Supreme Court's landmark ruling legalizing same sex "marriage." According to *CBN News*, more than 100 religious freedom bills have been proposed in thirty-four states that would protect Christians and others from lawsuits simply for objecting to gay marriage.

You may have heard about *New York Times* writer Nicholas Kristof who admitted that liberal intolerance is rampant, saying liberals practically demand people think like them. So much for diversity of thought. *BreakPoint*'s Eric Metaxas did an excellent commentary on censorship last March, explaining how Kristof said what most of us already knew: gatekeepers in academia and the media typically look down on those with different views.

> "We progressives believe in diversity, and we want women,
> blacks, Latinos, gays and Muslims at the table – so long as
> they aren't conservatives." – Nicholas Kristof

The majority of elite media, for example, are liberal, with less than 7 percent admitting they are conservative. They have voted for or contributed to Democratic candidates in practically every single election. Kristof cites studies in his article showing an average of 8.5 percent of humanities professors and less than one in ten social studies professors are conservative, while about 20 percent identify as Marxists. Though he believes evangelical Christians and conservatives deserve a fair shake, he is more concerned about diversity in education today.

Those entities which are educating and shaping young minds, conditioning public opinion, and forcing change on a docile citizenry are now helping roll out the "T" portion of the LGBTQ agenda. Transgenderism takes it much further than same-sex marriage ever could by changing our language and redefining terms that describe human beings. Though it will not change eternal truth, removing God and erasing gender distinctions will eventually change what it means to be human.

It's all about marketing, perception, influence, and of course, politics. While many of us have been busy with our own lives in the last few decades, the Left has been quietly plotting, lobbying, and changing laws to protect individuals who identify as transgender under claims of "civil rights" or nondiscrimination laws.

Years before Bruce Jenner changed his name to "Caitlyn" in 2015 and was featured on the covers of *People*, *Glamour*, *Sports Illustrated*, and others, coal was being shoveled into the engine of the transgender train. Throwing in the towel of reason, the cover of *People* proudly proclaimed to millions of subscribers (and everyone who saw it in a supermarket rack) that Caitlyn Jenner is "Living as a woman every day – and feeling elated!"

Years before Oprah Winfrey used her influence in 2008 to contribute to the cause when she interviewed what was irresponsibly promoted as "the first pregnant man," Hollywood actress Hillary Swank won an Oscar for her portrayal of a girl who had a "sexual identity crisis" in *Boys Don't Cry*. The film was based on the tragic, true story of Teena Brandon (aka Brandon Teena) who was murdered in 1993.

And years before this, cross-dressing and transgenderism had been portrayed on network television shows such as *Mash* (1972 – 1983), and in many movies including the cult classic *The Rocky Horror Picture Show* (1975) and *Psycho* (1960). In the earliest days of TV, Milton Berle was one of the first to dress as a female character on his comedy/variety program *The Milton Berle Show* (1954 – 1959).

And a few years prior to that, the first so-called "sex change" took place in New York and in 1952, one headline read: "Bronx 'Boy' is now a Girl." Author and entertainer Christine Jorgensen (formerly George) died in 1989, but became the first American to undergo the controversial surgery and hormone treatments in Denmark. Upon his (aka her) return, Christine became a celebrity.

Sadly, we rarely hear of the downside or negative effects and consequences of this gender confusion and rebellion being promoted today. Here's one sobering fact: 41 percent of the transgender population will attempt suicide. Please let this sink in. When man attempts to replace God the Creator and redefine truth, there will always be severe repercussions for individuals and nations – and eventually, judgment.

This movement has not had enough resistance from the people. Activists have absolutely no hesitation pressuring politicians and using the courts to change public restroom laws and practices of the whole country by imposing the LGBT agenda and its will on the entire population.

> 2016 HEADLINE 1: "Target Stores Open Restrooms to Those Identifying as Transgender"

> HEADLINE 2 (months later): "Target Corp. Spends $20 million on One-person Bathrooms after Transgender Stunt Sparks Boycott"

Have you heard in the media the argument against transgender accommodations? The following stories are pretty self-explanatory, so rather than get into redundant detail, here are the actual headlines to relevant news items: (Hat tip to the American Family Association)[12]

> Dallas, TX: Man wanted for taking photos inside Target changing room

> Eugene, OR: Convicted Sex Offender Accused of Looking Up Girls' Skirts in Target

> Bedford Police Dept.: Man Arrested for Recording Juvenile Girls in Target Store

> CBS-DFW: Shopper Upset Man Allowed To Use Women's Dressing Room

> NY Daily News: Seattle man undresses in women's locker room to test new transgender bathroom rule

---

12   AFA.net, "Sign the Boycott Target Pledge!" April 20, 2016, *www.afa.net/action-alerts/ sign-the-boycott-target-pledge/.*

LifeSite News: Sexual Predator jailed after claiming to be transgender to assault women in shelter

The Mercury News: Sex offender wearing fake breasts, wig, arrested for loitering in women's restroom

Fox4 News: 'Peeping Tom' records underage girl changing at Frisco Target

NY Times: Transgender Woman is charged with voyeurism at Idaho Target

Fox25 Boston: Police searching for man caught peeping in Revere Target

What's the point? The Left argues transgender individuals do not have equal rights, they're not protected, old bathroom policies "discriminate" against them, and even that it's dangerous (due to potential depression and suicide attempts) to have laws stating everyone must use the restroom according to their *biological sex at birth* (which is for all practical purposes unchangeable).

As we continue discussing evidence of the negative effects of new bathroom policies, remember something else: people do not need ideas on new ways to do evil or to sin (Romans 1:30). Criminals often get ideas from Hollywood, but in this case, predators are being tempted and almost welcomed to act on their lusts as the number of incidents taking place in public facilities is growing.

Of the following dozen headlines from last year, some are incidents involving predators committing criminal actions in public restrooms. The others may involve transgender women (men) or men dressed as women (cross-dressing). These reports may or may not have been a result of the new public policy regarding bathroom bills. (Hat tip to Breitbart News)[13]

Seattle, WA – man changes in women's locker room, cites new gender rule

---

13   Warner Todd Huston, "Twenty-Five Stories Proving Target's Pro-Transgender Bathroom Policy is Dangerous to Women and Children," April 23, 2016, *www.breitbart.com/big-government/2016/04/23/twenty-stories-proving-targets-pro-transgender-bathroom-policy-danger-women-children/.*

Woodbridge, VA – Man Dressed as a Woman Arrested for Spying into Bathroom Stall

Smyrna, TN – Man charged for allegedly filming in multiple women's restrooms

Palmdale, CA – Palmdale man arrested for videotaping in women's bathroom at Macy's

Miami, FL – Man arrested after camera found in shopping center restroom

Quarryville, PA – Man Accused of Peeping in Women's Restroom also Faces Child Porn Charges

Logan County, OK – Edmond man arrested for recording child in shower

Fullerton, CA – Man arrested for filming people in Chapman Univ. unisex bathroom

Toronto, ON – Sexual predator jailed after claiming to be transgender to assault women in shelter

Wilton Manors, FL – Another victim comes forward in video voyeurism case

Martinsville, IN – Former Chili's Mgr. Arrested after Videotaping Women in Restroom

Brea, CA – Man Arrested after Allegedly Filming at Least 7 People in Unisex Bathroom at Starbucks

After reading these headlines, we can better understand the mindset of those who justify the controversial policies that threaten women and children. The Left endorses practically all that is ungodly. You might be wondering how so many people in the country could fall for the lies, exaggerations, accusations, and promotion of nihilism (traditional values and beliefs are unfounded and useless; there are no objective moral truths). First, it's part of the LGBTQ mothership, and second, it's called deception.

MORE CELEBRITIES SPEAK

In an appearance on *The Ellen DeGeneres Show* early this year, Margaret Sanger-admirer Katie Couric, now working for Yahoo, again showed why she lost the respect of so many news consumers in the country. She was invited by DeGeneres to discuss her documentary on the *National Geographic Channel*, "Gender Revolution," which aired in February.

NBC News said the new film explores the "evolving concept of gender." *The Huffington Post* called it a "Groundbreaking Educational Resource about Gender," and *Think Progress* said Couric "explains transgender identities in compelling detail."

Couric emphasized "a whole new vocabulary" that exists, and she said in today's world, "it's much more open and accepted, I think, for people to not fall into this binary that I was raised . . . with this boy, girl, blue, pink;" but her next point reveals her vivid imagination: "Just because you operate on a child and tell that child you're a certain gender, that doesn't necessarily coincide with who that person feels he or she actually is. . . . In the later stages of development, it's when your brain is wired, and sometimes a surge of testosterone can make a female fetus feel as if that baby is male or that person is male."[14]

At this point, DeGeneres chimed in and took it a step further by saying, "like you're in the wrong body." Couric continued: "And the opposite, if there's not enough testosterone."

Look at what Couric said. Even in the womb, a baby can *feel* like a different gender. This is awful science, but there's a partial truth here. Couric may have inadvertently angered her Planned Parenthood allies by implying what research has proven: babies in the womb are human persons. (From the earliest stages of development, preborn babies can also feel pain.)

Next, co-host of *The* [Liberal] *View* Whoopi Goldberg and her One Ho Productions produced a transgender model-centered reality television show *Strut*, on the Oxygen channel. Goldberg, an extremely well-liked and extremely liberal entertainer, has equated the very real

---

14   Katie Yoder, "Abortion Sympathizer, Katie Couric: Even a 'Female Fetus' Can 'Feel' Male," February 3, 2017, *www.newsbusters.org/blogs/culture/katie-yoder/2017/02/03/abortion-sympathizer-katie-couric-even-female-fetus-can-feel.*

civil rights struggle black people faced in America with the plight of transgender individuals.

> "It's like everything else in the world – people weren't ready for [black people] to be free from slavery," she says. "They weren't ready for integration. They weren't ready for gay people to get married. And yet, here we are. Times are moving forward. Whether you like it or understand it is not the point."

Oxygen Media's VP of programming said transgenders "will empower viewers," and described *Strut* as following "a group of inspiring and resilient trailblazers who are working to change the modeling industry, and the world around them, by simply being true to themselves." Notice how many people emphasize the importance of being true to themselves, the way of man and their desires, rather than being true to God, how He created us, and His purpose for us.

For those unaware, NBCUniversal has been pivotal in pushing LGBTQ content for decades. They hosted television's first lesbian wedding on *Friends* in 1996, as well as the groundbreaking successes *Will and Grace* and *Queer Eye for the Straight Guy*. For multiple years, Comcast and NBCUniversal were given kudos from the radical Human Rights Campaign who named them one of America's best places to work for LGBT individuals.

Since we're addressing some celebrities who endorse moral relativism, let's look closer at the "pregnant man" promoted so effusively by Oprah Winfrey. A 2012 headline read: "The 'Pregnant Man' Finalizes Bitter Three-Year Divorce."

I bet most people reading this have not heard about this story. Time for a reality check. We may never know how many people were encouraged to dis God, embrace relativism, be unhappy with themselves, change their names, inject hormones or take drugs, and have surgical procedures to mutilate the physical body God gave them at birth. Whether she did it for ratings and money or because she really believed the lie, Oprah gave the "T" ideology a massive platform in 2008.

If we cannot change who we are, the gender in which we are born, our DNA, and the truth, then wasn't the so-called first "pregnant man" simply a lesbian or transgender? If Thomas Beatie kept her lower body private parts in order to have children, then in good conscience, is this person truly a man? I follow a simple rule of thumb: if someone legally changes their name, then out of respect, call them by their legal name. I have a difficult time, however, going along with the crowd and justifying the lie that they also changed their sex.

After all, if God designed us and assigned our gender, who are we to "reassign" it? Please consider these questions whenever you hear or read the words "gender reassignment surgery." Be forewarned that you may be called "phobic" for questioning culture.

Born (as a woman) in Hawaii in 1974, Thomas Beatie (Tracy LaGondino) says she always felt like she wanted to be a man. In her twenties, she began having testosterone injections, giving her facial hair, a lower voice, and altered sexual organs. Surgeries followed.

New York Times headline: "He's Pregnant. You're Speechless." In this June 2008 article, an activist stated this was a "neat human-interest story" and the couple was simply "using the reproductive capabilities" at their disposal. I give credit to the writer, Guy Trebay, for his insight about their need to change our language before they could successfully influence and change our thinking. Keep in mind this was about ten years ago:

> Yet as the first pregnant transman to go public, Mr. Beatie has exposed a mass audience to alterations in the outlines of gender that may be outpacing our comprehension. In the discussions that followed his announcement, what became poignantly clear is that **there is no good language yet to discuss his situation**, words like an all-purpose pronoun to describe an idea as complex as a pregnant man (emphasis added).

Remember, much of the advancement of the LGBTQ agenda depends on the successful implementation of strategic words as well as the redefinition of other words. Intolerant!

Why the explosion of gender terminology? Their goal is to change society. One writer suggested that the two-sex, binary gender system is inadequate for understanding all humans. And it appears we will soon live by their rules or be penalized for "misgendering." Seriously.

Leave it to New York City's Commission on Human Rights and Bill de Blasio's bureaucrats. According to the May 2016 article in *The Washington Times*, businesses failing to address customers by their preferred gender pronouns and titles (misgendering) are in violation of the law and could be subject to penalties of up to $250,000. You read that right.

Regardless of an individual's appearance or sex at birth, you must now call them by their preferred name or pronoun. Who on earth comes up with this new language? The "alternative pronoun systems" are developed by leftist change agents in academia and LGBTQ communities. Is this not a form of fascism, a word they wrongly use to attack Donald Trump, Republicans, and Christians?

New York is requiring people to use words that convey the idea that gender is a matter of self-perception rather than anatomy. They can be politically correct, but we cannot be biologically correct. It doesn't seem fair.

University of California Los Angeles (UCLA) School of Law Professor Eugene Volokh questioned how this is permissible under the First Amendment. In his Conspiracy Blog, he wrote, "So people can basically force us – on pain of massive legal liability – to say what they want us to say, whether or not we want to endorse the political message associated with the term, and whether or not we think it's a lie."[15]

As expected, the federal government is on the same page as de Blasio. That same week, President Obama issued his order compelling public schools nationwide to accommodate transgender people by regulating locker rooms and restrooms on the basis of gender identity. What did most Democrats do? Just like the media, they turned the other way and said, "Look at Hillary Clinton, she's so wonderful and so presidential."

It's hard to believe it's been three years since Facebook rolled out a complete glossary of over fifty new gender options. *ABC News* listed fifty-eight. I've seen even more in other reports, and it's enough to make your eyes cross.

Facebook has massive influence with over 1.8 billion users worldwide,

---

15   Bradford Richardson, "New York businesses face hefty penalties for 'misgendering' customers," May 18, 2016, *www.washingtontimes.com/news/2016/may/18/de-blasio-fine-businesses-wrong-gender-pronouns/*.

but is its popularity dangerous because it is promoting humanism? Now working for Apple, Facebook's former software engineer Brielle Harrison worked on the pronoun project. Married to a very understanding woman for about ten years. "Brielle," according to *The Blaze*, was undergoing "gender transformation," from male to female, and stated:

> "All too often transgender people like myself and other
> gender nonconforming people are given this binary option,
> do you want to be male or female? What is your gender?
> And it's kind of disheartening because none of those let us
> tell others who we really are. This really changes that, and
> for the first time I get to go to the site and specify to all the
> people I know what my gender is."

Rather than calling it insane, we'd be more effective in society if we know and communicate the facts, and remain undaunted as we lovingly speak the truth. I feel sorry for those who are struggling, because most people who fall into this thought process and lifestyle do so because, for whatever reason, they are unhappy with who they truly are and do not like the person they see in the mirror. They fail to see they have value in God's eyes.

One word we had better get to know as truth in this debate is "binary." According to medical science, human sexuality is binary and a child has either an "XY" chromosomal pattern or an "XX" pattern. We are given these genetic markers which indicate a design that allows us the capacity for reproduction. Due to sin on this earth, there are rare biological disorders in sexual development, but these are deviations from the norm.

NAT GEO SPEAKS

I believe *National Geographic Magazine* revealed their allegiance by its child exploitation and promotion of sexual confusion in its January 2017 edition, "Gender Revolution." Featured on the cover is a nine-year-old boy, Avery, whose mother says he identifies as a girl. The cover caption reads: "The best thing about being a girl is, now I don't have to pretend to be a boy." According to Avery's mother, he became depressed and angry after age three, but the "darkness lifted" when the child put on a princess dress.

As if to justify its actions, *National Geographic*'s editor writes, "Beliefs about gender are shifting rapidly and radically." But just because people's opinions and beliefs are always moving does not mean truth is changing. On the Nat Geo website, they claim their exploration of gender "doesn't come with a political agenda," but their assumption seems to be "there is no God."

Since political issues *are* moral issues, do you believe their claim? Is *National Geographic* innocent and ignorant or do they have an agenda? Curiously, nowhere in the magazine or its online "research" do they even hint at a biblical worldview of gender and sexuality. The fact of intelligent design and the belief that God is the Creator of mankind must have escaped their notice, or perhaps Nat Geo ran out of time in their "exploration" of the facts.

How can you do a thorough investigation on human life and development without examining as much of the evidence, history, and science about creation as possible? You simply cannot.

Their advice to parents was to make sure "your young child's environment reflects diversity in gender roles and opportunities for everyone," and they even tried to falsely claim that gender identity "can't be changed by any interventions." So don't even try to encourage your child according to their God-given, biological sex. Wow. Scripture teaches the very opposite and guides us to bring up our children *in the discipline and instruction of the Lord* (Ephesians 6:4), as well as to *Train up a child in the way he should go, Even when he is old he will not depart from it* (Proverbs 22:6).

The article ends by asking Avery what the ideal world would be like, and he said that there would be no more bullying. One reader's comment on the Nat Geo cover photo may sum up mankind's futile quest to be our own gods: "As long as you're happy and aren't hurting anyone, then do or be whatever you want." (More on Aleister Crowley's "Do What Thou Wilt" later!)

What conclusions does the author come to? Let children and adults define themselves. Aside from saying American culture is "lurching toward a gender-neutral society" and suggesting that even scientists and scholars can't offer us much clarity, the readers are left with a rhetorical question: "Why should we cling to the rigid characterization of men and women?" And there you have it – from a magazine that's been in publication for 128 years.

Why refuse to at least crack open a Bible which has been proven to be historically reliable and accurate, and that most people would consider – if not inerrant and true – an excellent source of information relating to the world and to mankind? Because part of this wicked agenda is to downplay the truth and minimize or erase the differences between male and female.

The Holy Scriptures do not flow and change with the culture. Yes, God created us in His image and we are fearfully and wonderfully made, but equal doesn't mean identical. They are twisting and distorting the truth in order to deceive people, and sadly, they are succeeding.

Perhaps even more disturbing is one of the photos Nat Geo posted on its Facebook page with the caption, "Sometimes our children lead the way." Is it good parenting advice to let children make life-altering decisions that will affect their physical and mental health as well as their finances? If my folks allowed me to "lead the way" when I was a kid, I can't imagine how messed up my life would be right now.

The picture had what appeared to be a teenage girl with long blonde hair on the left standing next to a lesbian woman with very short hair wearing a black t-shirt. They both held pictures of their younger selves: in the photo on the left was a six-year-old boy with dark brown hair, and in the photo on the right was a woman with long blonde hair. So what's the story?

Corey is now fourteen, and according to Nat Geo, "socially transitioned" to a girl in the past few years. He gave his mom, Erica (who apparently now goes by Eric) the courage to begin her own transition from female to male. After her first shot of testosterone, Erica said she finally felt "complete." The photo description continued: "They are moving in opposite directions but toward their true selves." What a blatant lie of the devil. Naturally, the picture had hundreds of thousands of "likes."

SELECTED EVENTS ON THE TRANSGENDER TIMELINE

The groundwork for this agenda was prepared long ago. Seeds of deception were planted and watered, and we've witnessed some of the rotten fruit produced. For those who think this movement is a recent one, let's look at some key events from over the years.

1952: Mentioned earlier in this chapter, Christine Jorgensen became a celebrity and an advocate for transgenderism as he was the first American to have a "sex change."

1954: *The Milton Berle Show* began its five-year television run; one of the routines on his comedy show featured Berle cross-dressing.

1960: Alfred Hitchcock's *Psycho* featured a cross-dressing murderer (Anthony Perkins) who had a split personality, identifying so strongly with his jealous and controlling mother that he became her.

1964: After "transitioning" from a man to a woman, activist and businessman Reed Erickson created an educational foundation donating millions of dollars to the gay and transgender cause. (This may be offensive to some, but as one doctor said, "A mutilated male pumped full of estrogen remains just that – a mutilated male pumped full of estrogen.")

1966: Physician Harry Benjamin published "The Transsexual Phenomenon," a groundbreaking book that outlined how transgender people could "transition" medically.

1969: The Stonewall Inn was a gay club in New York City and some attendees rioted because of frequent raids on gay clubs. Many in the LGBT community, including transgenders, joined in several days of violent demonstrations. The Stonewall Riots are widely considered to have sparked the LGBT "rights" movement. In fact, a few even consider this an event that "changed the world."

1972: Sweden becomes the first nation in the world to legalize "gender reassignment" surgery.

1973: The American Psychiatric Association (APA) caved to pressure from LGBT activists and the APA removed homosexuality from its lexicon of disorders simply by vote of the membership.

1975: Minneapolis became the first city to pass a law prohibiting discrimination against transgender people.

1977: Renee Richards (formerly Richard Raskind) sued the U.S. Tennis Association for the right to play professional tennis as a woman and won the case in the New York Supreme Court. Divorced after five years of marriage and the father of a son, he began cross-dressing in college, later received hormone injections, and eventually had "sex reassignment" surgery. *He now regrets having the surgery and discourages others from doing so.

1983: The sitcom *Mash* airs its final episode after an eleven-year run. One of the main characters, Corporal Klinger (Jamie Farr) was a cross-dresser.

1986: Activist Louis Sullivan founded FTM International (Female to Male), and was a pioneer of the grassroots movement identifying herself as a "female to male transsexual." Sullivan influenced the modern understanding of sexual orientation and gender identity as distinct, unrelated concepts. She died of HIV in San Francisco in 1991.

1987: The American Psychiatric Association added "gender identity disorder" as a classification for transgender people to a revision of "The Diagnostic and Statistical Manual of Mental Disorders."

1992: The first International Conference on Transgender Law and Employment Policy was held in Houston, the first of six gatherings where activists, especially lawyers, from around the country met and laid the groundwork for the transgender movement.

1995: The "grandmother of the transgender movement," Phyllis Frye, and Riki Anne Wilchins, creator of advocacy group GenderPAC, held the first transgender lobbying day in Washington, D.C. *Frye would become the nation's first openly transgender judge in Houston in 2010.

1999: The movie *Boys Don't Cry* was released, based on the true story of

Teena Brandon (Brandon Teena) who struggled with an identity crisis and was murdered in Nebraska in 1993.

2002: The Transgender Law Center was founded "to change law, policy, and attitudes" so that regardless of a person's gender identity and expression, discrimination would not be an issue. It is a self-proclaimed San Francisco-based "civil rights organization advocating for transgender communities."

2004: San Francisco hosted its very first "Trans March."

2006: The first transgender woman was elected to Hawaii's Board of Education.

2008: Crystal Dixon, an employee of the University of Toledo, was fired after writing a column critical of comparing "homosexual rights" to the noble civil rights movement. A black Christian, she argued that those choosing to embrace a homosexual lifestyle are not "civil rights victims." Dixon appealed her case to the U.S. Supreme Court and in 2012, a three-judge panel of the Sixth U.S. Circuit Court of Appeals ruled against her, stating the school's interest in promoting its values and policies outweighed Dixon's free-speech rights.

2008: *America's Next Top Model* featured a transgender contestant, Isis King.

2008: Stu Rasmussen was elected mayor of Silverton, Oregon, becoming the first openly transgender mayor in the country.

2009: Chastity Bono announced her transition to the public and is now Chaz.

2010: President Obama boasted the first presidential transgender appointee, naming Amanda Simpson senior technical advisor in a bureau within the Commerce Department.

2012: Russell Braly, an Arkansas transgender student fought and won the right to use the ladies' washroom, saying the state recognizes him as a woman since he legally changed his name (he now goes by Jennifer) and gender. Even though he did not have surgery to complete the "transition," Braly said, "I feel like I should be treated equally as a woman because that's what I'm transitioning into."

2012: The Miss Universe pageant opened competition to transgender contestants.

2013: As mentioned earlier, the American Psychiatric Association was pressured to update its manual of mental disorders and replaced the term "gender identity disorder" with "gender dysphoria."

2014: Under President Obama, the Department of Health and Human Services reversed a Medicare policy in place since 1981. Medicare must now cover sex-reassignment surgery.

2014: Laverne Cox became the first transgender person to appear on the cover of *Time Magazine*, and the first transgender to be nominated for an Emmy (*Orange is the New Black*).

2014: Obama's Justice Department under Attorney General Eric Holder declared that Title VII of the Civil Rights Act of 1964 applied to claims of discrimination based on gender identity.

2015: Bruce Jenner became the most high-profile face of the transgender movement as he changed his name to Caitlyn. Jenner was an Olympic gold medalist, author, actor, and reality-television star, and discussed his transition to a woman in an article in *Vanity Fair*. Soon after, *Glamour Magazine* named him Woman of the Year, and ESPN named him the Arthur Ashe Courage Award winner at the ESPY Awards.

2015: President Obama was the first U.S. president to mention transgender people in a State of the Union address, saying, "That's why we defend free speech and advocate for . . . people who are lesbian, gay, bisexual or transgender."

2015: At Harvard University, the school's faculty of arts and sciences registration tool expanded the number of pronouns students could use to identify as "transgender." They can now state a preference for "ze, hir, hirs" or "they, them, theirs."

2015: The Obama administration (the Pentagon) lifted a ban on military service by transgender people allowing them to serve openly. There may be thousands of transgender people in uniform throughout the U.S. military.

2015: Former policy adviser at the National Center for Transgender Equality, Raffi Freedman-Gurspan was appointed to serve as an outreach and recruitment director on President Obama's staff.

2016: News leaked out regarding the Obama administration approving the use of federal funding for transgender "genital reconstruction" operations under the Affordable Care Act. The Obama HHS "nondiscrimination mandate" would have forced doctors to perform surgeries they believe would cause people irreparable harm. Not only that, but this provision would also apply to federal civil rights laws and call for medical plans and insurers to cover the procedures.

2017: The Cub Scouts finally gave in to LGBT activist pressure, and a young girl from New Jersey, Jodi Maldonado (who identifies as a boy and goes by the name Joe), won a court case and can now go on camping trips with the boys. So now the Boy Scouts will allow a child in their programs based upon the gender listed on the application rather than their birth certificate.

2017: Naturally, *Time* focused their March 16 cover story on the "changing meaning of gender and sexuality," featuring an article by San Francisco Bureau Chief Katy Steinmetz. In *Time*'s marketing of gender confusion, I mean, fluidity, the article was titled "Beyond He or She." (This just three years after featuring Laverne Cox on its cover in 2014.)

Even with sixty gender types now, according to Facebook, over 30 percent of young people surveyed said that number of options is "just about right" or even too few! Along with other social media platforms such as YouTube, Snapchat, and Twitter, it is much easier to spread deception and gather support. Most liberal news media outlets are on the bandwagon with Hollywood normalizing gender deviation.

This will be the defining issue for the next generation and beyond. In the next chapter, we will address this agenda with truth from the medical and psychological community as well as a few testimonies from people with sex-change regret, including a young man who now says, "I can't believe what I've done to my life." You will not hear this in the mainstream media.

Chapter 4

Truth and Facts Don't Care About Feelings and Trends

Therefore, my beloved brothers, be ye steadfast, unmovable, always abounding in the work of the Lord, forasmuch as ye know that your labour is not in vain in the Lord.
(1 Corinthians 15:58)

"It is the duty of the Christian scholar to look difficulties and objections squarely in the face. Nothing is to be gained by overlooking, evading or shrinking from them. Truth has no cause to fear scrutiny, however rigid." – John W. Haley

As I was putting finishing touches on this book, I noticed a story from Canada where a parent who does not identify as male or female ("Non-Binary Trans") is fighting for the right to register their baby as "Gender Unknown." They claim that a biological examination is "restrictive" and cannot uncover the child's true identity. The province of British Columbia provided the child with a health card with a "U" for gender, meaning "undetermined."

In another story out of Portland, Oregon, a self-proclaimed "gay trans man" (aka "woman") named Reece is raising two children with a gay man and the NBC headline states, "There's No One Path to Creating Family." The couple proudly declared, "We know a lot of transgender men who have babies. We have several in our close circle of friends so it does not seem that strange to us."

When we toss biblical truth and morality out the window, something has to fill the void.

Rush Limbaugh rightfully stated that this whole culture war is about obliterating morality. Recent events have plenty of good people scratching their heads because they don't know how to defend the position of normalcy and truth without getting shouted down. Limbaugh said liberalism is determined to wipe out the concept of morality, believing that no one has the right to define it, adding:

> "Nobody can write laws that are based on morality and
> have them apply to everybody, because your morality may
> differ from mine, and there isn't any universal morality; . . .
> So something as simple as morality and right and wrong
> has now become politicized, and therefore illegitimate,
> 'cause you don't have the right to tell somebody what's right
> and wrong. . . . The only way they can win this war is by
> obliterating the concepts of right versus wrong, 'cause they
> are wrong, and they know it."[16]

Let's remember to pray for those who don't believe, because someone probably prayed for you and me when we didn't deserve God's grace.

But God demonstrates His own love toward us, in that while
we were yet sinners, Christ died for us. (Romans 5:8)

Though we now have a better understanding of the redefinition of tolerance, there is much work ahead because we are dealing with people who need Christ and who think their intolerance is rightly justified.

The word *tolerance* does not mean we should put up with everything and just keep our objections to ourselves. It comes from the Latin words *tolerare* (meaning "to allow, bear, or suffer"), and *tollere* ("to lift up"), and true tolerance implies bearing with other people (Ephesians 4:2; Colossians 3:13) and their beliefs. The original meaning is negative, similar to the idea of putting up with a bad migraine headache – you definitely want it to stop.

God's Word teaches that Christians have a responsibility to avoid

---

16   Susan Jones, "Limbaugh: Obliterating Morality Has Been What the Culture War is
     All About," CNS News, April 22, 2016, *www.cnsnews.com/news/article/susan-jones/*
     limbaugh-culture-war-about-obliterating-morality-and-right-versus-wrong.

sin, having nothing to do with evil and those who practice it. Jesus loved all people, but He did not sin with sinners or back down in the face of religious hypocrisy. The Christian church is a main reason immorality is running rampant in America. We need to be loving examples of truth, yes, but we must also speak up.

In a Bible commentary on the book of Ephesians, Pastor John MacArthur declared, "Love that does not openly expose and oppose sin is not biblical love." He added:

> To ignore evil is to encourage it; to keep quiet about it is to help promote it. The verb translated as "expose" (from *elegchō*) can also carry the idea of reproof, correction, punishment, or discipline. We are to confront sin with intolerance. Unfortunately, many Christians are barely able to keep their own spiritual and moral houses in order that they do not have the discernment, inclination, or power to confront evil in the church or in society at large.
>
> Sadly, many Christians do not confront evil because they do not take it seriously. They laugh and joke about unadulterated wickedness – things that are immoral and ungodly in the extreme. They recognize the sinfulness of those things and would likely never participate in them; but they enjoy them vicariously. In so doing, they not only fail to be an influence against evil but are instead influenced by it – contaminated to the extent that they think and talk about it without exposing and rebuking it.[17]

Most of us do not have a problem with freedom, or with progressive individuals or corporations refusing to do business with a state, or artists refusing to perform based on their conscience and personal beliefs. We should, however, have a problem with them insisting a baker, florist, pastor, bed and breakfast owner, photographer, etc. cannot also deny service due to *their* conscience and personal beliefs! This includes biblical beliefs about who created us and how we were created.

But from the beginning of creation, God made them male

17   John MacArthur, "When Silence is Sinful," Feb. 20, 2014, *www.gty.org/library/blog/B140220/when-silence-is-sinful*.

*and female. For this reason a man shall leave his father and
mother and the two shall become one flesh; so they are no
longer two, but one flesh.* (Mark 10:6-8)

It's obvious the transgender movement did not come out of nowhere,
but it sure is picking up speed and too many of us didn't see it coming.
It has been a very clever, gradual progression and some chose not to
see it. We didn't want to believe that Christianity was no longer driving
our culture and influencing America.

We may never know how much Hollywood has influenced public
opinion, but after reading the transgender timeline in the last chapter,
we have a much better idea. One movie that probably had more impact
than we realize was *Boys Don't Cry.*

"Teena R. Brandon, December 12, 1972 – December 31, 1993, Daughter,
Sister, & Friend" (actual tombstone inscription, Lincoln, Nebraska)

For reasons I will explain, I am choosing to use her birth name.
Hollywood may have gotten some of the story wrong, but was it on
purpose? According to reports, when Teena was a young girl she was
sexually molested by an uncle or other relative. Her mother, JoAnn, said
Teena sought counseling in 1991, and began to dress in men's clothing
and date women as a defense strategy. "She pretended she was a man
so no other man could touch her."

Boys Don't Cry was the story of "Brandon Teena" from the angle of
a confused transgender. Though it is true Teena pretended to be a boy
and had at least one serious girlfriend, some declare she was simply a
lesbian. Some say she was a transsexual.

Part of the problem is too many opportunistic activists jumped at
the chance to raise awareness for their cause, many of them insisting on
referring to Brandon as "he" or "him" when she did not legally change
her name and did not ever attempt to "transition" to the opposite sex.
Some say she was a cross-dresser, but at least one report stated she did
not even wear men's clothing, but mainly wore large or baggy women's
clothes to cover her body and make her look less appealing to men.

In her taped interview with Sheriff Charles Laux, when she reported
being raped (by the two men that murdered her just six days later),
Brandon admitted being confused and said, "I have a sexual identity

crisis." The men threatened her if she reported the rape, and Teena's mother later sued the county and Sheriff Laux for not taking her daughter seriously and failing to prevent the murder. Eventually, she won the case as the judge determined Laux's questioning of Teena was "demeaning, accusatory, and intimidating."

My heart broke as I listened to the entire interview, and God's heart must ache as well for all the sexually broken, hurting, confused people today who have bought lies and are conditioned to believe they would be happier if they changed "who they are." I know Jesus loves them and died for them, and those who have sowed the lies will one day be judged for leading so many astray.

Though many stories and links have been scrubbed from search engines, you can still find some inconvenient (for the LGBTQ activists) information that does not quite seem to line up with their story or the film's portrayal of certain facts. For example, *People* and *Variety* were at least two magazines that reported, albeit briefly, that Brandon's mother, JoAnn, was upset after Hillary Swank won an Oscar for Best Actress and thanked "Brandon Teena" in her acceptance speech instead of "Teena Brandon," her given legal name.

Swank was "truly saddened" after hearing about JoAnn Brandon's reaction and said, "She can't see what Brandon has done for everyone in our society. But my heart goes out to her, to lose a daughter. . . . I never tried to define her [Teena] as a lesbian."[18]

From more than one report, it appears that JoAnn Brandon has severe asthma and/or was disabled and could not work. At the time *Boys Don't Cry* was released, she had some issues (one report states she was "outraged") by the film's portrayal of Teena. Before she won the court case and was finally awarded financial compensation, she apparently had a fund set up to pay for Teena's funeral but received minimal contributions at the time. She was angry that Hollywood was profiting from her daughter's death while she struggled to pay the bills.

She last spoke to Teena on December 30, the day before her death. Her mother said that she had clearly spoken to a woman, adding, "I knew who she was. She said she had to get her head back together. She wanted

---

18   Army Archerd, "Swank Upset by Oscar Fallout," *Variety,* March 30, 2000, *variety.com/2000/ voices/columns/ swank-upset-by-oscar-fallout-1117780062/.*

to come back to her old life and her old life was Teena Brandon." One of the convicted murderers is still on death row and we may never know all the details, but some LGBTQ advocates insist they have the facts.[19]

(Note: *Boys Don't Cry* is by no means an appropriate film for families, and its R rating is well deserved in every applicable area.)

The gender identity agenda and transgender train (movement) seeks to erase the image of God in man if it were possible, and to redefine humanity on their terms.

Writing for *Crisis Magazine* in February 2017, author and professor Paul Kengor talked about the Boy Scouts of America opening their doors to girls declaring themselves to be boys – for the moment anyway. I agree with him that the Left has momentum after remaking sexuality, marriage, family, and now gender in their own image. This is another "capitulation to our culture's human-nature re-definers." Kengor writes:

> A girl has 74 trillion X chromosomes in her body. . . . Thus, a seven-year-old girl who calls herself a boy does so despite the reality that she has 74 trillion X chromosomes vs. ZERO Y chromosomes. To repeat: ZERO Y chromosomes. Biological reality could not be more stacked against whatever she might be feeling. 74 trillion vs. zero are utterly enormous odds. You've heard the saying that every fiber in your body tells you something? Imagine every chromosome in your body telling you something. What they tell you is your gender. You don't tell your body your gender; your body tells you your gender.
>
> Yes, I understand that perverse political correctness and radical-leftist ideology has warped and disordered our culture, but secular liberalism cannot alter the absolute laws of nature. Call it that pesky Natural Law thing.[20]

MEDICAL PROFESSIONALS SPEAK

The American Psychiatric Association considers transgenderism a

19   History vs. Hollywood, *Boys Don't Cry*, 1999, *www.historyvshollywood.com/reelfaces/boysdontcry.php*.

20   Paul Kengor, "Girl Boy Scouts ... and 71 Other 'Gender' Options," February 9, 2017, *www.crisismagazine.com/ 2017/girl-boy-scouts-71-gender-options*.

mental health issue, but as mentioned earlier, due to pressure from LGBTQ activists, the APA has been defining the condition as "gender dysphoria" since 2013. Another time the APA was forced to alter a medical classification or definition was in 1973 when they dropped homosexuality as a mental illness.

Some will argue that it is best or healthy for parents to encourage children to explore "who they are" and not force them to be limited to their biological sex. Studies show that out of all children who do experience "gender dysphoria" (a distressed state arising from conflict between a person's gender identity and the sex the person was identified as having at birth), 94 percent of them will grow out of it and lead normal, healthy adult lives.

According to the American College of Pediatricians (ACPeds), "Conditioning children into believing a lifetime of chemical and surgical impersonation of the opposite sex is normal, is child abuse." ACPeds also made strong recommendations that teachers and politicians reject any propaganda which could cause children to go down this dangerous road, saying, "Endorsing gender discordance as normal via public education and legal policies will confuse children and parents, leading more children to . . . be given puberty-blocking drugs. This, in turn, virtually ensures they will 'choose' a lifetime of carcinogenic and otherwise toxic cross-sex hormones."[21]

Most medical doctors and scientists agree that there has been no conclusive research revealing a transgender gene or hormonal study proving the transgender philosophy, but that hasn't stopped the madness. Millions of people suffer from mental illnesses and the loving thing to do is counsel them, not enable them. To conclude that a person needs cosmetic surgery to cure their gender dysphoria is not based on sound science.

But sadly, political gain is too lucrative, and we know legislation is often driven not by truth or medical research, but by the desire to make money and to further an agenda. In the case of making insurance money available for expensive cosmetic surgeries and hormone

---

21 American College of Pediatricians, "Gender Ideology Harms Children," January 2017, *www.acpeds.org/the-college-speaks/position-statements/gender-ideology-harms-children.*

treatments, is it fair to the taxpayer who helps fund Obamacare and has to pay for medical insurance?

Where children are concerned, the American College of Pediatricians urges legislators, educators, and health care professionals to "reject all policies that condition children to accept as normal a life of chemical and surgical impersonation of the opposite sex. Facts – not ideology – determine reality."

Under the page heading "Gender Ideology Harms Children," here are major guidelines from the medical profession on the ACPeds website:

> Human sexuality is an objective biological binary trait: "XY" and "XX" are genetic markers of male and female, respectively – not genetic markers of a disorder.
>
> No one is born with a gender. Everyone is born with a biological sex.
>
> When an otherwise healthy biological boy believes he is a girl, or an otherwise healthy biological girl believes she is a boy, an objective psychological problem exists that lies in the mind not the body, and it should be treated as such.
>
> Puberty is not a disease and puberty-blocking hormones can be dangerous.
>
> As many as 98% of gender confused boys and 88% of gender confused girls eventually accept their biological sex after naturally passing through puberty.
>
> Pre-pubertal children diagnosed with gender dysphoria may be given puberty blockers as young as eleven, and will require cross-sex hormones in later adolescence to continue impersonating the opposite sex. . . . In addition, cross-sex hormones (testosterone and estrogen) are associated with dangerous health risks including but not limited to cardiac disease, high blood pressure, blood clots, stroke, diabetes, and cancer.
>
> Rates of suicide are nearly twenty times greater among

adults who use cross-sex hormones and undergo sex reassignment surgery.

ACPeds President Michelle Cretella said that affirming so-called transgender children means sterilizing them as young as eleven years old.

Despite these facts and other easily accessible medical information available to those seeking truth, the peddlers of deception plow forward. Why do LGBTQ activists seem so callous and indifferent toward children who should be protected? The agenda may be stronger than their conscience.

Their ultimate aim is power and control by obliterating Christian influence and resistance, as this gender-neutral push could eventually reach their demonically inspired goal: to wipe out the standard of the traditional family unit and the true meaning of marriage. There seems to be a lot coming at us, but always remember that we have the truth on our side, and *If God is for us, who can be against us?* (Romans 8:31 ESV).

That being said, do we think most people in Hollywood, the liberal media, the U.S. Department of Education, or leftists in government care about truth or about the consequences of this ideology? Don't let the rhetoric surrounding this issue distract you from the fact that we are performing a dangerous experiment on today's children.

One email subject line reads: "I wish I listened to you," addressed to a Mr. Walt Heyer. The young person opened up about his heartbreaking experience as a victim of the agenda.

> I'm only in my mid [twenties]. I transitioned in my teens
> and had surgery. I was [too] young to make such a decision.
> I've sunken into such a deep regret. I don't even feel trans-
> gender anymore. I feel like my old self. I am happy with a
> female appearance but that is all I really needed. I feel like I
> was brainwashed by the transgender agenda and by gender
> norm expectations. I would do anything to [have] my penis
> back. My feelings were confusing and I thought they would
> never go away. I'm just a guy who's really in touch with
> my feminine side. I can't believe what I've done to my life.
> And now I have no choice but to take hormones forever. I
> don't know what to do. I feel like I'm losing my mind. All

I would have had to do was discontinue my hormones and everything would have been alright. I honestly feel 100% normal and okay . . . if only I had never had that surgery.[22]

A FORMER TRANSGENDER SPEAKS

Commenting on the magazines and media promoting transgenderism, Walt Heyer said the previously mentioned cover of *National Geographic* is a glossy reminder of the brokenness of transgender ideology. In his January 2017 article, Heyer re-emphasizes the point that even when they are affirmed, accepted, and loved, transgender individuals remain traumatized even after surgeries and many attempt suicide, "which indicates that the issues they struggle with run deeper than a change in gender identity can rectify."

He begins the article by quoting Psychiatrist Richard Corradi who calls transgenderism "a contagion of mass delusion." Heyer states that the LGBTQ army probably loves the Nat Geo gender issue:[23]

"But for me, one who was restored after living for eight years as a female transgender, the cover photo is a sad and painful reminder of a lost childhood, a family ripped apart, and a marriage that did not survive."

Walt Heyer makes another excellent point: that photo shows only one moment in time and cannot possible show young Avery's future. One photo does not give a long-range perspective of the consequences of Avery and his parents' choices.

Heyer continues:

"I was a cross-dressing boy at age nine, but – after years of pain and self-delusion – my cross-dressing stopped decades later, when I realized that the idea of changing sexes is pure fantasy. Cross-dressing initially felt zany, fun, exhilarating, and wonderfully affirming of my belief that I should have been born a girl. But after many decades of trying to comprehend the gender confusion that persisted even after

---

22 Walt Heyer, "The Experiment on Our Children: Doctors Don't Know Who the Real Trans Kids Are," June 12, 2017, *www.thepublicdiscourse.com/2017/06/19512/*.

23 Walt Heyer, "A Nine-Year-Old Boy is Spreading a 'Contagion of Mass Delusion,'" January 5, 2017, *www.thepublicdiscourse.com/2017/01/18465/*.

my sex transition, I came to understand that my grandmother's cross-dressing of me was emotional child abuse.
The psychological harm grew as years went by."

Heyer also said he sought out a gender therapist who would affirm him
and who approved people for gender reassignment surgery. Due to
political correctness and the extreme safeguarding of people's feelings
at all costs, we are abandoning the ability to call what is fake "fake"
and what is real "real." Avery's photos are a source of revenue for Nat
Geo and a strategic tool for the LGBTQ lobby.

Moreover, the magazine failed to include interviews with people
who have had their lives destroyed by the long-term consequences of
transgenderism. Heyer states:

"I turned to Christ and away from transgenderism. I
wanted to be obedient to the Lord. Obedience is giving up
what I want in order to live the life Christ wants. I had to
stop living in defiance of God and stop demanding that
the church, God, and everyone else make accommodations
for my delusions. Demanding that people use my preferred
female pronoun name was childish."

He also said cross-dressing eroded his true gender and his teenage
years, "ripped apart my marriage and ended my career." So how did he
break through the bondage? Through prayer, the power of Christ, and
counselling. (Hoping to help others, his website is *SexChangeRegret.
com*, and blog *WaltHeyer.com*)

One of the best ways to conclude this very important topic is to
provide you with some excellent and, most importantly, biblically
based information from the Christian Medical and Dental Association
(CMDA). This is from their Transgender Identification Ethics Statement.

CHRISTIAN MEDICAL PROFESSION SPEAKS

CMDA affirms the historic and enduring Christian understanding
of humankind as having been created male and female. CMDA has
concerns about recent usage of the term "gender" to emphasize an
identity other than one's biological sex. CMDA holds that attempts to

alter gender surgically or hormonally . . . are medically inappropriate, as they repudiate nature, are unsupported by the witness of Scripture. Accordingly, CMDA opposes medical assistance with gender transition on the following grounds.

A. Biblical – God created humanity as male and female (Genesis 1:27; 5:2; Matthew 19:4; Mark 10:6). Men and women are morally and spiritually equal (Galatians 3:28) and are created to have roles that are in some respects alike and in other respects wonderfully complementary (Ephesians 5).

B. Biological – Sex is an objective biological fact that is determined genetically at conception by the allocation of X and Y chromosomes to one's genome, immutable throughout one's lifetime. Procreation requires genetic contributions from both one man and one woman.

C. Social – Inclination to identify with the opposite gender may have biological, familial, and social origins that are not of the making of particular individuals. Social movements which contend that gender is decided by choice are mistaken in defining gender, not by nature, but according to desire. Authentic personal identity consists in social gender expression that is congruent with one's natural biological sex. CMDA recognizes that this traditional view has become counter-cultural; however, CMDA affirms that God's design transcends culture.

D. Medical – Among individuals who identify as transgender, use cross-sex hormones, and undergo sex-reassignment surgery, there is well-documented increased incidence of depression, anxiety, suicidal ideation, substance abuse, and risky sexual behaviors.

E. Ethical – Medicine rests on science and should not be held captive to desires or demands that contradict biological reality. Sex-reassignment operations are physically harmful because they disregard normal human anatomy and function. The medical status of gender identity disorder as a mental or psychosocial disorder should not be discarded on the basis of social activism. The purpose of medicine is to heal the sick, not to collaborate with psychosocial disorders.

CMDA Recommendations for the Christian Community and Nondiscrimination

A person struggling with gender identity should evoke neither scorn nor enmity, but rather our concern, compassion, help, and understanding. The Christian community is to be a refuge of love for all who are broken – including sexually broken – not to affirm their sin, nor to condemn or castigate, but to shepherd them to Jesus, who alone can forgive, heal, restore, and redirect to a godly, honorable, and virtuous way of life.

(It seems their final recommendations below deal with the one-way tolerance we've addressed.)

Mutual respect and civil discourse are cornerstones of a free society. Those who hold to a biblical or traditional view of human sexuality should be permitted to question transgender dogma free from exclusion, oppression, or unjust discrimination. CMDA affirms that health care professionals should not be coerced or mandated to provide or refer for services that they believe to be morally wrong or harmful to patients. Health care professionals must not be prevented from providing counseling and support to patients who are experiencing confusion in regard to gender orientation.[24]

Use this information as a resource you can refer to when needed as these debates continue in our culture and in our personal lives, including conversations with family, friends, foes, and on social media. The short answer to this epic dilemma is Jesus. He is the only one who can save, heal, and break free those who are in bondage to sin and oppression.

So Jesus was saying to those Jews who had believed Him, "If you continue in My word, then you are truly disciples of Mine; and you will know the truth, and the truth will make you free." (John 8:31-32)

---

24   Christian Medical & Dental Associations, "Transgender Identification Ethics Statement," *cmda.org/resources/publication/transgender-identification-ethics-statement.*

The transgender "T" in LGBTQ was custom built into the agenda, patiently waiting for the right time to be rolled out. There is truly nothing new under the sun. Preparations needed to be done prior to implementing the Left's ideology. As part of the groundwork, they and their counterparts before them sought to minimize our nation's pillars: God, truth, marriage, family, and history. It seemed like quite the undertaking. The agenda to them seemed like a dream at one time. But they were patient, persistent, and focused on the long term while incremental progress was made.

Chapter 5

Lies of the Left (Pelosi Politics)

By this we know that we have come to know Him, if we keep His commandments. The one who says, "I have come to know Him," and does not keep His commandments, is a liar, and the truth is not in him. I have not written to you because you do not know the truth, but because you do know it, and because no lie is of the truth. (1 John 2:3-4, 21)

"Ironically, it is the skeptic who blindly trusts in wild assertions to escape the one thing their belief system fears most: the risen Lord and Savior Jesus Christ." – Tim Chaffey

On January 20, 2017, when President Donald Trump was about to be inaugurated, House Minority Leader, Nancy Pelosi, appeared on *MSNBC* and claimed Democrats do the will of God while Republicans dishonor Him. Wow, interesting take – please tell us more, Nancy! Pelosi was digging herself a hole as she tried explaining why so many religious and rural Americans no longer support the Democratic Party. Apparently, she thinks Democrats are doing God's work, but aren't getting the credit, or something like that.

Perhaps realizing the growing disconnect between the Left and hardworking citizens, *Morning Joe* host Joe Scarborough asked Pelosi how the Dems can "connect with the middle American who sometimes feel they're looked down on because of their faith or their values." Excellent question.

There certainly is an elite bubble in which many wealthy liberals operate. Most are not only far removed but also out of touch with the average American, and they have an attitude of superiority to prove it. We've seen it from Hollywood celebrities, the music industry, and of course, from our own government. And by the way, Republicans are not all excluded from this as some are fighting the Christians and true conservatives within that party.

Hillary Clinton revealed her attitude toward tens of millions of voters when during a campaign speech in September 2016 she said, "You could put half of Trump supporters in what I call the basket of deplorables. . . . The racist, sexist, homophobic, xenophobic, Islamophobic – you name it."

But what she said in April of 2015 is even more alarming because it exposes a big part of her worldview. Speaking at a women's summit in New York City, Hillary Clinton stated, "Yes, we've cut the maternal mortality rate in half, but far too many women are still denied critical access to reproductive health care and safe childbirth. . . . Laws have to be backed up with resources and political will. **And deep-seated cultural codes, religious beliefs and structural biases have to be changed**" (emphasis added).

If we believe the Bible is true, then abortion is wrong, life begins at conception, and every life is a gift from God. This means that in Hillary Clinton's view, we're biased and we must change. And thanks to WikiLeaks, it wasn't surprising to hear that in her emails, Clinton's campaign staff routinely mocked traditional Christians.

This is all consistent with godless progressive thinking. When campaigning for president, then-Senator Obama talked to supporters in San Francisco about American citizens in places like Pennsylvania and "a lot of small towns in the Midwest" that were frustrated about jobs and the economy. Obama went on to say, "And it's not surprising then that they get bitter, they cling to guns or religion or antipathy to people who aren't like them or anti-immigrant sentiment or anti-trade sentiment as a way to explain their frustrations."

Going back to the January 20 interview, Nancy Pelosi responded by implying that people in rural America feel isolated, from what I'm not sure, and many of them, "don't think that Democrats are people of faith." Maybe because they observe the overall fruit of your party's policies?

When answering Scarborough's question, she referred either to helping the poor or perhaps to climate change and the environment, accusing Republicans of hypocrisy: "I say they pray in church on Sunday and prey on people the rest of the week, and while we're [Democrats] doing the Lord's work by ministering to the needs of God's creation, they are ignoring those needs, which is to dishonor the God who made them."

Let's examine truth and morality according to the book of Pelosi.

So, is it the Lord's work to make sure a woman can legally eliminate the life of her baby up until the very moment of delivery – and use taxpayer money to help pay for it? Is it the Lord's work to force charities (Little Sisters of the Poor, for example) and Christian nonprofits to pay for abortion-inducing drugs even though it goes against their religious beliefs and conscience? Is it the Lord's work to prevent children and families, particularly inner-city parents from choosing a charter school or private school for their kids? Is it the Lord's work to threaten the religious freedom of those who believe marriage is the union of one man and one woman and would rather not use their artistry or business to promote a same-sex wedding?

Is it the Lord's work to cater to a fraction of the population and promote transgender bathroom policies over the safety of women and young children? Is it the Lord's work to disobey the laws of the land by defending sanctuary cities that break current immigration laws and fail to protect legal U.S. citizens, some of whom have been attacked, robbed, or even murdered by criminal aliens?

I am not defending Republicans here, but if you make a claim about doing God's work, you had better have the facts and policies to back that up. If Democrats claim to be more "Christian" than Republicans, why did they remove God from their party platform and literally boo the proposal to add God back in during the Democratic National Convention in September 2012?

Thinking the Democrats should get more credit for their good works, Pelosi also said, "We don't wear our religion on our sleeves and maybe we should." But it is obvious they already are wearing their religion on their sleeves – it's just not the religion she's claiming. Pelosi is Catholic, and according to her church's teachings, she's either a bad example of one or is a non-practicing Catholic. But let's be clear: the religion of the Left is Liberalism.

They are loyal to this cult and to a god that celebrates pagan morality. And they've been busy working to remove the true God and to eradicate our Judeo-Christian values from the public square.

BUT THEY INSISTED IT WAS NOT AN AGENDA

Another gem Nancy Pelosi left us was in 2010 when her party quickly rammed the massive Obamacare bill through Congress without a single Republican vote and she infamously stated, "But we have to pass the bill so that you can find out what is in it."

If the people and policy really mattered, there would have been more open debate and clearer explanations of the legislation. But it wasn't about doing the right thing. This was about power. If government can control the nation's health care, it can control many other things, such as the teaching of sex education (you don't want to know what this now includes) to the youngest children possible in public schools, which falls under their definition of "health."

On April 28, 2016, Nancy Pelosi came right out and admitted what many of us already knew: they had an agenda to transform America all along. In a press conference for the so-called "Equality Act," which we'll get to in a few minutes, she admitted that same-sex marriage isn't nearly as popular as they insist it is. The people were duped.

Pelosi said when Barack Obama became president and the Democrats came into the majority, their goal was to make homosexual "marriage" the law of the land. With thirty states having protections on God-ordained, natural marriage through the votes of millions of people per state, the Democrats could not accomplish this goal "legislatively," so they worked to achieve it through the courts.

Referring to the Supreme Court decision in 2015 that said all state bans on same-sex marriage were unconstitutional, Pelosi boasted:

> "We had four points – it was a four-legged stool of what we wanted to accomplish – to pass a fully inclusive hate crimes

legislation. Another piece of our agenda was to promote marriage equality in our country. Legislatively, we couldn't really succeed, but from the courts and the rest, and public opinion, of course, in the actual courts and in the court of public opinion, that victory has been won."[25]

Indicating the fact that she realizes the power and influence liberals have, notice she said, "and public opinion, of course." Naturally. They're winning because they never give up, they've flipped the courts and the media, have redefined words and gotten people to accept their meanings, and they've framed the debate while staying on offense. They have redefined truth.

According to the Obama/Pelosi/Reid Democrats, the second "leg" was the successful repeal of Don't Ask, Don't Tell (DADT) endorsing open homosexuality in the United States military. Pelosi proudly admitted that "would not have happened without the president's leadership and courage."

It may not have happened without the propaganda machine of the anti-Christian media. They sure played their part to alter public opinion on homosexuality. Gallup did a poll several years ago asking Americans to guess the percentage of gays and lesbians in the U.S. population. Ready?

Women and young adults think the gay population is about 30 percent and a quarter of all those polled guessed it was over 25 percent. What's the truth? LGBTQ individuals make up less than 4 percent of our population. Four. THIS is an example of the one-sided influence of Hollywood and the media.

The third leg of the perverse agenda was so-called marriage equality, and the fourth leg was something that freedom-loving citizens had better be paying attention to: the goal to pass the Employment Non-Discrimination Act (ENDA).

You may be wondering if this is something new, but in 2009, the Obama administration wasted no time and immediately got to work implementing pro-gay policies. The goals just mentioned above were

25   Penny Star, "Pelosi: Court Gave Us Victory on Same-Sex Marriage We Could Not Get 'Legislatively'" (CNS News, April 28, 2016) *www.cnsnews.com/news/article/penny-starr/ pelosi-same-sex-marriage-high-court-gave-us-victory-we-could-not-achieve.*

listed on the official White House website. They may have tried to hide the agenda fifty or twenty-five years ago, but there's no need to hide it any longer.

Liberals have fought to use the federal government to expand homosexual adoptions of children, as well as to implement and promote sex education and contraception in government schools. Don't say Obama was inept or unintelligent. He accomplished more in a very short time to transform the character, morality, and perception of America than perhaps any other president.

The following goals were also openly listed on the Obama White House's website:

> Protect cross-dressing and transgenderism in the workplace (including schools) through federal law, pass Employment Non-Discrimination Act (ENDA) to prohibit "discrimination based on sexual orientation or gender identity or expression," and expand hate crime statutes which includes giving the federal government the power to prosecute those crimes. . . . repeal the Defense of Marriage Act (DOMA), and push for full civil unions and federal recognition of homosexual couples, plus benefits equal to actual marriage.

This partial list should give you an idea of how committed they are to their goals, and once they are accomplished, they set new ones or work to expand the goals that were once just dreams.

The Democrats held the press conference at the Capitol in Washington for ENDA and announced they sent a letter to the head of the House Judiciary Committee urging him to set up a hearing for the so-called Equality Act, or H.R.3185.

Pelosi declared ENDA was "a very important piece of the agenda," and since the Democrats were seeing such momentum and success in the advancement of all the LGBT goals, she stated, "We saw the opportunity to do something bigger." She's right about this because it would hugely impact the entire country, punishing anyone who disagreed with same-sex marriage for moral reasons, and religious liberty protections would almost cease to exist.

The Democrats set out to expand on ENDA, and the Equality Act would – believe it or not – amend the Civil Rights Act of 1964 to include "sexual orientation" and "gender identity" as protected classes! (The current law bans discrimination based on color, race, religion, and sex.)

In his Washington Watch update, Tony Perkins of the Family Research Council called this Equality Act "the most radical piece of sexual orientation, gender identity legislation ever introduced," and added:

> "Together with the media, the Left did quite a snow job
> on Americans on the issue of marriage. Over time, they
> managed to create this phony impression of support – even
> when the ballot boxes and state laws told a different story.
> . . . they're owning up to the fact that they had to force
> the redefinition of marriage on the country illegitimately.
> While Americans are processing that bombshell, the
> Left is already moving on to the next target: a genderless
> America."[26]

A few areas of culture that would be directly impacted by the Equality Act are employment, public accommodations, education, federal programs, and the Religious Freedom Restoration Act.

Remember when so many pundits and promoters of same-sex marriage kept insisting that they simply wanted to "live and let live"? Some of us who are informed and who understand the wicked heart of mankind knew it wouldn't stop with legalizing same-sex marriage, but few listened. The LGBTQ and its allies practically forced the celebration of sin on the country.

Though liberal activists are the minority by far, they have the loudest voices, and if they can't change your thinking and behavior, they'll gladly shout you down and cut off open debate. It should be noted that not everyone on the Left is heartless, hostile, and agenda-driven, but the activists make up for those who simply do want to live their lives in peace and not force their views on us all.

To quote Francis Schaeffer again:

> "The thinkables of the eighties and nineties will certainly

---

26 Tony Perkins, "'Popular Opinion' Isn't So Popular After All!," Family Research Council Washington Update, April 29, 2016, *www.frc.org/ updatearticle/20160429/popular-opinion*.

include things which most people today find unthinkable and immoral, even unimaginable and too extreme to suggest. Yet – since they do not have some overriding principle that takes them beyond relativistic thinking – when these become thinkable and acceptable in the eighties and nineties, most people will not even remember that they were unthinkable in the seventies. They will slide into each new thinkable without a jolt."[27]

For the few who still may wonder how we got here, we might trace the incremental transfer of influence from Christianity to immorality to several historical decades in the last 100 years. In my previous books, I've written about dozens of individuals who have had a negative, damaging impact on our culture including eugenicist, feminist, and racist Margaret Sanger, founder of Planned Parenthood and the one who coined the term "birth control." Her abortion crusade really took off in the early 1920s, and in the '30s she teamed up with eugenicist Ernst Rüdin, one of Adolf Hitler's top promoters of sterilization.

Humanist, college professor, and progressive philosopher John Dewey is known as "the father of American education," and is revered still today. He led the National Education Association down the path toward socialism starting in the 1930s and beyond, particularly after travelling to Russia and returning inspired by their education approach based on collectivism.

In the 1940s and '50s, atheist, bisexual, and pedophile Alfred Kinsey was a biologist who pioneered perversion through Indiana University, and his twisted "research" still influences many in education and government today. Considered by some to be the "father of the sexual revolution," few have attempted to investigate how he came up with his findings on the sexuality of minors and very young children.

Sanger promoted adultery and the sexual liberation of women. Dewey promoted social studies and the removal of God in education. Kinsey promoted and justified animalistic, unrestrained expressions of sex regardless of age or environment. And these are just three people

---

27   Francis A. Schaeffer and C. Everett Koop, *Whatever Happened to the Human Race*, *The Complete Works of Francis A. Schaeffer, A Christian Worldview*, Vol. 5 (Winchester, Il: Crossway, 1982), 283.

who literally helped drive the morality and worldview of Americans into the gutter.

By the early 1960s, Americans' opinions had been influenced to begin accepting ideas about sex that our great-grandparents would have found disgraceful and embarrassing. Bible reading and voluntary prayer were taken out of schools, and attitudes toward rock and roll, drugs, and of course, sex, radically shifted, which led to the famous Woodstock Music Festival. They say it was about "love, peace, and music," but it was open rebellion against God, authority, and societal norms.

It was only natural for liberals to adapt to the changing culture while conservatives generally remained true to traditional ideas of education, entertainment, and government. It's interesting to note that prior to the '60s, the word "gay" was not used to describe homosexuals. If not for the religious commitment of atheists, Democrats, progressives, and socialists, do you think the acceptance of homosexuality would be on the fast track it's on today? *That* is the effect of liberalism. As recently as 2012, same-sex marriage was illegal in thirty-two states and an over-whelming majority of Americans voted to defend marriage between one man and one woman.

Pastor Gary Gilley of Southern View Chapel in Illinois wrote a detailed article on homosexuality, "The Most Pressing Issue of Our Time," stating the LGBT community now demands respect and full acceptance of their behavior, and Christians who believe in God's Word as their foundation and final authority are in a most difficult place.

Gilley accurately writes about the fact that homosexuality has evolved from an act or behavior to: (1) a thing in itself, classified as a disorder needing treatment for healing/change, then (2) to an orientation, a political movement, and finally, (3) to identity and, thus, a "right."

> If we live in obedience to written revelation [Scripture], we cannot accept homosexual behavior as anything less than immorality. Yet, if we speak against the homosexual lifestyle, we are accused of hatred, judgmentalism and homophobia.

> Add to this the fact that most Christians have never

seriously examined the biblical teachings on homosexuality and issues are now arising that have rarely been seriously debated throughout church history, then we can readily see why the faithful children of God are being squeezed. They find themselves between the immovable Word of God and its clear teachings on all forms of immorality, including homosexuality – and the changing Western culture, which now sees homosexuality as perfectly acceptable and normal, as it does most other forms of immorality. Christians are quickly becoming marginalized.[28]

Why is it important to resist the "anything goes" religion of the Left?

Sexual sin hurts other people as well as ourselves, and sin in any form is against a holy God and His moral law. The homosexual lifestyle is not an unforgivable sin nor is it the worst of sins. Idolatry, lying, stealing, lust, coveting, and taking God's name in vain are all sins, but adultery, abortion, pornography, homosexuality, pedophilia, and rape are very serious sins in God's eyes, as these sexual sins have horrible, destructive consequences.

And as we know from the countless thousands of *former* homosexuals, it is very much possible to repent and be set free from the chains of this sin. So why do we spend so much time discussing it? Because the Left uses the LGBTQ movement as a battering ram to force change and drive out Christianity and its positive influence from the public square in order to control society.

None of us are without sin and we all need a Savior. Sin is the very thing that separates us from our Creator, and the reason Jesus Christ suffered and died.

> *It is a trustworthy statement, deserving full acceptance, that Christ Jesus came into the world to save sinners, among whom I am foremost of all. Yet for this reason I found mercy, so that in me as the foremost, Jesus Christ might demonstrate His perfect patience as an example for those who would believe in Him for eternal life.* (1 Timothy 1:15-16)

---

28 Gary Gilley, "Homosexuality, The Most Pressing Issue of Our Times," (Volume 21, Issue 6, Nov/Dec 2015) http://tottministries.org/homosexuality-the-most-pressing-issue-of-our-times/

We must address the lies and promote truth, biblical morality, religious freedom, and conservativism in our society, but this won't come without a price.

Again, Jesus warned His followers that if the world hates us, remember they hated Him first (John 15:18). This does not change or even redirect our mission and purpose on this earth.

Pastor Gary Gilley put it this way:

> "The world has changed so rapidly that many of us are getting whiplash. The church has been put in a unique and difficult position by standing for the truth which has been thoroughly rejected by the majority. But in darkness, light shines best. May the church not cave to the demands of the many but honor the Lord who has set them free from the bondage of darkness."

We can honor the Lord by living for Him even though immorality is advancing. Speaking the truth in love often involves confrontation and exposing the works of darkness. Authentic faith demands our obedience, that we not stay silent about evil agendas, and that we keep on believing in the midst of fierce opposition.

One very important key to momentum, and oftentimes, to victory, is understanding the fact that influence changes everything. We're heading in one direction or the other as a church and nation; there is no neutral ground in the spiritual realm or in this natural, physical realm. So what way are we headed?

Chapter 6

Fighting for Religious Freedom

But whenever a person turns to the Lord, the veil is taken away. Now the Lord is the Spirit, and where the Spirit of the Lord is, there is liberty. (2 Corinthians 3:16-17)

"We need to stand up now. It's me today, but it could be you tomorrow. When our children ask us why we don't have a free America anymore, we'll have to say we did nothing. Civil liberties travel together." – Barronelle Stutzman

At the 2017 National Prayer Breakfast, one of the things President Donald Trump promised is that he would "get rid of and totally destroy the Johnson Amendment." Out of necessity, religious freedom has become a hot topic in America. In light of recent court cases in which the livelihood of Christian business owners has been ruined and their lives threatened, religious freedom is not faring too well.

In the last year, hundreds of people have written about the Johnson Amendment, but before June of 2016, it was rarely mentioned. I had written about it in detail in my book *The Cost of Our Silence*, in a chapter called "The Separation of Christianity and State." I shared a book excerpt that quickly became the most popular blog on my website.

Then-candidate Donald Trump brought up the Johnson Amendment while he was campaigning and said it should be repealed. I'm glad he did, not just because I believe the law is unconstitutional, but because people began searching the Internet using terms such as "the Johnson law," "Lyndon Johnson Amendment," "1954 Johnson bill," and "The Johnson Amendment."

The reason I was thrilled is that the next day, I happened to check my website traffic and there was an incredible spike in hits, especially those referred by Google. At that time, I typed in "The Johnson Amendment" and I was surprised to see my website come up in the top five or ten search results, depending on the search engine. So thank you, Donald Trump, for the exposure and some unexpected book sales!

It's eye opening if you think about how this unchallenged law has been on the books since 1954, a law that limits what religious leaders can say through threat of fine or taxation. Because there were conservative nonprofit groups speaking out against his run for reelection in the Texas senate, Johnson slipped his amendment into a tax code overhaul bill being debated at the time.

The amendment created a change in the U.S. tax code, which prohibited tax-exempt organizations from endorsing or opposing political candidates or from making campaign contributions to specific candidates. Johnson got away with it. The law allegedly threatens churches and other nonprofit organizations with the possibility of losing their 501(c) tax status. The Left has used it to bully Christian pastors into silence, but church leaders must understand the First Amendment freedoms they still have.

The ACLU and other liberal groups have used the Johnson Amendment as a boogeyman to instill fear into churches and nonprofits. The Secular Coalition for America, the ACLU, and Americans United for Separation of Church and State are among groups opposing any change to the law. It's interesting to note one of the groups that came against Lyndon Johnson in 1954 stated that he was too soft on communism, and ACLU founder, Roger Baldwin, was an open supporter of communism.

Some have gone so far as to refer to the Johnson Amendment as a "Christian Gag Rule." It is true, many church leaders have been gagged, but they put the gag on themselves. Let me explain. I hope Congress does repeal the law, but I also don't believe it prevents church leaders from talking about politics. Through the years, too many religious leaders have willingly decided to avoid talking about *anything* controversial – including political and social issues.

The Left has enjoyed the church's silence on these moral issues. Politics affect legislation and implementation of laws, many of which affect the entire nation. It is crucial that religious leaders lead. These important issues must be addressed regardless of government threat.

It is true and well documented that under the Obama administration the IRS widely discriminated against conservative and Christian groups, especially leading up to President Obama's reelection. Many were buried in red tape while others were denied their nonprofit status for years while liberal groups coasted through the application process. After their corruption was exposed a few years later, the IRS barely got a slap on the wrist and the public had long moved on. The profiling by the IRS also extended to Christian and Jewish charities.

Franklin Graham had faced IRS investigations for his two organizations, Samaritan's Purse and the Billy Graham Evangelistic Association (BGEA). Prior to the elections back in the fall of 2012, BGEA ran national ads in papers encouraging citizens to vote their biblical values, specifically mentioning marriage and Israel. Exactly one month after the elections, both of Graham's organizations were notified by the IRS they would be audited.

After evidence came in from across the country of other groups being discriminated against, and Franklin Graham learned in 2013 the IRS admitted that "it had targeted not-for-profit organizations," he called it "chilling." In a letter to President Obama requesting immediate action be taken, Graham stated:

> "Unfortunately, while these audits not only wasted tax-
> payer money, they wasted money contributed by donors for
> ministry purposes as we had to spend precious resources
> servicing IRS agents in our offices. I am bringing this
> to your attention because I believe that someone in the
> administration was targeting and attempting to intimidate
> us. This is morally wrong and unethical – indeed some
> would call it 'un-American.'"[29]

---

29   Franklin Graham, "Document: Graham Writes Obama About IRS Profiling," CNN, May

Let's be crystal clear. Even if Donald Trump and the Republican-controlled Congress decide not to *fully* repeal the Johnson Amendment for whatever reason, pastors, church leaders, and nonprofits can still speak out about candidates, politics, government, Planned Parenthood corruption, the vital subject of protecting life in the womb, natural marriage, or anything else!

Basically, the current law limits only two things: churches and non-profits cannot endorse a candidate, and they cannot donate to or raise money for a candidate from the church pulpit.

Nonprofit organizations including churches can hand out or send out voter guides on the issues and even hold voter registration drives at church. As for informing Christian citizens, churches at this very moment have the right, privilege, and responsibility to preach what Scripture teaches about the brokenness of sin and pornography, and the anguish of abortion. Churches must encourage healthy marriages, purity, and abstinence, and expose the lies of homosexuality and transgenderism.

Much ground has been given up and millions of church-going believers of all denominations have followed the lead of their pastor, priest, or reverend who decided years ago to be silent. The best-selling book of all time still has the answers. All the information and wisdom we need regarding life, salvation, morality, and how to live is within the Bible's pages.

Jesus told Christians to be the salt of the earth, so one question is, are we preserving America? Salt is a dietary mineral used to flavor and preserve food, and it is needed by most every creature on the planet. America needs Christianity in order to become strong again. It is unhealthy and even dangerous to not have enough salt intake because it regulates the water content in our bodies. So yes, salt provides a healthy balance, adds flavor, and is a preservative.

Unfortunately, what we have seen is a dramatic lack of salt and light in our culture. I've also traveled enough to have been in services at hundreds of churches across the country and the disappointing conclusion is that we have watered down the Word of God, and have

---

14, 2013, *www.cnn.com/ interactive/2013/05/politics/irs-graham-letter/.*

accepted a lukewarm, country-club Christianity. (To the remnant, stay strong, friends!)

Regardless of what happens with the Johnson Amendment, we must as the church get back to the stable underpinnings of scriptural truth and have the loving boldness to confront sin, whether it be in the culture or within the church. When we lift up the name of Jesus as the final answer and ultimate authority, we can trust Him with the results, that He will draw people to saving grace.

A day before President Trump made his remarks at the 2017 prayer breakfast in Washington, a bill was introduced in Congress that was referred to as a fix to the Johnson Amendment and would allow a church or nonprofit to freely discuss politics with few limitations.

The language in the newly introduced Free Speech Fairness Act proposes to "allow charitable organizations to make statements relating to political campaigns if such statements are made in the ordinary course of carrying out its tax-exempt purpose." The act was introduced in the House by a Southern Baptist pastor, a Catholic, and a co-chair of the Congressional Prayer Caucus. Though not perfect, this is a step in the right direction.

I am not suggesting pastors and religious leaders endorse candidates. Christian citizens should know the Bible, be informed, and *already* know where each candidate stands, but under the Constitution, pastors should be allowed to make endorsements. That being said, they wouldn't have to *if* they had already been preaching the whole counsel of God and speaking about the most pressing issues of the day including politics.

One of those issues impossible to ignore because it is already being used to infringe upon our religious freedoms is the use of non-discrimination laws. I realize that so many acronyms are being thrown around today that it's very hard to keep up, but I recently read about another new one: SOGI. These "Sexual Orientation and Gender Identity" laws create new protected classes of people based on behavior and inclination, not biological realities of race and sex.

Liberal and progressive activists are pressuring state and federal governments to expand protections under existing civil rights laws. Their aim is to bar discrimination in the areas of employment, housing, and public accommodations. We've already seen how these kinds of so-called protections affect religious freedom, and these efforts must be discouraged and resisted.

Peter Sprigg, senior fellow for policy studies at the Family Research Council, laid out in extensive detail a dozen reasons why anyone who believes in freedom should oppose these laws. Without listing the compelling, detailed arguments for each of the following, here they are:

Sexual orientation and gender identity are unlike most other characteristics protected in civil rights laws.

- SOGI laws increase government interference in the free market.

- SOGI laws would mandate the employment of homosexual and transgendered persons in inappropriate occupations.

- SOGI laws force some businesses to violate their moral and religious convictions.

- Religious exemptions do not adequately protect people of faith.

- Gender identity laws undermine the rights of businesses to set dress and grooming standards.

- Gender identity laws would violate the privacy of others.

- SOGI laws can lead to costly lawsuits against businesses.

- SOGI laws are unnecessary.

- Sexual orientation laws pave the way for legalization of counterfeit same-sex "marriage."

- SOGI laws "legislate morality" – the "morality" of the sexual revolution.

- SOGI laws prepare the way for reverse discrimination.[30]

Christians have been colliding with the redefinition of truth, the most

---

30 Peter Sprigg, "Sexual Orientation and Gender Identity (SOGI) Laws: A Threat to Free Markets and Freedom of Conscience and Religion," Family Research Council, *www.frc. org/issuebrief/sexual-orientation-and-gender-identity-sogi-laws-a-threat-to-free-markets-and-freedom-of-conscience-and-religion.*

blatant being creation and gender identity. Sexual freedom, found nowhere in the U.S. Constitution, is in the process of overthrowing religious freedom which is, in fact, guaranteed in the Constitution. We are not denying anyone's lifestyle, but the Left aims to deny our rights to live according to our faith.

It is not good enough for them to simply disagree with our biblical worldview; they now wish to conform public opinion to their claim that Christianity is false. If this weren't enough, they insist we are the discriminators, and the fact we can even believe something like the Bible supposedly proves we are full of hate.

People much more knowledgeable than me have pointed to a lack of evidence that SOGI laws are even needed. Where are all the alleged cases of discrimination? You'd think the media would be all over each and every case, but regardless, the Left has fabricated a need. Have you heard about cases in which individuals from the LGBTQ community have been turned away by a major employer, hotel chain, or restaurant?

I am not suggesting there is no bullying or discrimination toward those who identify as LGBTQ, and I am certainly not denying that innocent people have been abused and even murdered. But let's get this straight once and for all: it is not Bible-believing, practicing Christians who are doing the bullying, discriminating, and killing. Some may claim they are Christian, but by their actions they clearly are not.

And since there are always exceptions and extremists in every people group or religion, please do not lump us all together. You will not convince me or those who know the truth and are informed, that we are bigoted, intolerant, irrational, and hateful just because we believe the Holy Bible and are trying to live a life pleasing to God. Please go sell that somewhere else; your accusations are becoming tedious.

Ryan Anderson from the Heritage Foundation came out with an exhaustive report on this new hot topic of SOGI policies and religious liberty. I agree with him that at their core, "SOGI laws are not about the freedom of LGBT people to engage in certain actions, but about coercing and penalizing people who in good conscience cannot endorse those actions."[31]

31   Ryan T. Anderson, "How to Think about Sexual Orientation and Gender Identity Policies and Religious Freedom," Heritage Foundation, February 13, 2017,

When five progressive Supreme Court judges ignored the will of over 51 million Americans in more than thirty states (those were just the ones who voted!) by ruling against protecting marriage between one man and one woman, it was clear we had arrived at a historic moment – one that many of us predicted was coming but hesitated to admit.

Some Christians are concerned that more cases will be decided and laws will be passed that could be used against us, perhaps forcing us into a position of choosing whether to disobey God and our conscience or disobey an immoral law.

One obvious example of a person who was caught in the middle of this debate is Kentucky Clerk Kim Davis in 2015. She spent six days in jail for refusing to issue marriage licenses to homosexuals. Citing religious objections and matters of conscience, and that her new job duties conflicted with God's moral law, Davis stated, "To issue a marriage license which conflicts with God's definition of marriage, with my name affixed to the certificate, would violate my conscience."

Davis, a relatively new Christian at the time, was elected to her position as Rowan County Clerk and was sworn in before the Supreme Court ruled in favor of same-sex marriage, and also at a time when *75 percent* of Kentucky citizens supported natural marriage between one man and one woman. But that didn't matter to the activists and agitators.

Here's a crucial takeaway from that case: a citizen was imprisoned – in America – for exercising her Christian faith and freedom of conscience. Until the past decade, our nation has always protected religious freedom for Christians and non-Christians alike. That time is passing quickly.

One pastor said that encouraging homosexual behavior is "participating in someone's destruction," and by doing her government job, Kim Davis would have blessed (with her authority and signature) a union leading to eternal and possible physical destruction.

Here are some points to consider on the topic of Christians and civil disobedience:

- Christians should resist a government that commands

---

www.heritage.org/marriage-and-family/report/
how-think-about-sexual-orientation-and-gender-identity-sogi-policies-and.

or compels evil and should work nonviolently within the laws of the land to change a government that permits evil.

- Civil disobedience is permitted when the government's laws or commands are in direct violation of God's laws and commands.

- If a Christian disobeys an evil government, unless he can flee from the government, he should accept that government's punishment (consequences) for his actions.

- Christians are certainly permitted to work to install new government leaders within the laws that have been established.[32]

It must be noted that being faithful to God and biblical standards does not exempt anyone from civil punishment no matter how righteous they deem their cause. As an example, let's remember a much more famous example of a man who believed that a just human law must square with the law of God. Dr. Martin Luther King Jr. expressed his thoughts on the matter when he stated, "One has not only a legal but a moral responsibility to obey just laws. Conversely, one has a moral responsibility to disobey unjust laws. I agree with St. Augustine that 'an unjust law is no law at all.' . . . An unjust law is a code that is out of harmony with the moral law . . . [and] is a human law that is not rooted in eternal law and natural law."

This quote is from a letter King wrote in the Birmingham city jail in 1963 when he was arrested for civil disobedience. He directed the letter to fellow clergymen who believed King should have waited for the racial equality issue to be resolved by the courts. Waiting, of course, is always an option. This is a biblical concept, but so is the idea of actively waiting, by taking steps of faith while asking God for further direction.

In September 2016, the U.S. Commission on Civil Rights released its report on religious freedom and non-discrimination. The chair of the commission, Martin Castro, wrote the report, which included this alarming statement: "The phrases 'religious liberty' and 'religious

---

32   GotQuestions.org, "When is civil disobedience allowed for a Christian?" *www.gotques-tions.org/civil-disobedience.html.*

freedom' will stand for nothing except hypocrisy so long as they remain code words for discrimination, intolerance, racism, sexism, homophobia, Islamophobia, Christian supremacy, or any form of intolerance."[33]

Do you still think there is middle ground and we can just get along, coexist, or compromise? We can no longer take our first freedom for granted. Nor should we take truth for granted.

FINAL THOUGHTS

Thomas Jefferson and many others warned against tyranny in America if a decision is rendered that is *not* born out of the will of the people through the political process and their elected representatives. Our founders knew the importance and power of fair elections. To naively say something is the law of the land because the court decided it is to surrender to judicial tyranny.

Those who established this land and fought the Revolutionary War to gain our independence believed the church had a right and responsibility to influence society for good. They may never have imagined government could be so empowered as to censor Christians and restrict their expressions of genuine faith.

Since many of our founders and earliest American patriots gained theological training at universities (the earliest universities taught the Bible and prepared men for ministry), many of them became pastors. They most likely would not comprehend today's anti-Christian system of academia and government.

Writing for *The Stream*, Deacon Keith Fournier stated:

> We have accepted the secular supremacist spin used to interpret our founding documents by progressives like Harvard Professor Mark Tushnet, who sees orthodox Christians as the moral equivalent of the defeated Nazis and Japanese – discredited losers who must be crushed without mercy or respite. It is people with views like Tushnet's who end up on our nation's highest courts. And we let them beat us down. We numbly accept the notion

---

33   Mark A. Kellner, "'Religious Freedom,' 'Liberty,' Just 'Code Words' for Intolerance, U.S. Civil Rights chairman says," Washington Times, September 8, 2016, *www.washingtontimes. com/news/2016/sep/8/religious-freedom-religious-liberty-just-code-word/.*

that a bloated agency of the federal government, drunk
with free-flowing power, is the arbiter of interpreting
my religious freedoms and yours. That was not what our
nation's founders intended.[34]

The bottom line for true believers is obedience to what the Bible teaches,
which includes loving others while preaching God's Word to a dying
world. It used to be commonplace for pastors to preach about political issues and candidates. These were actually referred to as "election
sermons." Moreover, some Christians believe we should eliminate all
tax-exempt statuses on churches because they question whether it is
biblical. After all, regarding the temple tax in Israel, Jesus once said,
*Render to Caesar the things that are Caesar's; and to God the things that
are God's* (Matthew 22:21).

Nothing, and I emphasize, nothing should hinder us from speaking about the truth and the gospel of Jesus Christ, and obeying the call
of God to advance His kingdom in order to save others from eternal
damnation. For those of us who believe the Bible and are striving to
please God rather than man, we need to encourage our pastors and
leaders as we ask ourselves a couple of questions:

> Are we prepared to live in these last days and share the gos-
> pel knowing that expressions of our faith in public will be
> increasingly hated and threatened?

> Are we willing to sacrifice comfort, reputation, and secu-
> rity in this world for our Lord, Savior, and King as well as
> for eternal rewards?

We have been blessed with incredible freedoms in America – freedoms
many other nations and peoples only dream about. But if we have
accepted the forgiveness of God and have trusted in Christ alone to save
us, then our true freedom comes not from government or country, but
from having our chains of sin broken forever. Because, as Jesus once
said, *So if the Son makes you free, you will be free indeed* (John 8:36).

Free and faithful witnesses should be living according to the Bible
and impacting others. But sadly, the remnant of disciples – those who

---

34   Deacon Keith Fournier, "Trump is Right: Repeal the Johnson Amendment that Muzzles
     Pastors," July 20, 2016, *stream.org/trump-right-repeal-johnson-amendment-muzzles-pastors/*.

are loving, discerning, practicing Christians – understand the world is changing and our country is changing, and since our country is changing, our culture is changing. But sadly, since our culture is changing (for the worse), the church is changing as a result. "Conforming" might be a better word. It should be the other way around, but moral relativism is winning because we are close to surrendering the truth war.

Chapter 7

Relativism in the Church

For by Him all things were created, both in the heavens and on earth, visible and invisible, whether thrones or dominions or rulers or authorities – all things have been created through Him and for Him. He is before all things, and in Him all things hold together. (Colossians 1:16-17)

"The devil's alternative credo often has a few carefully chosen elements of truth in the mix – but always diluted and thoroughly blended with falsehoods, contradictions, misinterpretations, distortions, and every other imaginable perversion of reality. Add it all up and the bottom line is a big lie." – John MacArthur

A person's worldview indicates what he or she believes about truth and moral absolutes. It provides the lens through which we see all things, and how we treat people and make important decisions. The Bible teaches that our hope in Christ is *an anchor of the soul* (Hebrews 6:19) and our worldview is the linchpin on which our faith and our lives are based.

The fight for religious freedom is part of this war on truth and, unfortunately, the church has given up much ground. The Left knows exactly what they believe, but we often struggle with defining our Christian worldview. Why? What do we believe regarding the deity of Christ? This starting point affects everything.

> *But of the Son He says, "Your throne, O God, is forever and ever, And the righteous scepter is the scepter of His kingdom."* (Hebrews 1:8)

Many believers agree Jesus is God forever, but prefer focusing on the here and now. And this is part of our problem as Christians. Our indifference has allowed godlessness and relativism to advance. We pursue either the things of God or the things of man.

Barna Research surveyed Americans last year on moral absolutes and found only 35 percent of people believe moral truth is absolute. Barna concluded that "Christian morality is being ushered out of American social structures and off the cultural mainstage," and this results in the broader culture trying to fill the void.

A few key findings include:

- Just 59% of practicing Christians believe moral truth is absolute.

- Seventy-six percent (76%) of Christians agree that the best way to "find yourself" is by looking within yourself. (91% of the general public agrees.)

- Forty percent (40%) of practicing Christians agree that "any kind of sexual expression between two consenting adults is acceptable." (69% of Americans)

- Sixty-seven percent (67%) of Christians agree that the "highest goal of life is to enjoy it as much as possible." (84% of people overall)[35]

This further proves the degree to which Americans pledge allegiance to the "morality of self-fulfillment," a new moral code that has all but replaced Christianity as the culture's moral norm. The greatest good is "finding yourself" and living life in pursuit of pleasure. This is not what the Bible teaches and yet two-thirds of Christians are living for today rather than seeking first the kingdom of God and His righteousness (Matthew 6:33).

Can you see why we're in trouble? Most Christians do say they

---

35   Barna Research, "The End of Absolutes: America's New Moral Code," May 25, 2016, *www. barna.com/research/ the-end-of-absolutes-americas-new-moral-code/.*

are concerned about immorality in America, but the church has not equipped them to deal with the onslaught of evil and the growing tide of secularism. Since so many Christians are on a happiness quest instead of seeking the truth, why should the world be any different?

No wonder people are confused about the very nature and origins of humanity. It is vital that we not be obtuse about our biblical worldview and the truth. Many Americans profess to be saved and yet, these same folks often say there are many ways to heaven, the meaning of sin has changed, or Jesus is not God.

Tragically, even today's church appears confused about exactly what the Bible teaches, but God is not the author of confusion (1 Corinthians 14:33). Americans generally have more than one Bible in their comfortable homes, but prefer not to study God's Word because it would interfere with how they want to live.

Religion and culture expert Dr. Alex McFarland declares Jesus is the fact on whom all other facts rest. In the context of creation and the deity of Jesus Christ, he stated:

> A powerful Being initiated a beginning and intentionally caused the world around us. The cosmos has purpose and is not all that there is. If the subject matter of John 1 corresponds to reality (and the case for the Bible's absolute trustworthiness is compelling), then atheism, secularism, moral relativism, and politically correct pluralism are all false. God is real, life has purpose, and yes, humans are accountable.
>
> Therefore, if Jesus did indeed come from heaven, is divine, and shows us the way to God, everything changes. A culture that has tethered itself to godlessness is investing itself in that which is false.[36]

I'll let you decide whether America as a whole is tethered to Christ or to something else. Simply put, moral *absolutism* emerges from a theistic worldview, whereas moral relativism is based on an atheistic worldview

---

36   Alex McFarland, "Jesus: The Fact On Whom All Other Facts Rest," December 20, 2016, *alexmcfarland.com/ media/jesus-the-fact-on-whom-all-other-facts-rest/*.

and holds the idea that conflicting beliefs can be true. (What is moral for me may be immoral for you, etc.)

The secular progressive agenda is based upon the presumption that there is no God, and while some liberals may claim to believe in a god, they generally disbelieve the Bible and certainly do not think there is only one true God. Therefore, they cannot possibly accept Jesus for who He is or what He taught.

Since they are the ones reshaping our culture by hammering away to their heart's desires, we should pay attention to who they are, what they say, and what ideas they are promoting. The Left has worked nonstop to change America in part by chipping away at its Christian foundation and infiltrating these seven areas: government, arts and entertainment, education, media, business, religion, and the family.

This is why I spend so much time focusing on the church and what Christians believe and do. I'm not saying we aren't concerned about immorality, I'm saying it doesn't bother us as much as it used to or we'd be living much differently. And if we did, America would be a better country.

We like the idea of being religious and appearing righteous without having to fully live out the requirements in the Bible. We enjoy our public monuments, but we're not big fans of the Ten Commandments. After all, holiness and sanctification are hard work. It is much more convenient to do good deeds, plus it helps us feel better about ourselves.

As Christians, are we really that different from average Americans who believe they are good people? Research also indicates the sad reality that only about half of professing evangelical Christians think abortion and sex outside of traditional marriage are sins.

Hard to believe? Let's look at some related findings by LifeWay Research in a survey of Americans on "The State of Theology." From what we are learning, there should be deep concern about the biblical illiteracy of Christians in all denominations.

In his *BreakPoint* commentary on the subject, Eric Metaxas summed it up this way:

> Seventy percent of Americans agree there's only one true
> God—one in essence, three in person: Father, Son, and

Holy Spirit. Yet almost the same number believe God accepts the worship of all other religions, even those that deny the Trinity or worship other deities.

Sixty-one percent correctly say Jesus is both human and divine, but half think that He's also "the first and greatest being created by God," rather than existing eternally, as Scripture and the ancient creeds of the faith teach.

More bizarre contradictions emerged: Over sixty percent of Americans say that God, Who cannot err, is the Author of the Bible. Yet fewer than half are willing to affirm that the Bible God wrote is "one hundred percent accurate in all it teaches." . . . Perhaps most oddly, half of Americans believe that only those who accept Jesus will be saved, yet sixty percent also say everyone will eventually make it to Heaven.[37]

Confused? Welcome to American Christianity!

People's opinions about the Bible can be surprising, and we're talking about people who sit in the pews and soft seats every weekend. Aside from the solid remnant of believers, some churches operate more like a social club or corporation rather than a hospital for sinners or rescue ship for those spiritually drowning.

Christianity has also become a bit confusing to a watching world. What people seem to be following is humanism, moral relativism, New Age, Universalism, their own desires, or a religion of works, none of which can be justified or defended with Scripture. The evangelical and Protestant Church was compromised many decades ago and obviously weakened. One result is there are countless souls sitting in our churches who are not even saved or don't really believe the doctrine of the church they attend.

It is imperative that Bible-believing Christians evangelize as many as possible – within our churches – because many have been deceived among us. Moreover, outside church walls across the country, the numbers of atheists, gnostics, New Agers, as well as other religions are

---

37   Eric Metaxas, "Americans Fail Theology 101," Breakpoint Commentary, October 6, 2016, *www.breakpoint.org/ 2016/10/americans-fail-theology-101/.*

growing, particularly among young people. The Left and those who are hostile toward Christianity are "evangelizing" our culture as well as our churches. Which side is making more converts?

Regarding historic, fundamental Christian teachings, and America's departure from the faith , the survey also shows that both unbelievers and evangelicals don't really understand the concept of doctrine itself. Moreover, decades ago, we thought bigger churches were part of the solution, but this has only watered down the Word of God even more. We have a whole new generation of immature believers who do not know Scripture well, let alone how to give an answer (1 Peter 3:15) as to why they believe what they believe.

Modern megachurches have also encouraged cotton-candy Christianity and "your best life now" faith. (If we can live our best lives now on this earth, then why should we think about heaven and eternity?) With growing churches and more building programs, numbers may be increasing at larger churches, but Christian maturity and disciple-ship is suffering. I've seen it. The bigger the church, the more difficult it is to follow up with people individually and promote accountability. This is quite common in America. We have lost some of our focus on the gospel, sin, making disciples, preaching repentance, prophecy, and building stronger believers.

With more churches in the U.S. than convenience stores, gas stations, and motels combined, (over 300,000), the problem in America is not that we have too few churches, and it's not that we have too few members. The problem is that we have too few disciples and too many pretenders "professing" Christianity.

Another survey suggests only 3 percent of those claiming some form of the Christian religion "have surrendered control of their life to God, submitted to His will for their life, and devoted themselves to loving and serving God and other people." Three percent. If you have not fully surrendered to the Lord, please put this book down and spend as much time in prayer with the Father as you need to. Study the Bible. You will not be disappointed.

If you are uncertain about your faith, ask the Lord for help. I've heard folks refer to unbelievers or non-Christians optimistically as "pre-Christians." I like that, because if we really love people, we sincerely want them to be saved and to turn from their wicked ways and trust Jesus. The God of hope can reach anybody.

We've all heard people demand of Christians more respect, tolerance, and acceptance. We hear people argue for peace and coexistence as they point to other religions or sexual behaviors. They are indirectly suggesting the Bible is not true and Christianity is just another path. We've also heard people, including Oprah, ask, "How can there be only one way to God?"

Doesn't God want us to be happy? It's one excuse after another not to trust in Jesus Christ.

> *But a natural man does not accept the things of the Spirit of*
> *God, for they are foolishness to him; and he cannot under-*
> *stand them, because they are spiritually appraised. Because*
> *the foolishness of God is wiser than men, and the weakness*
> *of God is stronger than men.* (1 Corinthians 2:14; 1:25)

We live in such touchy-feely, emotion-driven times that it is easy to understand why people are avoiding hard facts and absolutes. Many in our culture overemphasize tolerance, empathy, and compassion, and esteem these as the highest of values. To be clear, these are not bad things, but why should they be higher in value than truth and whether God exists?

Our feelings change and shift with moods, circumstances, and relationships. Should our feelings be the final arbiter of truth? There must be objective evidence apart from our personal experience, something outside ourselves that determines what is true, or we're in a lot of trouble.

People place feelings, fads, philosophies, or other religions alongside Christianity as if to imply that all spiritual paths are valid – except, of course, the Christian faith. To them, religious freedom doesn't apply to Christians. By the way, have you heard many people criticize Islam for being too "exclusive" or for being intolerant? I didn't think so.

Why do folks generally shy away from God and an honest pursuit of truth? Because they would rather not hear the real answers. Asking whether or not the Bible is true and getting people to think is always a great starting point. The problem is if they acknowledge it's true, then they'd have to live differently.

Natasha Crain contributes to Cross Examined Ministry, an outstanding resource to equip believers, and wrote a fascinating article last year, "An Open Letter to an Atheist." She made many excellent points and asked good questions such as:

> What if there are eternal consequences for what you believe?

> Would it be more loving for Christians to tell others about that [heaven and hell], or to stay silent in the fear that the truth might bother you?

> Is the message that Jesus is the only way to God frightening to you? If so, I encourage you to really dig deep and understand why it would be frightening to you if there was really just one objective truth.[38]

Remember discussing the armor of God and spiritual warfare? The Bible has much to say about what Christians can do to prepare for Enemy attacks, and to take more of a proactive position rather than a defensive one. The Left in America wants the Judeo-Christian God obliterated. They and the "useful idiots" that follow them are at war with Christians and our value system, traditional Americans, natural law, six thousand years of world history, as well as reasonable moral boundaries.

When moral relativism negatively affects the moral relativist, however, they cry foul, which reveals a convenient double standard. Here are a few examples: when someone lies to, cheats on, physically harms, steals from, or commits a crime against God deniers, they demand justice and the perpetrator punished to the full extent of the law. But what moral law are they referring to?

If you are against immigration laws and believe anyone should be allowed to come into an American town or city, it may not always end well. If you defend city governments who are breaking federal immigration law, and if you support sanctuary cities for illegal or criminal

---

38   CrossExamined.org Apologetics Ministry, *crossexamined.org/*.

aliens, why do you change your tune if a violent act is carried out against you or someone you love?

Writing about this topic for Christian Apologetics and Research Ministry (CARM), Robin Schumacher stated that moral relativists have a major problem in that they cannot answer this simple question: is there anything wrong with an action and, if so, why? Schumacher writes:

> "In contrast to the moral relativist whose worldview is secular humanism, the Christian worldview provides a solid standard and authority that can be confidently referenced and followed. The Creator God, who has revealed Himself in His Word, is both the standard and authority for morals. From God's nature comes pure good that serves as the straight line by which all crooked lines can be corrected."[39]

The godless thought process is one that goes along with the idea of a "post-truth" culture, and one huge problem in the church may be too many Christians cannot defend the faith against moral relativistic thinking. It's no wonder we become defensive at the slightest accusation, which is a major tactic of the Left.

The more aggressively something is marketed, even if it was at one time unthinkable, the less likely we are to resist. I'm not sure what the next trend or sin of choice will be, but if our nation continues down this road where truth is no longer an objective reality, there's no telling where we'll end up. One thing is certain – it won't be good.

Christians have a secure, unchanging foundation on which to base our truth claims and, on this stable ground, we can trust that God is the eternal and ultimate authority, not man. Thankfully, objective truth exists because we have His Word and we will need to rely on His promises and truth more than ever in the coming days.

Informed Christians are not surprised by cultural shifts, forgotten history, and surveys, but it is understandable that many of us are deeply disappointed in the direction of the church and our country. Thankfully, we trust in an unshakable God, we know He is still working, and we can be confident that truth never changes. God will do what He said He is going to do.

---

39   Robin Schumacher, "What Is Moral Relativism?"C.A.R.M. (no date), *carm.org/moral-relativism*.

Chapter 8

Israel's True Prophetic History

Remember the former things long past, for I am God, and there is no other; I am God, and there is no one like Me, declaring the end from the beginning, and from ancient times things which have not been done, saying, 'My purpose will be established, and I will accomplish all My good pleasure.' (Isaiah 46:9-10)

"The truth is incontrovertible. Malice may attack it. Ignorance may deride it, but in the end, there it is."
– Winston Churchill

True history might be covered-up or rewritten, but it can never be erased. The year 2017 marks the fiftieth anniversary of the reunification of Jerusalem. Next year is the seventieth anniversary of Israel becoming a state (1948). No matter what happens with our religious freedoms or because of world governments, no matter what man does, no matter what catastrophic events take place, and no matter what this world can throw at us, God is still sovereign over all people, events, and things. As we know from Scripture, this includes the nation of Israel.

We are not on earth for ourselves but for God's purposes. As born-again Christians, we are called to be His ambassadors and messengers. God's faithfulness throughout the Bible encourages us because we know we can trust that He will make good on the remaining prophecies regarding Israel, the return of Christ, and the end times. If God says something will happen, it will. He spoke through the prophet Zechariah saying, *Thus says the LORD, 'I will return to Zion and will dwell in the midst of Jerusalem. Then Jerusalem will be called the City of Truth, and the mountain of the LORD of hosts will be called the Holy Mountain'* (Zechariah 8:3).

Remember Jesus said that His words will remain forever? We would be wise to keep in step with the Holy Spirit and pay attention to the signs of the times. World leaders are scheming and nations are preparing for war. The Enemy is advancing and the stage is being set for the Antichrist. Where does America come into play in the last days and how much depends on our support for Israel?

> *It will come about in that day that I will make Jerusalem a heavy stone for all the peoples; all who lift it will be severely injured. And all the nations of the earth will be gathered against it.* (Zechariah 12:3)

According to the Scriptures, a remnant of Jews will be saved, but we also know things will get bad for Israel before they get better, as this prophecy became all too real on December 23, 2016. As Christians all around the world were preparing for Christmas, the United Nations pounced on an opportunity to condemn Israel for settlement construction, and the United Nations Security Council voted unanimously to deny the Jewish historic connection to the holy temple mount and the Western Wall. With the UN vote, parts of Jerusalem suddenly became "occupied territory," shrinking Israel back to its indefensible 1967 borders.

In its annual anti-Semitism report, the Simon Wiesenthal Center ranked President Obama's refusal to veto the anti-Israel UN resolution, the "most anti-Semitic incident of 2016." The Center declared America's decision to abstain on the resolution "the most stunning UN attack on Israel" that ends up "reversing decades-long U.S. policy" of defending the Jewish State.[40]

Two top Israeli officials accused the Obama administration of facilitating or orchestrating the resolution behind the scenes. Prime Minister Benjamin Netanyahu rejected the move and decided to suspend Israel's

---

40   Valerie Richardson, "Obama's refusal to veto anti-Israel UN vote ranked most anti-Semitic incident of 2016," 12/27/16, *www.washingtontimes.com/news/2016/dec/27/obama-refusal-israel-vote-most-anti-semitic-2016/*.

cooperation with the committee that was created to promote so-called "cultural understanding." Due to America's involvement, our nation will face repercussions for turning its back on Israel.

Following the resolution, Republican senators in the U.S. submitted a letter to the Obama administration asking "to join Israel in suspending ties to UNESCO." Two major reasons the UN has not achieved world domination are Israel and the United States. It is clear that due to these two democracies, forces of evil are ramping up against Jesus Christ, in our country and worldwide.

Netanyahu said that the "scandalous decision to the effect that the Jewish People have no connection to the Temple Mount, or to Jerusalem at all, is contradicted by the Bible and the entire historical record." When he met with President Trump in Washington, D.C. and spoke briefly at a press conference, he stated, "The reason why Jews are called Jews is because we are from Judea."

The attempt by the UN to redefine three thousand years of Israel's history – on the site believed by archaeologists and biblical scholars to be the location of the original Jewish temples built in Old Testament times – was waged via UNESCO's 24-to-6 pro-Muslim vote in support of the resolution sponsored by Arab nations. For those who understand prophecy, this is not shocking.

> Why do the nations rage, And the people plot a vain
> thing? The kings of the earth set themselves, And the rul-
> ers take counsel together, Against the LORD and against His
> Anointed. (Psalm 2:1-2 NKJV)

This psalm also talks about God laughing from heaven at Israel's enemies, and it ends up with a warning to worship the Lord in reverence because His wrath may soon be kindled.

Now with a pro-Israel U.S. president, we can already see the difference in the relationship between America and Israel, our biggest ally. Netanyahu looks relieved during meetings with Trump. The living God will either have mercy on us by delaying His judgment and giving more people time to repent, or He will give us what we deserve.

Though we do not know what the Trump administration or world leaders will do, we know who is in control and this should give us some comfort. King Solomon wrote, *The king's heart is like channels of water in the hand of the LORD; He turns it wherever He wishes. There is no wisdom and no understanding and no counsel against the LORD* (Proverbs 21:1, 30).

So whether it's Netanyahu, Trump, Obama, Putin, Iran's Ahmadinejad, Turkey's Erdoğan, Kim Jong Un, or Germany's Angela Merkel, we can be assured that nothing takes place and no leader comes to power apart from God allowing it to happen.

The Lord seems to be setting the stage for His return like never before. A coalition of nations is rising up against Israel just as predicted, and most are Muslim nations. Similar to Old Testament times, the very existence of Israel and the Jews produces an almost irrational hatred. Hitler tried wiping out the Jews and so will the Antichrist during the future tribulation. News reports often mention the global conflict over Israel and much of the history seems to go back to the land. Why do Iran and other Muslim nations hate Israel and why all the fuss over borders?

It all goes back to the promises God made to Abraham, Isaac, and Jacob. But Muslims – descendants of Sarah's maidservant, Hagar – have lived in hostility toward their brothers from the beginning.

> *And I will make you a great nation, And I will bless you,*
> *And make your name great; And so you shall be a blessing;*
> *And I will bless those who bless you, And the one who curses*
> *you I will curse. And in you all the families of the earth will*
> *be blessed. The LORD appeared to Abram and said, "To your*
> *descendants I will give this land." So he built an altar there*
> *to the LORD who had appeared to him.* (Genesis 12:2-3, 7)

AND

> *For all the land which you see, I will give it to you and to*
> *your descendants forever.* (Genesis 13:15)

In addition, the book of Deuteronomy (32:8-9) also indicates the Palestinians are the occupiers because the Palestinian National Authority did not exist until 1967, and there has never been a Palestinian state.

Let's revisit some history. In 1947 – 48, the Arab states tried to destroy the tiny Jewish state formed by the United Nations partition plan. Then in 1948, the nation Israel was born in one day, as prophesied in Isaiah 66:8. This was unprecedented, and it's just as important to understand that Israel was not "created" in 1948. The nation was re-gathered according to God's will, not the work of men. The new government of Israel proclaimed the new state on May 14, 1948.

According to historical records, just before the start of the Jewish Sabbath on Friday, May 14, David Ben-Gurion read a 979-word declaration of independence in front of a small audience at the Tel Aviv Art Museum, concluding, "The state of Israel is established! The meeting is ended." At midnight, British rule over Palestine lapsed, and minutes later, White House spokesman Charlie Ross announced U.S. recognition. The chief rabbi of Israel later told Harry Truman, "God put you in your mother's womb so you would be the instrument to bring the rebirth of Israel."

That day, God did use President Harry Truman to acknowledge the new Jewish government. The first nation to recognize the state of Israel was America. You can look up a copy of this typewritten document with handwritten corrections that Truman signed:

"This government has been informed that a Jewish State has been proclaimed in Palestine, and recognition has been requested by the provisional government thereof.

The United States recognizes the provisional government as the de facto authority of the new State of Israel.

Harry Truman

Approved, May 14, 1948"

Over five million Jews returned to Israel, and as predicted, the remnant was restored (Isaiah 11:11-12; Ezekiel 37:21-22; 38:8). Never before in history has a people been dispersed throughout the world and then returned to their homeland from the north, south, east, and west (Isaiah 43:5-6), and the emigration of Jews to Israel from other nations continues today.

The majority of Arabs and Muslims are enemies of Israel and want the nation destroyed. Obviously, they don't believe Israel has a right to exist. This is the key to the entire Middle East conflict. Author and talk show host Dennis Prager adds:

> "Those who deny this and ascribe the conflict to other reasons, such as 'Israeli occupation,' 'Jewish settlements,' a 'cycle of violence,' 'the Zionist lobby' and the like, do so despite the fact that Israel's enemies regularly announce the reason for the conflict. The Iranian regime, Hezbollah, Hamas and the Palestinians – in their public opinion polls, in their anti-Semitic school curricula and media, in their election of Hamas, in their support for terror against Israeli civilians in pre-1967 borders – as well as their Muslim supporters around the world, all want the Jewish state annihilated."[41]

In 1967, surrounding nations attacked Israel, but the Jewish people were able to regain full control of Jerusalem during what is known as the Six-Day War. On June 7 of that year, the Israeli army broke through and returned Jerusalem to the Jewish people for the first time in 1,897 years. This coordinated attack happened before Israel ever had a single settler in Palestinian land and in the West Bank.

Two months after the war however, from June 5 – 10, 1967, Arab countries met in Sudan and on September 1 that year, announced their famous motto against Israel: "No peace, no recognition, no negotiations."

Before we get to some fascinating history regarding Israel and involving America, be reminded that Scripture alludes to a coming invasion of Israel according to the Old Testament prophet Ezekiel in chapters 38 and 39. There is another reason Muslims are motivated to take Jerusalem. In his book *The Middle East Meltdown: The Coming Islamic Invasion of Israel*, Dr. Andy Woods writes:

> "In Islam, Jerusalem is the city from which Muhammad supposedly ascended back to Allah. In the Quran, the word 'Jerusalem' isn't even found a single time. On the other hand, in the Bible, the word 'Jerusalem' or 'Zion' is used around 1,000 times. . . . According to Islamic doctrine,

---

41   Dennis Prager, "The Middle East conflict is hard to solve but easy to explain," 7/18/06, *www.dennisprager.com/ the-middle-east-conflict-is-hard-to-solve-but-easy-to-explain/.*

once Islam has ruled over a territory, it irrevocably belongs to Allah. Consequently, any nation that exists (besides an Islamic nation) over a territory that Islam once ruled is viewed as a usurper and disrespecting of Allah."[42]

So, here's Israel, controlling less than 1 percent of all Middle Eastern territory and surrounded by twenty-two hostile Arab and Islamic dictatorships. In fact, Arab nations have approximately 640 times more land than Israel, the only democracy in the region. There have always been battles over the land regardless of what God said about it.

In Joshua 13:6-7, God declares:

> *All the inhabitants of the hill country from Lebanon as far*
> *as Misrephoth-maim, all the Sidonians, I will drive them*
> *out from before the sons of Israel; only allot it to Israel for*
> *an inheritance as I have commanded you. Now therefore,*
> *apportion this land for an inheritance to the nine tribes and*
> *the half-tribe of Manasseh.*

The children of Israel were promised a reasonable allotment of land. Today, the nation is about one-nineteenth the size of California, surrounded by over twenty hostile Arab nations sixty times Israel's population. Do you see the big picture here? How can anyone believe the propaganda suggesting Israel is responsible for all the problems in the Middle East?

Since 1948, Israel has sought peace with neighboring dictatorships that tell the world Israel doesn't have a right to exist and must be wiped off the face of the earth. The Quran commands Muslims to take over territories and force people to submit to Islamic control. (The word *Islam* actually means "submission.")

Centuries before Israel became a nation, history shows how miraculous it was for the people to return to what was a dry, barren wasteland. Due to their disobedience, God had judged the people, they were scattered throughout the known world, and the place was a literal desert. Imagine people in Isaiah's time hearing the following words:

> *The afflicted and needy are seeking water, but there is none,*
> *And their tongue is parched with thirst; I, the LORD, will*

---

42   Andy Woods, *The Middle East Meltdown: The Coming Islamic Invasion of Israel* (Taos, NM: Dispensational Publishing Company, 2016), 59-60.

answer them Myself, As the God of Israel I will not forsake
them. "I will open rivers on the bare heights And springs in
the midst of the valleys; I will make the wilderness a pool of
water And the dry land fountains of water. "I will put the
cedar in the wilderness, The acacia and the myrtle and the
olive tree; I will place the juniper in the desert Together with
the box tree and the cypress, That they may see and recog-
nize, And consider and gain insight as well, That the hand
of the LORD *has done this, And the Holy One of Israel has*
created it. (Isaiah 41:17-20)

God fulfilled His promise to open up rivers, springs, and fountains of
waters, and in the last hundred years, approximately one billion trees
have been planted in Israel. Other prophecies were fulfilled as well,
including *Israel will blossom and sprout, and . . . fill the whole earth*
with fruit (Isaiah 27:6; 35:1-2). Israel now exports fresh produce to the
world to the tune of 800 million dollars each year, including over 200
million dollars from flowers and plants.

According to the prophets Amos and Joel (approximately 800 BC),
God would restore the people so they could rebuild ruined cities (Amos
9:13-15; Joel 3:18). They would plant vineyards and gardens and enjoy
the land, and God promised they would never again be uprooted from
their land. Plenty of psalms also remind us of what God has done for
His people.

Remember His wonders which He has done, His mar-
vels and the judgments uttered by His mouth, O seed of
Abraham, His servant, O sons of Jacob, His chosen ones! He
is the LORD *our God; His judgments are in all the earth. He*
has remembered His covenant forever, The word which He
commanded to a thousand generations, The covenant which
He made with Abraham, and His oath to Isaac. Then He
confirmed it to Jacob for a statute, To Israel as an everlasting
covenant, Saying, "To you I will give the land of Canaan as
the portion of your inheritance." (Psalm 105:5-11)

God swore an oath and confirmed a covenant, but just as predicted, the city of Jerusalem was destroyed and trampled underfoot by the Gentiles (Luke 21:24) in AD 70. Also, according to prophecies, Jerusalem would be – and was – rebuilt on its own ruins (Jeremiah 30:18; Zechariah 12:6) and eventually reestablished in 1948. It had to be God! Christians who understand from Scripture or personal experience that the Lord is faithful, know absolutely nothing is impossible for Him. God orchestrates a myriad of circumstances, events, and lives to accomplish what He desires, and He did just that for the nation of Israel in more recent history.

It happened in 1973.

The fourth Arab-Israeli war began on October 6 in a coordinated, surprise attack by Egyptian and Syrian forces on Israel. Many Jewish soldiers were away from their posts observing Yom Kippur, and with the help of Soviet weapons, the Arab states had a clear advantage. Iraq and Jordan joined in as well. During the holiest of days on the Jewish calendar when much of the nation virtually shuts down, Israel could not have been more vulnerable.

Some advanced concern about possible attacks existed, but "Israeli intelligence was not able to determine conclusively that an attack was imminent." (Reminds me of American intelligence in the days leading up to December 7, 1941, at Pearl Harbor.) Once fully mobilized, the Israel Defense Forces slowly pushed back the Arabs at a heavy cost to both sides. Israel was vastly outnumbered in manpower and weaponry, with some reports suggesting less than 200 Israeli tanks faced over 1,400 Syrian tanks. Near the Suez Canal, less than 1,000 Israeli infantry were up against tens of thousands of Egyptian soldiers.

Just days into the war, Minister of Defense for Israel Moshe Dayan, a hero in the Six-Day War, started talking about pulling back and even a possible surrender. According to another report, Prime Minister of Israel Golda Meir, known for her strength and determination, resisted surrender but secretly had an aid secure lethal pills from her doctor in case Israel's enemies prevailed. Though weapons and ammunition supplies were dangerously low, reserve troops bought more time and the tide slowly seemed to turn in Israel's favor. However, with Russia helping the Arabs, it seemed a nearly insurmountable undertaking. Golda Meir turned to the United States and the Nixon administration.

Apparently, Richard Nixon and his Secretary of State, Henry Kissinger, didn't exactly love the Jews. You may consider that an understatement as some describe them both as anti-Semites. Regardless, while Kissinger was in talks with various countries about a cease-fire, Nixon was dealing with economic issues in America as well as a strategy to help facilitate peace in the Middle East. An aide later said Nixon's forte was "this kind of multi-dimensional diplomatic chess."

As a young boy, Richard Nixon's Christian (and Quaker) mother told him that one day he would be in a powerful position, and a situation would arise where Israel and the Jews needed his help. When it did, he was to help them. At 3:00 a.m. on October 6, 1973, Golda Meir called U.S. President Richard Nixon and asked for help. It is reported that Nixon said he heard the prophetic voice of his mother as he listened to Meir's plea.

By the time she hung up, Golda Meir would soon have the weapons her country needed. That swung the pendulum to Israel's favor and brought an end to the Yom Kippur War. The U.S. Air Force launched Operation Nickel Grass, which sent some twenty-two thousand tons of jet aircraft, tanks, ammunition, and other equipment to Israel. Another thirty-three thousand pounds of materiel arrived by sea.

Had Nixon not acted so decisively, who knows how it would have ended. Some in his own administration disagreed with helping Israel, and it risked Nixon's reputation at the time as well as the American economy. Prime Minister Golda Meir and Nixon kept in frequent contact throughout the ordeal. For the rest of Meir's life, she referred to Nixon as "my president," and said, "For generations to come, all will be told of the miracle of the immense planes from the United States bringing in the material that meant life to our people." (Hat tip to Dr. Andy Woods and Dorothy Von Lehe)

God can use world leaders and yes, even U.S. presidents for His purposes, to bless the nation of Israel and to accomplish His will.

*We give thanks to You, O God, we give thanks, For Your
name is near; Men declare Your wondrous works. "When I
select an appointed time, It is I who judge with equity. The
earth and all who dwell in it melt; It is I who have firmly set*

its pillars. Selah. For not from the east, nor from the west,
Nor from the desert comes exaltation; But God is the Judge;
He puts down one and exalts another. (Psalm 75:1-3, 6-7)

The Lord will use whomever He needs to cause *all things to work together for good to those who love God and are called according to His purpose* (Romans 8:28).

Dennis Prager adds a few more post-war historical facts, further explaining why the conflict in the Middle East really is easy to understand:

> Though nearly all of the Sinai remained in Israel's hands, the boost in Egyptian self-confidence [for the successful surprise attack on Israel] enabled Egypt's visionary president, Anwar Sadat, four years later (Nov. 1977), to do the unimaginable for an Arab leader: He visited Israel and addressed its parliament in Jerusalem. As a result, in 1978, Israel and Egypt signed a peace treaty in return for which Israel gave all of the oil-rich Sinai Peninsula back to Egypt.
>
> Three years later, in 1981, Sadat was assassinated by Egyptian Muslims, a killing welcomed by most Arabs, including the PLO (Palestine Liberation Organization). Why welcomed? Because Sadat had done the unforgivable – recognized Israel and made peace with it.[43]

Palestinians do not want a two-state solution, and they do not want negotiations or peace talks with Israel. Their imbedded ideology demands they destroy Israel so there is no Jewish state. To Muslims, any other option is compromise, or worse, failure.

Israel is one of the most advanced countries on earth in many ways: its culture, economy, medical advances, technology, and its decency as a society. The blind anti-Semitism of many in the West is truly astounding. The Jews are not some bloodthirsty, controlling, manipulative people. A secular nation that needs Jesus Christ and certainly not perfect by any means, the Jewish people are far from violent or war hungry; they are a family-oriented, yielding, and docile people. Israel has offered peace and land to other nations in the past, but Middle East tensions remain.

---

43   Dennis Prager, "The Middle East conflict is hard to solve but easy to explain," 7/18/06, *www.dennisprager.com/ the-middle-east-conflict-is-hard-to-solve-but-easy-to-explain/.*

Even in America today, you may notice more anti-Semitism from people, many of whom have never learned the truth about world history and the plight of the Jews. They have believed the anti-Israel sentiment in much of the world media and anything having to do with the UN. This is why, in a video message congratulating President Trump after he was elected, Netanyahu called him "a great friend of Israel," and said, "Over the years, you have expressed your support consistently, and I deeply appreciate it."

I'm wondering if most Americans are neutral towards Israel. Some have fallen for the deception of what is known as "Replacement Theology," which essentially teaches that the Christian church has replaced Israel in God's plan. Adherents claim the Jews are no longer God's chosen people and that He does not have specific plans for the nation of Israel.

While this may not be an issue of salvation, it is a hugely important biblical issue affecting how we live, whom we support, and what we believe. If God judged the nation of Israel and there is no future for the Jews other than coming to Christ, how in the world do you explain the history of divine intervention and supernatural survival of the Jewish people over thousands of years? Under Replacement Theology, the term *Israel* in the New Testament supposedly refers to the church.

Of all people, followers of Jesus Christ should understand that the Christian church was started by Jews, we are an extension of the promise, and that we have been "grafted in" to the root of the olive tree (see Romans 11). We should be pro-Israel, which means we should love the Jewish people. Why? It is clear God loves Israel and His people are close to His heart.

> *Because He loved your fathers, therefore He chose their descendants after them. And He personally brought you from Egypt by His great power, driving out from before you nations greater and mightier than you, to bring you in and to give you their land for an inheritance, as it is today. Know therefore today, and take it to your heart, that the* LORD, *He is God in heaven above and on the earth below; there is no other.* (Deuteronomy 4:37-39)

Author Jim Fletcher at Rapture Ready emphasizes the importance of holding the Jewish people and Israel in high esteem. Writing about the above verses in Deuteronomy, he states:

> "God is addressing the Jewish people, not the Church or the 'True Israel.' He is making specific statements and promises to the physical line of descendants that began with Abraham, Isaac, and Jacob; and remember too, Isaac was the 'child of the promise.' I am pro-Israel first because I love the Jews. That's it. Everything else flows from that: a love for prophecy, a love for modern Israel, etc. I am not pro-Israel to 'get a blessing' or because they are 'an important ally in the Middle East.'"[44]

Prime Minister Netanyahu seems to have a renewed confidence in the relationship between Israel and America once again. For most of us, it is a welcomed improvement. The Obama administration turned its back on Israel and even tried impacting their election in 2015. The media there did not give Netanyahu a chance to win reelection and even had him down six points in the polls, but we all know how that turned out. It's also not surprising the American media had Donald Trump more than six points down in the polls leading up to the election. Apparently, God had different plans for both Israel and the United States.

Scripture teaches that God will either bless or curse (or judge) nations for their treatment of His people. Can decisions by the Trump administration make up for those of the past eight years? Who really knows, but the 2016 presidential election sent shockwaves around the world. Think about this for a minute. It would seem insane for political parties to nominate two of the worst potential candidates, both with the highest negatives in election history, to run for president. But that is exactly what happened.

Donald Trump had plenty to overcome, including his own flaws and bad habits, narcissism, and years of baggage. He had to face and defeat strong, viable candidates such as Carson, Cruz, Rubio, Walker, Paul, Bush, Fiorina, Perry, and Kasich. He bested the Clinton machine and a biased, complicit media that campaigned against him. He overcame George Soros's money, manufactured protests, and skewed polls, the

---

44   Jim Fletcher, "Do You Like Jews?" 3/5/2017, *www.raptureready.com/category/israel-watch/*.

"Never Trump" camp, as well as pro-Hillary, dishonest debate moderators, and some believe voter fraud. The odds seemed insurmountable. Some claim it was Russia. I say it was God.

The 2016 election cycle was bizarre, historic, and often hard to watch, but don't forget that Washington outsider and billionaire Donald Trump was fairly and legally elected by American citizens to be the forty-fifth president of the United States.

That number 45 is interesting. According to Bible prophecy in Isaiah 45, God anointed and raised up a pagan king, Cyrus, to stand for Israel and work on behalf of His people. I am not necessarily saying Trump is a modern-day Cyrus, but as we know by now, God will use whomever He will.

In the book of Daniel, the Scripture reads, *Praise be to the name of God for ever and ever; wisdom and power are his. He changes times and seasons; he deposes kings and raises up others. He gives wisdom to the wise and knowledge to the discerning. He reveals deep and hidden things* (Daniel 2:20-22a).

If we really do believe God and know He is sovereign over all events and circumstances, we should trust Him and ask for wisdom for the days ahead. One concern I have is that some will get comfortable or complacent just because Hillary lost. Though I do not fully understand how God can be so patient with America, the truth is He seems to have given us a bit more time to repent, revive, and return to being about the Lord's business. Many are using the word "reprieve."

Maybe Franklin Graham was right that God intervened in the 2016 election. All I know is our time is still short. God will either have mercy on us by delaying His full judgment a bit longer, or He will allow the church to continue following the path of the lukewarm Laodiceans of Revelation 3. If we continue on our current course of apathy, we're toast.

Though we can't be certain if God has been working in Donald Trump's heart, we do know Vice President Mike Pence is a godly man. There are also pastors and other people of faith in Trump's circle of influence, so we'll see what happens. Let's pray and hope for the best, but the key is to keep our eyes on Israel!

At the Constitutional Convention in 1787, Benjamin Franklin wrote to George Washington: "I have lived, Sir, a long time and the longer I live, the more convincing proofs I see of this truth – that God governs in the affairs of men. And if a sparrow cannot fall to the ground without His notice, is it probable that an empire can rise without His aid? We have been assured, Sir, in the sacred writings that 'except the Lord build the house, they labor in vain that build it.'"

God cares about the hearts of people. We're here to tell others the good news about Jesus Christ and to be shining examples of Him in society. The entire Bible from Genesis through Psalms and all the way to Revelation points to and supports the return and future reign of the Messiah, the God of Israel, the King of Kings, Jesus Christ.

We have an abundance of compelling reasons to trust in the living God who has a plan. For one, we still need to refer to prophecy. The Bible consists of so many specific predictions fulfilled which cannot be logically explained apart from divine inspiration. And the best is yet to come.

> Behold, a day is coming for the LORD when the spoil taken
> from you will be divided among you. For I will gather all the
> nations against Jerusalem to battle, and the city will be cap-
> tured, the houses plundered, the women ravished and half
> of the city exiled, but the rest of the people will not be cut off
> from the city. Then the LORD will go forth and fight against
> those nations, as when He fights on a day of battle. In that
> day His feet will stand on the Mount of Olives, which is in
> front of Jerusalem on the east; and the Mount of Olives will
> be split in its middle from east to west by a very large valley,
> so that half of the mountain will move toward the north and
> the other half toward the south. And the LORD will be king
> over all the earth; in that day the LORD will be the only one,
> and His name the only one. (Zechariah 14:1-4, 9)

Now that we have our eternal perspective back, let's return to the business at hand: the fight for truth in our churches and culture.

Chapter 9

Can Natural Marriage Be Saved?

Marriage is to be held in honor among all, and the marriage bed is to be undefiled; for fornicators and adulterers God will judge (Hebrews 13:4).

"As God by creation made two of one, so again by marriage He made one of two." – Thomas Adams

God is sovereign over Israel; He has allowed moral relativism in the American church, the spread of the transgender agenda, the threat to our religious freedoms, and obviously, He is also sovereign over the attacks on marriage and truth.

Some might say the task to repair the damage done to the institution of marriage and our society is formidable while others say it is impossible. It is true that marriage is on shaky ground in America, but your marriage and mine do not have to be. There's part of the solution – help encourage and strengthen Christian marriages and all God-ordained unions between one man and one woman. The marriage covenant must be considered sacred and our word must be our bond ("Till death do us part").

Marriage must be held in high esteem once again, and to make good progress in this endeavor, it will take plenty of effort – starting in our churches. As with any other pivotal issue, there is heavy spiritual warfare involved. Every happy and healthy, successful society has strong marriages, families, and children. How is America doing?

Here are some of the many things coming against marriage today: easy divorce, increasing pornography and adultery, the LGBT agenda, leftist courts, cohabitation, dependency on welfare, people getting married later in life, prime time television and movies, the radical feminist movement, technology and social media robbing family time, young people's attitudes about marriage – you get the idea.

As daunting as it may be to right the ship again by reversing course or at least patching up the holes and bailing out all the excess water, we know that with God all things are possible. If, however, we do not clearly identify the obstacles, opponents, and problems as well as learn from the past, the work we do to save the institution of marriage and marriages in America will be less effective.

Nearly forty years ago, in 1979 to be exact, this is how *Webster's New Collegiate Dictionary* defined *marriage*:

> "a. the state of being married; b. the mutual relation of husband and wife; wedlock; c. the institution whereby men and women are joined in a special kind of social and legal dependence for the purpose of founding and maintaining a family; the rite by which the married status is effected; union."

Using the online definitions from *Merriam-Webster* and Dictionary. com, here is how marriage is defined today, in 2017:

> "a. the state of being united as spouses in a consensual and contractual relationship recognized by law; the mutual relation of married persons.

> "b. any of the diverse forms of interpersonal union established in various parts of the world to form a familial bond that is recognized legally, religiously, or socially, granting the participating partners mutual conjugal rights and responsibilities, and including opposite-sex marriage, same-sex marriage, plural marriage, and arranged marriage."

Since we've already answered the question of whether or not God changes (He does not) and whether or not Scripture changes (it does not), do not be discouraged when people's beliefs and attitudes change, and when laws change. We must revisit and reestablish what is true, moral, and historically accurate. Why? Because our culture has been bombarded with what is false, immoral, and historically inaccurate.

We can safely say many things were already going south before five liberal judges changed how this nation was to look at marriage. Though it was one of many spokes in the wheel of the agenda, same-sex marriage is another harbinger of our declining society. Prior to the *Obergefell v. Hodges* – SCOTUS decision, the agenda was well underway to remove America's moral anchors and replace them with humanism and hedonism.

The goal of marriage activists and anarchists is not for gays and lesbians to be able to marry. The goal is to destroy the family unit, eliminate all marriage, and render the term *marriage* meaningless. Do I exaggerate? Since I've read stories about a woman marrying herself, someone else marrying their two cats, a woman marrying a dolphin, a man marrying his dog, a man marrying a video game character, and another man marrying a robot, I think we're well on the way to meaninglessness.

Much has been argued and debated in this intense battle over the definition of marriage in America. What has not been discussed enough is the fact that for many decades, both men and women in the U.S. have struggled with everything from adultery and pornography to idolatry and lying. We have loved pleasure more than God (2 Timothy 3:1-5), and as a result, we have pursued selfish gain.

We have dishonored our parents, forgotten the Sabbath, and most of us at one point in time have taken the Lord's name in vain (OMG!). We've coveted our neighbor's house, spouse, career, or lifestyle. We have either aborted our own babies (the Latin meaning of *fetus* is "off-spring"), known someone who has, or have approved of the murder of innocent life by our encouragement or our vote (that's six broken commandments so far).

We idolize our favorite athletes, celebrities, and political parties. We place so many things above the Lord our God, including activities and relationships, that we barely scrape a few minutes together to read a Scripture or mutter a quick prayer. Our divorce rates are too high and we're not setting the best example for the world. This must change.

Even in the Ashley Madison fiasco a few years back, in the 31 million users on its site, there were hundreds of pastors, deacons, elders, and church staff members on the list. If you don't remember the fallout, Ashley Madison is a dating site for married people and they experienced a data breach leading to the release of personal information of millions of users. Obviously, this led to many families either divorcing or trying to pick up the broken pieces of their lives.

Instead of discouraging more people from checking it out, hundreds of thousands of new users signed up even after the hackers leaked data on Ashley Madison clients! This is the world we live in today. Here's a company openly and proudly glorifying sin with the motto: "Life is short. Have an affair."

Tragically, some who were involved have already died in their sins without repenting to God, and the question that must be asked is – knowing they may spend eternity in hell – was it worth it? *But a man who commits adultery has no sense; whoever does so destroys himself* (Proverbs 6:32 NIV).

We cannot do the necessary work to repair and restore marriage in this nation if our own houses are in disorder. Consider this another heart check.

SAME-SEX MARRIAGE NOT THE FINAL OBJECTIVE

Regarding the agenda discussed in an earlier chapter, a strategy has been in the works to unify the LGBTQ movement with the Democrat Party, the media, minority groups, environmentalists, women, and progressive men to build a liberal voting bloc. The Left has already identified obstacles and threats to their goals. Not surprisingly, Christians, conservatives, and anyone who believes in traditional marriage and sexual boundaries are now a target.

In an article for *WorldNetDaily* (WND), Leo Hohmann revealed more disturbing information on the plans some folks have to expedite the transformation of the country. Four years ago in the liberal publication *The Nation*, four liberal women, three of them university professors, wrote an op-ed discussing LGBT obstacles and opportunities. Remember, this was **two years** *before* the Supreme Court's decision on marriage. In "What's Next for the LGBT Movement?" one of the women wrote, "Gay marriage is a done deal. It's only a question of how many barriers remain and how long it will take to have gay and lesbian marriages legally recognized in the United States."[45]

Can you imagine if Christians had this kind of commitment and confidence in sharing the gospel and in strengthening marriages and families? The truth is there are more and more people being deceived by this agenda. It has been stated openly that they aim to "work toward the elimination of marriage as an institution." I predicted the eventual legalization of same-sex marriage due to the nation's state and federal courts being infested with leftists and activist judges. What I did not see coming were the plans to completely eradicate marriage as a whole. This same article went on to say, "What next? Disestablish marriage. Get the state out of the business. Abolish the legal category; Freedom, equality, and the health of our liberal democratic polity depend on it."

In *The Daily Beast,* another writer seemed flabbergasted because there are Americans who *still* have a fundamental discomfort with LGBTQ people in their own social circles. According to a GLAAD poll, and who knows how they came up with this number, "More than 100 million Americans *still* say they're uncomfortable just seeing a gay co-worker's wedding photo."

Wow. They want change, and they want that change forced upon the rest of us. The Left has vast community organizing resources, and they intend on reeducating people in churches, schools, and families. One liberal activist group, Believe Out Loud, an online community for LGBT "Christians," admitted their agenda is to infiltrate churches, saying it has "a unique role to play in promoting this acceptance in the context of U.S. churches, particularly within Christianity."

Another lesbian journalist, Russian-American Masha Gessen, literally has three kids who have five parents, and she does not see why her kids shouldn't have five parents legally. She even admitted that homosexual activists were lying about their political agenda. She boldly declared,

45   Leo Hohmann, "LGBT Activists: Marriage Was Never The 'End Game,'" 6/30/2015, *www.wnd.com/2015/06/lgbt-activists-marriage-was-never-the-end-game/.*

"The institution of marriage is going to change, and it should change. And again, I don't think it should exist."[46]

You read that right. Marriage shouldn't even exist. Radicals like this need the love and grace of Jesus Christ. But radicals like this say that we're the ones on the wrong side.

In a radio interview, Gessen reiterated the fact that for them, same-sex marriage is not enough. "It's a no-brainer that (homosexual activists) should have the right to marry, but I also think equally that it's a no-brainer that the institution of marriage should not exist. . . . (F)ighting for gay marriage generally involves lying about what we are going to do with marriage when we get there – because we lie that the institution of marriage is not going to change, and that is a lie."

Your heart may be heavy as you read some of this, but it is the reality of the battle we face in culture and the church. Though I vehemently disagree with Gessen on marriage, I respect her candor.

This is completely different than an activist writing a hit piece on Christians such as the one Kate Arthur put out at BuzzFeed. I'm sure you heard about it. Arthur created a bogus controversy because – get this – the church that *Fixer Upper* stars, Chip and Joanna Gaines, attend – actually believes the Bible regarding marriage and homosexuality!

I love the way Chip Gaines responded in a blog post that he and his wife "refuse to be baited" into what essentially was a drummed-up witch hunt, and added, "Jo and I feel called to be bridge builders. We want to help initiate conversations between people that don't think alike," he said. "Listen to me, we do not all have to agree with each other. Disagreement is not the same thing as hate, don't believe that lie."[47]

Because the couple identify as evangelical Christians and have not stated a position on homosexuality, BuzzFeed decided to take matters into its own hands and look into the church they attend. Arthur checked the beliefs section of the church's website and pointed to a sermon by Pastor Jimmy Siebert, during which he emphasized God's design for marriage in Genesis:

---

46   Leo Hohmann, "LGBT Activists: Marriage Was Never The 'End Game,'" 6/30/2015, *www. wnd.com/2015/06/lgbt-activists-marriage-was-never-the-end-game/*.

47   Chip Gaines, "Chip's New Year's Revelation," 1/2/2017, *magnoliamarket.com/ chips-new-years-revelation/*.

"This is a clear biblical admonition. So if someone were to say, 'Marriage is defined in a different way,' let me just say: They are wrong,' he said. 'God defined marriage, not you and I. God defined masculine and feminine, male and female; Truth No. 2: God is able to give us power over every sin, including homosexuality. Lie No. 2: I am a homosexual in thought and action, and I cannot change.'"[48]

Pastor Siebert outlined that homosexuality is a sin, but Christ can set men free from any sin, no matter what it is. He also urged compassion for homosexuals and encouraged Christians to "lovingly, carefully bring them back to Scripture." *Cosmopolitan Magazine* tried to stir the pot at the time saying this was a "startling revelation." (I hope it never gets to the point when it is "startling" if Christians believe the truth of the Bible.)

Part of me wishes Chip Gaines would have publicly backed their pastor and church's doctrinal beliefs, but I do understand the angle he took. Jesus called us to love even those who disagree with us no matter how far they might go to attack us because of our Christian faith. This is one time where HGTV decided not to pursue the matter further.

The Benham Brothers were not given the same treatment in 2014 when the network cancelled their upcoming (at the time) HGTV show, *Flip It Forward*. The two Christian brothers were both fired because they are openly opposed to abortion and the agenda to redefine marriage.

They said what happened to the Gaineses was another hit piece by the "thought mafia," and said they are safe for now. They too agree this is our new reality in America, and if we live out our Christian faith and go against secular trends, we will be "targeted, vilified, and ultimately punished for not bowing the knee."

When we tell others what the Bible teaches about sin, we can mention lying, stealing, cussing, adultery, idolatry, coveting, murder, or abortion, but if we utter the word *homosexual*, it triggers people. What some of them hear us say or *pretend* to hear us say is, "I can't stand you pagan LGBTQ people, and in fact, I hate every one of you!"

---

48   Heather Clark, "We 'refuse to Be Baited': Fixer Upper Host Speaks After Controversy Over Church's Marriage Beliefs," 1/4/2017, *christiannews.net/2017/01/04/we-refuse-to-be-baited-fixer-upper-host-speaks-after-controversy-over-churchs-marriage-beliefs/*.

Or at least that's how their argument goes. In all fairness, however, not all activists are dishonest and agenda driven. One gay writer recently said the old strategy of journalists "shaming" people is not going to work anymore. In an op-ed in December 2016, Brandon Ambrosino wrote, "It is no longer okay – indeed, it never was – to write cutesy articles shaming religious people as homophobic for simply being one of the many millions of Americans in 2016 who attend a religious congregation that does not support same-sex marriage. That is not a good move for activism or journalism."[49]

He said conservatives shouldn't be mocked or fired. Ambrosino pointed out that after Trump accused the media of bias, stories like BuzzFeed's "hit piece" on Chip and Joanna Gaines proved to the world that he was right.

COHABITATION INCREASING, MARRIAGE DECREASING

What's interesting is the fact that one year after the SCOTUS made history by officially endorsing homosexuality, less than 10 percent (123,000 couples) of gay marriage advocates married a same-sex partner. The way the media and others portrayed their desperate plight, wouldn't you logically think the majority of gays and lesbians would have immediately flocked to the courthouses and wedding chapels of America to legalize their relationships?

But that is not what happened, nor has marriage significantly increased since. Why? There are many reasons, including one we've already stated: legal same-sex marriage was not their final objective. So let's look at a few other reasons for decreasing marriage numbers.

The divorce rate remains high, even among Christians, and we now see early statistics on gay and lesbian divorces as well. Even more disturbing is the fact that according to a Gallup poll, 72 percent of Americans now believe divorce is morally acceptable.[50]

This is an eye-opening trend in a nation once built on strong

---

49   Amy Furr, "Gay Writer: 'It's No Longer Okay' to Shame Religious People Who Oppose Same-Sex Marriage," 12/8/2016, *www.cnsnews.com/blog/amy-furr/ gay-writer-its-no-longer-okay-shame-religious-people-who-oppose-gay-marriage.*

50   Gallup, "Birth Control, Divorce top List of Morally Acceptable Issues," 6/8/2016, *www. gallup.com/poll/192404/ birth-control-divorce-top-list-morally-acceptable-issues.aspx.*

marriages, families, and churches. Another sad revelation is that many people believe waiting to get married before having sex is unnecessary, as 67 percent say sex between an unmarried man and woman is fine.

The same month as the Gallup poll, Barna's own research led to this conclusion: a majority of Americans now believe in cohabitation. Barna, in fact, referred to living together before marriage as "the new norm." A few reasons given for the increase in cohabitation were a secularizing culture, people delaying marriage, and changing expectations.[51]

The main excuse people give for cohabitation is to "test compatibility" (84 percent) prior to marriage. Though its acceptance is widespread in American culture, the research also suggests there are still large pockets of resistance to this changing ethic among religious communities and "those who adhere to more traditional values and premarital expectations."

As for the actual numbers, two thirds of adults (65 percent) either strongly agree or somewhat agree that it's a good idea to live with one's significant other before getting married, compared to one-third (35 percent) who either strongly or somewhat disagree.

One of the sadder statistics from the research is that for Christians surveyed, 41 percent think cohabitation is morally acceptable, and 48 percent of Christians live with or have previously lived with their boyfriend/girlfriend. This makes me wonder if we are all reading the same Holy Bible or if some professing believers are even reading God's Word at all!

Who is more culpable for destroying the sanctity of marriage in America? If we are being completely honest, more evidence points to the church in America as well as to average citizens, rather than gays and lesbians. We need to face the ugly fact that for half a century, we have generally focused more on our lifestyles, careers, money, houses, and entertainment than we have on our marriages.

We absolutely must educate and encourage the younger generation about healthy marriages. Anyone under thirty years old has to be told the truth: it isn't all about you and getting your needs met. We've

---

51   Barna, "Majority of Americans Now Believe in Cohabitation," 6/24/2016, *www.barna. com/research/majority-of-americans-now-believe-in-cohabitation/*.

learned (and some of us are still learning) the hard way that our own narcissism and self-obsession takes time to change.

I can understand why so many people choose to live together before getting married (some having no intention of marrying at all). It's what they think will make them happy. Isn't this the ultimate deciding factor? Will the other person (finally) be the perfect one to satisfy me? Will they serve me, please me sexually, make my life better, and make me their number one?

Marriage however, is about finding someone to commit to be with for the rest of your life, someone you will commit to serve and sacrifice for regardless of life's ups and downs. We do not need a test run (as if we are buying a new car that will meet our needs) in order to make the quality decision to love another person for life. We need a mature understanding of covenants, of what "I do" really means, and what true love really is.

Jesus said if anyone wants to follow Him, *he must deny himself* (Matthew 16:24). While speaking of His own self-sacrifice, Jesus told His disciples the hour had come for Him to be glorified, and said, *Unless a grain of wheat falls into the earth and dies, it remains alone; but if it dies, it bears much fruit* (John 12:24).

This goes against our human nature, to give up our own desires, wants, and lives, but a successful marriage is built upon principles of unconditional love, service, and sacrifice. This kind of godly attitude could possibly have helped salvage millions of struggling marriages. Let's take a deeper look at some historical trends.

Since around the early 1960s, the divorce rate in America increased over 100 percent to where more than one out of every two marriages ends in divorce. According to the U.S. Census Bureau, since 1960, the number of men who are married has declined from 70 percent to 55 percent.[52]

Moreover, the percentage of men who have never married is now at 35 percent. Data on women shows similar patterns. We also know people are postponing marriage, and the average age of men and women getting

---

52   U.S. Census, "Men's Marital Status," *www.census.gov/hhes/families/files/graphics/MS-1a.pdf*.

married is increasing. The median age at first marriage is almost thirty years of age for men and almost twenty-eight years of age for women.

Historically, this represents a dramatic change. For nearly a century, from 1890 to about 1990, the median age at first marriage had remained relatively stable. Women, for example, were getting married when they were between twenty and twenty-two years old. A key reason is not that marriage is less desirable necessarily, but that people are more concerned about losing their independence and adding marital "duties" to their lives, including the perceived "burden" of serving another person.

In a 2017 report at CNS News on how the culture of marriage is struggling in America and how this fact indicated future difficulties for the country, author and law professor Lynn Wardle wrote:

> For many persons, marriage has gone from being considered a marker of maturity, responsibility, and a respectable status to being a burdensome condition to be avoided for as long as possible. As the status of marriage declines, the number and rates of marriages drop, the timing of marriages is delayed, and the rate of non-marital births and childrearing rises. Over time, that results in more children being born and raised in the more difficult, disadvantaged circumstances . . .

> Sadly, research confirms that the deterioration of the social status and desirability of marriage and marital family life are harbingers of future problems and distress for individuals (especially for children), as well as of chaos for families and societies.[53]

In 1957, very few couples lived together without being married, while sixty years later in 2017, the cohabitation rate for women prior to their first marriage is around 70 percent. These are not just cultural indicators; these are judgments on the Christian church and our lack of moral influence in America.

---

53   Lynn D. Wardle, "Culture of Marriage Struggling in 2017: A Harbinger of Future Difficulties for America," 2/24/2017, *www.cnsnews.com/commentary/lynn-wardle/ culture-marriage-struggling-2017-harbinger-future-difficulties-america.*

THE WEAKENING AMERICAN FAMILY

Countless books have been written on the subjects of family, improving marriages, better parenting, strengthening Christian families, raising good kids, and on and on. Maybe we should go back to the guidebook of all books and instruction manuals: the Bible.

Here are a couple of reminders: forgive, and remember that love endures all things.

> *Be kind to one another, tender-hearted, forgiving each other, just as God in Christ also has forgiven you.* (Ephesians 4:32)

> *Love is patient, love is kind and is not jealous; love does not brag and is not arrogant, does not act unbecomingly; it does not seek its own, is not provoked, does not take into account a wrong suffered.* (1 Corinthians 13:4-5)

Instead of studying and applying Scripture, we tend to look for quick fixes and other things to save us time, money, or energy. History has also proven we have too often relied on the government to solve some of these problems or to improve the country. A government-run program can sound good or even start with good intentions, but what often happens is programs grow more government, cost more than originally expected, and have a negative impact on people's lives.

President Lyndon Johnson's "Great Society" in 1965 looked great on paper, I'm sure. One thing it definitely accomplished was to send spending through the roof to unprecedented levels on health care, education, and welfare. The welfare spending in particular created a heavy financial tax burden on the people.

One of the Great Society welfare bills supposedly created to help widows with children has nearly destroyed the black family in America. Prior to this, churches, families, and communities cared for their own, so there are some who question the absolute necessity of this program to begin with. The program Aid to Families with Dependent Children (AFDC) was expanded to include aid to any woman with a child – as long as there was not a male in the household.

Author James Bowers explains this in his book *The Naked Truth*:

> "The theory was with the AFDC check coming in, they can

get by. Of course, the more children, the larger the government check. . . . Therefore, the message to young black women is to have as many illegitimate children as possible, and make absolutely sure you do not get married to the father!

"Not only a horrible situation, but think of all the young black children being raised without a father, or the young black males with no role model at all. Is it any wonder that many black boys gravitated to gangs and crime?"[54]

This program and others seemed to lead to the breaking up of black families in part by making husbands irrelevant. Hollywood is helping the cause as well, but that's for another chapter. One thing liberals figured out was that welfare helped buy votes. Apparently, 70 percent of unmarried women voted for Barack Obama, and politicians quickly realized this was a voting bloc to capitalize on. Into the so-called Affordable Care Act, the Democrats incorporated a section that rewarded women with tax advantages if they cohabitated but did *not* get married.

It makes sense that from 2010, the first full year of the Obama administration, through 2014, the number of births to unmarried mothers with less than a high school education climbed to 70 percent. For women with at least a bachelor's degree, unmarried births account for only 12 percent.[55]

There are many more things that have chiseled away at healthy families and marriages through the years, but Christians must protect marriage again. Most alarming is according to a National Center for Health Statistics report, an average of 75 percent of Americans agree with this statement: "It is okay to have and raise children when the parents are living together but not married."

One of the actual communist goals from 1958 was to discredit the family as an institution – to encourage promiscuity and easy divorce. (Check and check!) We are not advancing in our culture by accepting new views on sexuality and "gay" marriage. It's just the opposite. We

---

54   James C. Bowers, *The Naked Truth: The Naked Communist Revisited* (Manitou Springs, CO: Schwartz Report Press, 2011), 99.

55   Alysse ElHage, "Married Parenthood Remains the Best Path to a Stable Family," 3/8/2017, *ifstudies.org/blog/ married-parenthood-remains-the-best-path-to-a-stable-family.*

are regressing. In ancient Rome, the permissive sexual worldview for hundreds of years was quite oppressive, but think about how some of these attitudes are creeping into Western civilization today.

According to author and pastor Matthew Rueger, women and children were viewed as sexual objects and marital fidelity was foreign during those times. We cannot ignore this godless and unholy paganism that has cheapened our attitudes about the value of human beings. Rueger writes, "Slaves – male and female – could expect to be raped; there was widespread prostitution; and predatory homosexuality was common. Christian sexual morality might have been seen as repressive by the licentious, but it was a gift from God for their victims. . . . Contemporary views about sexuality are simply a revival of an older and much less loving view of the world."[56]

This brings us full circle in a way. Though homosexuality was common in many cultures, homosexual marriage was not. Families could not have been extended, for one thing. In many societies in world history, sexual sin has always existed in some form or other, but no surviving society has ever existed that recognized the legal marriage between two people of the same sex.

There may have been one other time in history, however, in which homosexual marriage was practiced or even legal. It was not in ancient Babylon, Greece, or Rome; it was in Noah's time.

Jesus said, *But of that day and hour no one knows, not even the angels of heaven, nor the Son, but the Father alone. For the coming of the Son of Man will be just like the days of Noah. For as in those days before the flood they were eating and drinking, marrying and giving in marriage, until the day that Noah entered the ark* (Matthew 24:36-38).

Is the state of marriage a sign we are getting closer to the end, which means judgment day?

In a radio interview discussing Faith2Action's 2016 documentary, *Light Wins*, which is about the LGBT movement and attacks on natural marriage, Texas Representative Louie Gohmert said even though homosexuality was rampant in Sodom and Gomorrah, it was not legal according to the Babylonian Talmud. Further commenting on Janet

56   Eric Metaxas, "Progressively Regressive Sexuality," 12/26/2016, *www.breakpoint.org/2016/09/progressively-regressive-sexuality/*.

Porter's documentary and information presented on the book of Jewish interpretation of Scriptures written one thousand years before Christ, Gohmert noted, "According to rabbinical writings, the only other time in history where homosexual unions were authorized as marriage was in the days of Noah."

Let's say this may or may not be the case. Is America still in trouble because of immorality, a lack of repentance in the church, and the breakdown of marriage and family?

CONCLUSION

So how do we respond to people who say we just need to "agree to dis-agree" on these pivotal moral issues? We can agree to disagree on sports teams, cars, the best restaurants, or who makes the best coffee, but on important doctrinal issues that affect people's salvation or a society's survival, we just cannot in good conscience let it go. We can respect others and still disagree, but the most important thing is the truth.

If they ask you why heterosexual marriage wasn't defined in the past, they need to know that historically, there was never a need to define marriage until now. It was always assumed to be between one man and one woman. This is clear in the Bible, in thousands of years of world history, as well as in ancient writings.

One argument that bugs me is when Christians say they have "evolved" on the issue of gay marriage. What they mean is that they are going along with what appears popular and less judgmental, and they have chosen the world over Jesus. Opinions and polls have shifted, but we serve a living God who never changes, and natural marriage is rooted in His Word.

Next argument: "How can you say you love others and be opposed to marriage equality?" Their question poses a false assumption. Nobody was discriminated against just because the law supported heterosexual marriage. We're already equal. The decision that was placed before the Supreme Court was whether or not – as a country – to redefine the his-torical and legal (and biblical) understanding that marriage is a lifelong commitment uniting one man and one woman.

How about, "Why can't we love whomever we want to love?" Go ahead.

Loving and living together wasn't illegal, so the issue wasn't whether you were legally allowed to love your partner or multiple partners.

Next, even with legalized same-sex marriage, I've heard some activists now say homosexuality needs to be removed from "your list of sins." Christians are not the writers and editors of God's Word. Believers are simply followers of Christ. Please take your demands to Him and see where it gets you.

Let's keep planting seeds of truth even if you don't think they are taking root. There's always hope – until a person dies, then it's over and the people they may have been trying to please in this life won't matter anymore. Marriage does matter because it matters to God, and we are His children.

Henry Ward Beecher once said, "The most important thing a father can do for his children is to love their mother."

We all make mistakes, but it's time to forgive and return to serving. Men of God, next to cultivating a strong relationship with the Lord, renew your commitment to your wife and strengthen your children's perception of marriage by loving their mom. Women of God, please be patient; keep encouraging your husband, especially when he tries to put God and spiritual things first.

Repentance is the first step to revival, and marriages in America desperately need it. Let's love and obey Jesus, love our spouses, and work together to model good Christian marriages.

> AND THE TWO SHALL BECOME ONE FLESH; *so they are no longer two, but one flesh. What therefore God has joined together, let no man separate* (Mark 10:8-9).

Chapter 10

The *Real* War on Women:
Lies about Life

Thus says the LORD, your Redeemer, who formed you from the womb: "I am the LORD, who made all things, who alone stretched out the heavens, who spread out the earth by myself" (Isaiah 44:24 ESV). And how has it happened to me, that the mother of my Lord would come to me? For behold, when the sound of your greeting reached my ears, the baby leaped in my womb for joy (Luke 1:43-44).

"Is it anything but society's moral confusion that says if you hold an infant's head inside the birth canal while inserting scissors and suction tips to extract its brain, you are completing a 'legitimate medical procedure,' but doing the same thing with the infant's head outside the canal is first-degree murder?" – Peter Heck

Did you know it costs only $120 to send an aborted baby's brain using FedEx Priority Overnight?

I'm not sure what is more disappointing: the fact that for years Planned Parenthood has been harvesting and selling the body parts of aborted babies and shipping them out to the highest bidder, or the fact that when the United States Senate published an enormously important five-hundred-page report exposing the abortion giant for criminal activity, the media collectively yawned and ignored the breaking story. They'd rather report on someone (an "activist") praying ("protesting") outside an abortion clinic than mention what goes on inside the clinic itself.

Another problem is that most Americans barely raise an eyebrow over this appalling practice – not only the snuffing out of innocent preborn lives, but also the selling of their body parts, perhaps the most disturbing revelation about the abortion business yet. I admit it; I'm angry. How have Christians reacted? Are we trying to share the awful truth? When was the last time you heard a sermon – or even a brief mention – on the issue of life in the womb? I thought murder was a moral issue and God valued every life.

God called it an abomination in the Old Testament, and yet today, women (and men) are throwing away their babies, sacrificing them on the altar of convenience and feminism. We have looked the other way as babies are ripped apart limb from limb, many women are physically injured or at least emotionally scarred for life, and some have died due to botched abortions. And not only is this legal, but it's funded by our tax dollars. Since abortion is essentially a sacrament to Democrats, and the Left owns the media, abortion is one of the least regulated industries in America. Kermit Gosnell's filthy clinic was not a unique case.

In fact, one high-volume abortion mill in St. Louis, Missouri, has injured women in at least sixty-four botched abortions and has over thirty-nine health violations. Fire department records and eyewitness accounts prove Planned Parenthood of St. Louis "uses emergency ambulance transports for [abortion] patients on average of once every six weeks dating back as far as 2009." There have been 210 incidents where this facility has been cited, most of them for safety or sanitary violations.[57]

Too many of us are no longer fazed by our culture of death.

Though the pro-life movement has had some recent success, there is much political ground to cover and regain, taking us all the way back to 1973. I quoted parts of the *Roe v. Wade* transcript in my previous book, including the debate over when life begins and what is considered a "viable" human life. Astonishingly, the court ruled that states

---

57 Cheryl Sullenger, "One Planned Parenthood Clinic Has Injured Women in 64 Botched Abortions, Has 39 Health Violations," 3/13/2017, *www.lifenews.com/2017/03/13/one-planned-parenthood-clinic-has-injured-women-in-64-botched-abortions-has-39-health-violations/*.

may only consider the potential well-being of the preborn baby (*fetus*) at the point of "viability," which they defined as the capacity to survive outside the womb.

Aside from the Bible, facts and research from biology and science via technology and modern medical research have pretty much destroyed the opinions of the men in black robes on the Supreme Court. Here's a quick question: if a person's heart is worth operating on at twenty-nine weeks in utero, why is it still legal to abort them?

A patient in Ohio recently underwent a pre-birth heart procedure. You read that right. The twenty-nine-week-old fetus needed an "aortic valvuloplasty," an operation that treats "hypoplastic left-heart syndrome," a condition occurring when the left side of the heart doesn't develop properly. Typically performed after the baby is born, the procedure involved threading a needle into the fetal heart, and was performed at University Hospitals Rainbow Babies and Children's Hospital in Cleveland by Dr. Aimee Armstrong and her team.[58]

There is so much evidence supporting life in the womb, but we have accommodated this culture of corruption. What do I mean by corruption? You mean other than killing human babies, making taxpayers and insurance plans pay for it, selling baby body parts, and marketing abortion "services" to public school kids as young as twelve with the help of the NEA? Out of fifty-six Planned Parenthood affiliates, the CEOs make an average salary of $238,000 a year. (Remember, this is a "non-profit" organization that clears about $50 million a year after expenses.)

According to the executive director of the American Life League, Jim Sedlak, "Six of those CEOs earn more than $400,000 a year, and one over a half million dollars. . . . When we looked at Planned Parenthood's national headquarters we found their CEO, Cecile Richards, now gets the incredible pay of $957,952 a year. In addition, top underlings' pay ranged from $300,000 to $500,000."[59]

Our great-grandparents or certainly our Founding Fathers would have revolted. Make no mistake: this is a battle of worldviews. Who

---

58   JoAnne Viviano, "In-utero heart operation on 29-week-old fetus is first in Ohio," 3/6/2017, *www.dispatch.com/ news/20170306/in-utero-heart-operation-on-29-week-old-fetus-is-first-in-ohio.*

59   Charlie Butts, "PP execs raking in six-figure salaries," 3/9/2017, *www.onenewsnow.com/pro-life/2017/03/09/pp-execs-raking-in-six-figure-salaries.*

should be born, how long should people be allowed to live, and who determines the quality, productivity, and value of human life? Isn't it God?

Pastor David Platt often stresses God's love for the unborn, and in a sermon stated, "Children are so precious. They are a treasure to be cherished. And yet, we live in a culture where children are a problem to be avoided."

Two-term leader of the Democratic Party Barack Obama declared he didn't want his daughters "punished with a baby" should they mess up and get pregnant. This is the exact opposite attitude taught throughout Scripture about the blessing and worth of every human life. Most of us have heard the argument by some of the most twisted pro-abortion activists insisting pregnancy is comparable to a disease that must be cured and thus, a baby is something to be removed.

Mother Theresa once said quite simply, "When a mother can kill her baby, what is left of civilization to save?" Before we dive into the shocking revelations from the United States Senate report on Planned Parenthood, I want to share a captivating story that proves how far our "civilized" society in America has fallen in regard to life and morality.

Author and university professor Peter Kreeft shared a story that not only paints a vivid picture, but also drives home the truth about the vast moral deficit in America. In his book *How to Win the Culture War*, he writes:

> I know a doctor who spent two years in the Congo winning the confidence of a dying tribe who would not trust outsiders and who were dying because of their bad diet. He was a dietitian, and he saved their lives. Once they knew this, they trusted him totally and asked him all sorts of questions about life in the West.

> They believed all the amazing things he told them, like flying to the moon, destroying whole cities with one bomb, but there were two things they literally could not believe. One was that in the West there are atheists – people who believe in no gods at all. ("Are these people blind and deaf? Have they never seen a leaf or heard a waterfall?")

The other thing was that in one nation alone (America), over a million mothers each year pay "doctors" to kill their babies before they are born. The reaction of the tribe was to giggle at this, which was their embarrassed way of trying to be polite, assuming it was a joke. They simply had no holding place in their minds for this concept, and expected every day that the doctor would tell them the point of the joke.[60]

And we are so ignorant and proud that we often refer to these people as *primitive*. Is it any wonder small Christian countries send missionaries to evangelize us in the decadent West? The first time I heard about this was in 2001. A pastor in California shared about missionaries flying into Los Angeles International Airport to reach Americans with the gospel. We need it! I believe we are ripe for God's judgment and abortion is a glaring indicator of our national depravity. One benchmark of a nation's holiness and righteousness is how its most vulnerable are treated.

And by the way, at the time of this writing, the Trump administration and Republicans are working on passing legislation to defund Planned Parenthood. I'm not holding my breath, but if this does happen, Hollywood will pick up the slack. There are celebrities now donating to the abortion giant such as Katy Perry who donated $10,000 and challenged others to do the same. You can always count on the entertainment industry to help promote your godless cause! One prime-time program, *Jane the Virgin*, even ran a banner on the bottom of the screen during the program with a hashtag and the words, "Support Planned Parenthood."

In one of the more disturbing displays of heartless, anti-Christian rebellion, on a season finale of the ABC show *Scandal*, they featured what was practically an hour-long Planned Parenthood advertisement. In the episode, the character Olivia (Kerry Washington) gets an abortion for convenience. Similar to many prime-time shows, *Scandal* has had no problem openly glorifying adultery and homosexuality while bashing Republicans and Christians, even telling one character to put his "bigoted Christian values" behind him.

During the scene in which Olivia is about to have an abortion,

---

60   Peter Kreeft, *How to Win the Culture War* (Downers Grove, IL: InterVarsity Press, 2002), 16.

surgical instruments are shown and as the abortionist begins the horrific procedure, the background music being played during the scene is the song "Silent Night." "Round yon virgin, mother and child; Holy infant, so tender and mild; Sleep in heavenly peace." Hollywood used abortion to mock the Savior of the world, who in real life was "born that man no more may die," to quote another Christmas song ("Hark! The Herald Angels Sing"). The show is another display of Hollywood's moral depravity, pushing the envelope of decency even further.

The media has also shown their cards and the evidence is beyond convicting; they simply refuse to report fairly on the horrors of the abortion industry. It was no surprise the talking heads as well as those in the print and online media virtually ignored the December 2016 breaking story on Planned Parenthood. At least some of them have admitted they don't want to write about these things because it will reflect negatively on abortion.

THE REPORT

The Senate Judiciary Committee published hundreds of condemning pages in the massive report on the practice of abortion clinics profiting from the sale of aborted fetuses. This investigation relied exclusively on documents obtained directly from Planned Parenthood and the complicit businesses doing the buying and selling (not on information from the troubling undercover videos by The Center for Medical Progress (CMP)).

First off, the law couldn't be clearer that it is illegal to make any money by selling the body parts of fetuses or body parts of any human being. The report shows Planned Parenthood willfully ignored and broke the law. What is shocking is hundreds if not thousands of Americans are part of these business transactions. These companies had contracts with Planned Parenthood and other abortion businesses to acquire specific body parts, and according to sources, the contracts were reviewed and altered by their accountants and lawyers.

This report is a journalist's dream. The problem in America is that there are so few true journalists in the profession working for the major networks and newspapers. Findings in this report are disturbing to anyone with a conscience. The Select Investigative Panel on Infant Lives urged law enforcement officials to prosecute the guilty parties involved: abortion facilities, universities who purchased parts for research, and fetal tissue companies.

One of the criminal referrals made by the panel was against the fetal tissue company StemExpress because it "may have destroyed documents that were the subject of congressional inquiries . . . and subpoenas." The panel also sent letters to the Texas attorney general and Department of Justice asking them to prosecute a late-term abortionist for allegedly murdering babies born alive.

The fact that this has been going on for years is bad enough. The fact that laws are being broken and few in the media report it usually means massive corruption is involved. There are four types of models of fetal tissue harvesting, and these can present problems when it comes to complying with federal laws. According to LifeSite News:

> "Laws potentially breached include those against the selling of human body parts, laws protecting human research subjects and patient privacy, 'laws regulating anatomical gifts for transplantation, therapy, research, and education; laws protecting late-term and born-alive infants'; and 'laws pertaining to public funding for fetal tissue research and abortion providers,' according to the final report.

> "Of particular concern to the Panel is the 'Late-Term Clinic Model' because of the 'intersection of late-term abortions, the potential for live births during the abortion procedure, and the transfer of tissues or whole cadavers from that clinic to research entities.'"[61]

American citizens deserve to know the truth about the abortion industry and who is breaking the law. In Planned Parenthood's case, they appear to be redefining "non-profit" right before our eyes. Representative Diane Black commented on the Select Panel's "relentless fact-finding investigation" over the last year and said it has "laid bare the grisly reality of

61   Claire Chretien, "Breaking: Congressional panel publishes final report on Planned Parenthood body parts scandal," 1/4/2017, www.lifesitenews.com/news/breaking-congressional-panel-publishes-final-report-on-planned-parenthood-b.

an abortion industry that is driven by profit, unconcerned by matters of basic ethics and, too often, noncompliant with the few laws we have to protect the safety of women and their unborn children."

The report concluded that human fetal tissue research is unproductive and has not produced a single medical treatment. It is not used to cure polio, mumps, and measles, nor is it used in modern vaccine production. Basically, baby body parts are not required "for the overwhelming majority of current research."

Still, the lengthy report provides troubling details including how some of the "technicians" spend their time dealing with the actual body parts. One company's own documents show how one technician harvested various body parts that they were able to sell for $6,825, which does not include additional costs per part for "shipping, disease testing, cleaning, and freezing." Every service is subject to separate fees. What a business! Three to four fetuses in a single morning of work. This reminds me again that the love of money is the root of all kinds of evil.

Journalist and filmmaker Phelim McAleer produced the Gosnell movie and co-authored a book about America's most prolific serial killer, abortionist Kermit Gosnell. McAleer said this report is an astonishing document and called it a "window into a very strange and very chilling world of selling baby parts." And "in this very creepy world, nothing goes to waste."

From the report, apparently Advanced Bioscience Resources, Inc. (ABR) is a company that has a cozy relationship with abortion clinics for obvious reasons. They detailed the basic job duties and daily activities of a technician from the time they obtained a twenty-week-old fetus at a Planned Parenthood clinic. For example:

> From that one fetus, ABR sold its brain to one customer for
> $325; both of its eyes for $325 each ($650 total) to a second
> customer; a portion of its liver for $325 to a third cus-
> tomer; its thymus for $325 and another portion of its liver
> to a fourth customer; and its lung for $325 to a fifth cus-
> tomer. These fees are merely the service fees for the speci-
> mens themselves; ABR separately charged each customer
> for shipping, disease, screening, cleaning, and freezing, as

applicable. So from that single fetus for which ABR paid a
mere $60, ABR charged its customers a total of $2,275 for
tissue specimens, plus additional charges for shipping and
disease screening.[62]

We know from the report the bills were paid. We've all seen invoices
with due dates and reminders to pay within thirty days, etc. The Senate
report provided a sampling of the thousands of invoices sent "back and
forth in the baby parts business." But what McAleer points out is the fact
that when you take a closer look you can see what is actually detailed in
the invoices – the "liver 2nd trimester," "brain 2nd trimester," the "eyes
(2) 2nd trimester." He concludes his article by saying the committee did
all the investigative work and the evidence is glaring. He stated, "They
have the contracts and the invoices, they have the internal documents.
But it has basically gone unreported. As the media frets about fake news
and a loss of credibility, they might think about covering stories that
challenge their beliefs and the beliefs of their friends."

In the horrifying trial of Philadelphia abortionist and mass murderer,
Kermit Gosnell, witnesses described baby abortion survivors "swim-
ming in toilets to get out." It was only after fifty-six days, letters to the
House of Representatives, and a public outcry, that all three major TV
networks finally mentioned the story.

Supporters of abortion do not see it the way you and I do, assuming
you are a Bible-believing Christian. They still see the issue as having to
do with *choice*, privacy, and women's health. Even after the compelling
undercover videos by David Daleiden and the CMP, pro-aborts argue
most women give their consent to allow abortion facilities to use the
remains of their fetuses.

That's the angle: "it's voluntary," they claim. I'd like to ask another
question for those open to reason and logic. If a woman who is two-
months pregnant is physically attacked and loses her unborn baby, can
the attacker be charged with manslaughter? What if the woman was
four-months pregnant? Six-months? How about eight-months pregnant?

In cases where both the woman and baby were killed, would the

---

62   Phelim McAleer, "The Senate Report on Planned Parenthood No One is Talking
      About," 12/20/2016, *townhall.com/columnists/phelimmcaleer/2016/12/20/
      the-senate-report-on-planned-parenthood-no-one-is-talking-about-n2261816*.

person be charged with double homicide, and if so, the more important question is why?

Currently there are thirty-eight states with fetal homicide laws, states that recognize the preborn or "unborn" child or fetus as a homicide victim. Signed into law in 2004, the Unborn Victims of Violence Act (Public Law 108-212) is a United States law recognizing a fetus in utero as a legal victim, if they are injured or killed during the commission of any of over sixty listed federal crimes of violence.

The most famous is Laci and Conner's Law, the bill named after Laci and Conner Peterson, the California mother and fetus whose deaths were widely publicized in 2003. Scott Peterson was convicted of double homicide under a fetal homicide law. Talk about a confused society. Some proponents of life, science, and biblical morality believe abortion is an act worthy of criminal charges as millions of babies have been "unborn victims of violence."

Another interesting case was decided in early 2017 when the Alabama Supreme Court unanimously ruled in defense of a woman's unborn baby in a wrongful death lawsuit. The Court stated that unborn children are human beings and are entitled to legal protection, "whether they have reached the ability to survive outside their mother's womb or not." This is huge!

Editor of LifeNews, Steven Ertelt reported:

> "The court largely based its decision on an amendment in Alabama's Homicide Act, which 'changed the definition of a 'person' who could be a victim of homicide to include 'an unborn child in utero at any stage of development, regardless of viability.' Alabama Supreme Court Justice Thomas Parker also wrote a concurring opinion, noting that the 'viability' standard in *Roe v. Wade* is faulty."[63]

Alabama became the seventh state to allow wrongful-death actions before the preborn child becomes viable. Still, some argue abortion is just one of many "medical services."

---

63   Steven Ertelt, "Alabama Supreme Court Rules Unborn Children Deserve Legal Protection," 1/4/2017, *www.lifenews.com/2017/01/04/alabama-supreme-court-rules-unborn-children-deserve-legal-protection/*.

THE THREE-PERCENT LIE

Here's how the 3-percent myth goes. Planned Parenthood repeatedly claims that abortion accounts for only 3 percent of its services. Who makes this claim? Leftists, abortion activists, the mainstream media, Hollywood, Democrats, and of course, Planned Parenthood employees. This claim is deceptive and disingenuous at best and a flat-out lie at worst.

One out of every eight Planned Parenthood customers gets an abortion. This equates to over 30 percent of the nation's abortions – or one abortion every ninety-seven seconds. Planned Parenthood manipulates its own data to cover up the fact that abortion accounts for the majority of its "services" for pregnant women.

Moreover, if a woman with an unwanted pregnancy goes into a Planned Parenthood facility, that preborn child is 160 times more likely to be poisoned, burned, or dismembered than allowed to be born and put up for adoption to a waiting family. (Planned Parenthood aborts 160 children for every one child it refers out for adoption.)

So, how do they come up with that 3-percent figure? Planned Parenthood divides the number of abortions they commit by the number of services the facilities provide. Services such as pregnancy tests, pap smears, breast exams, sexually transmitted infections (STI) testing, birth control, and others are – get this – counted equally with an abortion procedure. A pregnancy test can be $10 while an abortion can be upwards of $1,500 depending on gestation.

Are you still with me? So even though abortion is their moneymaker, the lion's share of their business and much more profitable, Planned Parenthood calculates contraception or a pregnancy test as equal (in value) to an abortion procedure. It's just one of many *services*. Even liberal websites and news outlets have debunked the 3-percent talking point. The *Washington Post* even gave Planned Parenthood "three Pinocchios" for their misleading claim. The abortion giant does this in order to justify its half a billion dollars in federal funding.

Live Action President Lila Rose called the 3-percent lie a clever marketing gimmick and a cover-up of its abortion-driven agenda. Rose states:

> "Planned Parenthood downplays abortion – falsely claiming that it only makes up three percent of its business

– and instead plays up its cancer screenings and so-called 'women's health care.' However, Planned Parenthood's own numbers prove it's an abortion corporation, focused on abortion, not on women's health care. Planned Parenthood doesn't perform a single mammogram, and it performs less than two percent of all women's cancer screenings in the United States, yet it commits over 30 percent of America's abortions."[64]

According to Live Action, numbers taken from Planned Parenthood's own data show just how low the percentage of its services are for actual women's health needs.

Planned Parenthood's U.S. market share for Pap tests is 0.97 percent. (It performed 271,539 tests out of 28.1 million tests nationwide in fiscal year 2014-2015.)

Planned Parenthood's market share for clinical breast exams is 1.8 percent (363,803 exams out of 20 million exams nationwide).

Planned Parenthood's market share for mammograms is 0.0 percent. (They do not do mammograms.)

Planned Parenthood's market share for abortions is 30.6 percent. (It committed 323,999 abortions out of approximately 1.06 million nationwide.)

Here's an example almost everyone can understand. Think of your favorite steakhouse. What do you go there for? Steak. But steak is just one of its products. Most steakhouses also serve chicken, fish, veggies, potatoes, dinner rolls, butter, fried food items, salad, salad dressing, appetizers, condiments, desserts, coffee, sodas, and all kinds of drinks.

A single steakhouse serves dozens of items from a side of corn to filet mignon. Now, there may be a difference in price of thirty dollars or so, but according to Planned Parenthood's math, both are counted as a single product. So along these lines, steak is a very small percentage of all the "products" a steakhouse serves. Now let's be real – very few

---

64   Becky Yeh, "New video debunks Planned Parenthood's 3 percent abortion myth," 9/4/2016, *www.liveactionnews.org/new-video-debunks-planned-parenthoods-3-percent-abortion-myth/*.

people are going to a steakhouse for salad, pasta, or just dessert, but to say steak is only 3 percent of what a steakhouse does is ridiculous.

Abortion accounts for over 90 percent of Planned Parenthood's services for pregnant women, but a majority of Americans still believe the lies. To Christians, much more important than the math is the morality of this issue, or in this case, the immorality of abortion.

Earlier this year, President Donald Trump made an offer to Planned Parenthood: stop doing abortions and you can keep your $500 million in federal tax dollars. The offer was turned down. Why? If abortion is such a small percentage of your *services* as you claim, why refuse the offer? Abortion is not a service "provided," it is an act of violence that ends a life. Whatever you think about him, President Trump is doing what no other president has been willing to do.

Cecile Richards replied to Trump by saying Planned Parenthood is "proud to provide abortion – a necessary service that's as vital to our mission as birth control or cancer screenings." Necessary? Vital to their mission of eliminating life? So vital to them it's worth risking a half a billion dollars. One argument liberals make is if Planned Parenthood were defunded, where would women go for *health care*?

There are approximately 13,540 women's clinics in the country providing comprehensive health care for women. You probably didn't hear about this in the media. Planned Parenthood has about 665 clinics. Some folks actually believe if the abortion leader loses its federal funding, women will be scrambling to find a clinic to help them, and even worse, some are convinced many women will be left out on the streets, so to speak.

Talk about fake news! Community health centers across the country exist to provide necessary care to millions of uninsured, working-poor, and jobless Americans. If Planned Parenthood's federal funding were to be discontinued, wouldn't the money be better allocated to help citizens get care at actual health centers that do provide a full range of services – without the corruption? By the way, nine thousand federally qualified health centers in the country provide comprehensive care (even mammograms) for women, and do not have the ethical issues Planned Parenthood has because these clinics do not perform abortions.

Planned Parenthood may be pro-abortion, but they aren't "pro-choice." American taxpayers don't have a choice but to be forced to subsidize abortion even if we believe it is immoral and goes against our conscience. One more disappointing fact is that from 2012 – 2016, employees of Planned Parenthood and its affiliates as well as political action entities devoted nearly $34 million to outside spending related to electing (or reelecting) pro-abortion Democrats across the country. Obviously, Barack Obama and Hillary Clinton were among the top recipients of our tax dollars – I mean, Planned Parenthood money.

NO APOLOGIES FOR THE GRIZZLY FACTS

In a YouTube video for the *Daily Wire*, author Ben Shapiro asks why the media keeps covering up the brutality of Planned Parenthood, ignoring the undercover videos showing its executives casually and callously discussing the harvesting and sale of aborted-baby body parts. Shapiro states, "Because it might make you uncomfortable; worse, it might make Democrats uncomfortable because Democrats love Planned Parenthood. The Democratic Party platform stands for the ability of a woman to crush her baby's head one minute before birth, and they want you to pay for it. It's actually in their platform."

The actual portion of their platform he is referring to reads, "The Democratic Party strongly and unequivocally supports *Roe v. Wade* and a woman's right to make decisions regarding her pregnancy including a safe and legal abortion regardless of ability to pay."

Shapiro also mentioned the fact that President Obama as a state senator in Illinois actually called for fully formed, living babies to be killed after birth. (See "Born-Alive Infants Protection Act.") The most radical liberals say that even if a baby survives an attempt on his or her life, the baby must be left to die because that (abortion) was the will of its mother. He said such a child was merely a fetus outside of the mother's womb.

Hillary Clinton says she's "proud to stand with Planned Parenthood," but after hearing about "doctors" selling baby organs, she pretended to find it "disturbing."

Shapiro doesn't hold back: "People who claim they're disturbed by the sale of baby organs, and are totally fine with the crushing of their heads are moral idiots. It's like saying you're disturbed by the whipping of American slaves, but not by anyone holding them as slaves in the first place."

The video continues with graphic descriptions of common abortion techniques. If it upsets you just reading this, imagine what the fetus endures. (It's now proven they feel pain.)

> During the first three months of pregnancy, doctors plunge a tube with an edged tip into the womb, they then use the suction power of the tube to literally tear apart the child while it's alive, and then they suck the pieces out of the mother's womb. This is called suction aspiration. Unpleasant? Try "dilation and curettage." In this version of abortion, doctors use a curette, which chops up the baby inside the womb and then scrapes it right out. As the baby grows, the methods of abortion get uglier and uglier.

> There's "dilation and evacuation," in which doctors use forceps to crush the baby including its brain and spine. The pieces are then removed. And as a last resort, doctors use partial-birth abortion. Democrats love partial-birth abortion. This is a procedure in which doctors use an ultrasound to find a baby's legs with the forceps. They pull it into the birth canal, they deliver the entire baby except for the head, and then they stab the baby in the skull with a scissors, insert a suction tube into the skull and suck out the brains. This is also the preferred method for ensuring that the internal organs are best preserved so Planned Parenthood can hock them to Big Pharma.[65]

Look at the church and our general lack of resistance to big abortion businesses. What will it take? Perhaps people need to witness the procedure. I agree with pro-life leader Father Frank Pavonne: "America will not resist abortion until America sees abortion."

Abortion is a selfish, violent act and in essence, a way for man to

---

65   Ben Shapiro, "Ben Shapiro: The Truth About Planned Parenthood," *The Daily Wire* YouTube, 8/20/2015, *www.youtube.com/watch?v=RhoFNmMeO8k*.

"play God" with human life. One baby's life destroyed is too many. If abortion is murder, if it is eliminating a human life, then abortion is an immoral act against the God who created that person in His image.

> Before I formed you in the womb I knew you; before you
> were born I sanctified you (Jeremiah 1:5 NKJV).

The lie about life is that abortion is a right and it liberates women, when in reality, most women deal with grief, guilt, regret, and years of deep anguish after having an abortion.

ETHICS OF EUTHANASIA AND ASSISTED SUICIDE

The logical progression of the abortion thought process is the devaluing of all life. Support for assisted suicide or euthanasia has also increased – even among churchgoers. Six states have legalized physician-assisted suicide in America.

Hollywood continues doing its part to influence the culture. A recent example is the 2016 movie *Me Before You*, which attempted to make assisted suicide romantic. The main character's death is depicted as noble, and yet, the message seems to be that the ultimate act of love – for those who are disabled – is death. How insensitive. Death is better than living with a disability? I know there are at least a few million Americans who would strongly disagree.

Here's a challenging question for some of us: if we believe it's wrong to kill human beings at the beginning of life via abortion, then why do some of us approve of killing people near the end of their lives? A majority of Americans – including four in ten professing evangelicals – want doctors to help terminally ill patients end their lives, and believe it is morally acceptable. LifeWay Research revealed last year that opposition to assisted suicide is lessening and the heart of the problem is our apathy and indifference as a "civilized" society.

Even the American Medical Association (AMA) has described physician-assisted suicide as a serious risk to society and "fundamentally incompatible with a physician's role as healer," but apparently millions of Americans disagree. Oregon was the first state in which it became legal in 1997, and there will be more to follow. One reason is that more people believe it's acceptable to ask for help to speed up the inevitable dying process, especially if a person is suffering. But doesn't this remove God's sovereignty?

Voters in Colorado were practically sold on Proposition 106 last year. It was cleverly titled "The End of Life Option Act." Of course! Who doesn't want options in life? But here's a big problem with these solutions that sound compassionate: most depressed people get better and some get permanently healed, so those who are suicidal could also be helped. Apparently, this law does not require psychiatric evaluation for patients requesting suicide.

In LifeWay Research's survey, 67 percent of Americans agree with the statement, "When a person is facing a painful terminal disease, it is morally acceptable to ask for a physician's aid in taking his or her own life." Sadly, even 38 percent of evangelical Christians agree.[66] Think about that; regardless of the reason, of Christians who profess to live by the precepts in the Bible, nearly four in ten say it is okay to get a doctor to help end a person's life.

Belgium has had fifteen years of legal euthanasia and some are saying the experiment has gone very wrong. "Mercy killing" is a false ideology. There have been cases in which a patient underwent "doctor-assisted dying" and was in a completely different, more-sound state of mind than when the approval papers were signed, but since it was legal, the doctors proceeded with the original wishes of the patient.

How about Canada? The debate up north is about ethics and safe-guards two years after Canada's Supreme Court legalized assisted sui-cide. Some are seeing a moneymaking opportunity to collect organs from donors for transplants or research from terminally ill patients. Some don't care about legal or moral issues. Due to the cost problems Canada has had with its health care system, some are pointing to esti-mates that assisted suicide may have led to the Canadian government saving nearly $138 million a year. How's that for motivation?

Assisted suicide is not a form of compassion, it is a form of control. It's easy to understand the moral dilemma because human beings are fragile and life is but a vapor. We are naturally fascinated with the idea that we can have more say over how and when we die, and according

---

66   Bob Smietana, "Opposition to Assisted Suicide Dies Out," 12/6/2016, *www.christianityto-day.com/gleanings/ 2016/december/opposition-to-assisted-suicide-dies-out-lifeway.html.*

to the survey, two-thirds say it is morally acceptable for terminally ill patients to ask their doctors for help in ending their lives.

A Gallup survey echoed the results. Up from 53 percent in 2013, the percentage of Americans saying physician-assisted suicide should be legal is around 68 percent. This debate will continue to be controversial for obvious reasons.

Traditional Christian teaching, however, says God the Creator holds the keys to life and death. According to the psalmist, our times are in His hands (Psalm 31:15), and in Psalm 138:8, *The LORD will accomplish what concerns me; Your lovingkindness, O LORD, is everlasting; Do not forsake the works of Your hands.*

And Psalm 139:16b states, *And in Your book they all were written, The days fashioned for me, When as yet there were none of them* (NKJV).

There are more Scriptures supporting the fact God created us, knows and cares for us (Nahum 1:7), knows the number of our days (Job 14:5), and promises to be with believers forever. I mention these because the argument for taking life into our own hands leads to a very slippery slope.

One activist in Australia claims assisted suicide is not just for the terminally ill; the option should be available to everyone. Philip Nitschke once wanted to make suicide pills available in supermarkets, even to "troubled teens." It may seem like an extreme position to believe that individuals have the right to dispose of their lives for any reason, but this has more support than most of us realize. Nitschke just launched "Exit Action," an advocacy group calling for death on demand or "unrestricted access to a peaceful death." He states, "Exit Action believes that a peaceful death, and access to the best euthanasia drugs, is a right of all competent adults, regardless of sickness or permission from the medical profession."[67]

His only sin, in the eyes of euthanasia movement leaders, is excess candor.

People often think they know best about life and death, and man has decided to call the shots. What could go wrong? Requesting doctors

---

67 Steven Ertelt, "Death on Demand: Euthanasia Activist Admits Assisted Suicide Not Just for Terminally Ill," 12/5/2016,
www.lifenews.com/2016/12/05/death-on-demand-euthanasia-activist-admits-assisted-suicide-not-jut-for-terminally-ill/.

to betray one of their most sacred oaths to do no harm and turn from their task of healing is not a decision to be taken lightly.

As difficult as it is to endure the suffering of a loved one, playing God is not the right answer. Tribulation produces perseverance, perseverance produces character, and character, hope (Romans 5:3-4).

There is an epidemic of deceit, and truth is found lacking in our culture. Will you help proclaim the eternal principles in God's Word about all life, and educate, expose, and raise awareness in your community? Will you encourage your pastor to talk about life in the womb from the pulpit?

It's important to the Lord of life and should be important to us. The question is, do we have the heart and perseverance to fight the battles to defend the most vulnerable – or are we too busy? Will our excuses hold any weight when we ultimately stand before God one day? From the unborn, the disabled, and the elderly, to the jobless, the homeless, or the hopeless, *every* human being is created in the image of God and worthy of dignity and respect.

Let's take Jesus at His Word and care enough for "the least of these" to speak on their behalf. Eternity in God's presence will bring us the ultimate healing and peace beyond anything this world can offer. And the rewards will be worth it.

> "He will wipe away every tear from their eyes; and there will no longer be any death; there will no longer be any mourning, or crying, or pain; the first things have passed away." And He who sits on the throne said, "Behold, I am making all things new." And He said, "Write, for these words are faithful and true." Then He said to me, "It is done. I am the Alpha and the Omega, the beginning and the end." (Revelation 21:4-6)

Chapter 11

Entertaining Demons in America: Women on the March

For I was very glad when brethren came and testified to your truth, that is, how you are walking in truth. I have no greater joy than this, to hear of my children walking in the truth. Beloved, do not imitate what is evil, but what is good. The one who does good is of God; the one who does evil has not seen God. (3 John 1:3-4, 11)

"One way to distinguish truth from all its counterfeits is by its modesty: truth demands only to be heard among others while its counterfeits demand others be silenced."
– Sydney Harris

Is it possible to walk in the truth and have one foot in the world? I tried this for years, and failed. The things we meditate on and allow into our soul affect us – leading us to do good or evil. When we watch most of the popular movies and television shows, and listen to the most popular music today, we are entertaining demonic spirits. What in the world are we allowing into our hearts, our minds, and our homes? Many Christians are quite defensive about the entertainment they consume. Why?

Those influenced (and some possessed) by demons are literally entertaining us. The Bible instructs us to protect, watch over, and guard our hearts with all diligence (Proverbs 4:23). One translation says do this "above all else" because everything we do flows from our hearts. It's quite possible that at some point in our lives, every one of us has failed to guard our hearts when it comes to amusement and entertainment.

So many things distract us, often leading to poor choices. Bad habits don't just fall out of the sky into our lives. Either we as Christians are disciplined in this area – striving to live counter-culturally – or culture is changing us. We're surrounded by narcissism, pride, technology, social media, self-exaltation, lies, and evil being called good, so let's look at today's influential entertainers and role models.

Selfie queen, Kim Kardashian, became wildly rich and famous, not for studying, working hard, and paying her dues – not for some great achievement, career accomplishment, or a contribution to society that helped others – but because people knew her name. She was famous thanks to her father, Robert, and O. J. Simpson, and she knew how to work the system in America.

What are her skills? Accumulation, self-promotion, and consumption, for starters. She reportedly spent $827,000 on gold-plated toilets for her mansion. The American public became fascinated with Kim and her family during the murder trial of Simpson in 1995. He and the late Robert Kardashian were close friends. Kim also grew up with wealthy heiress Paris Hilton who actually hired Kardashian to be her assistant during the reality TV show *The Simple Life* (2003 – 2007).

Apparently, the show was like *The Beverly Hillbillies* in reverse, where two rich Beverly Hills girls moved in with a small farm family in the Midwest for five weeks. Reality? The rich girls known for partying in Los Angeles attempted to do farming tasks – and the show lasted five years. (I don't know why either.)

Soon after that, Kim Kardashian was awarded $5 million in a settlement for her 2007 sex tape, and she used the money to propel her family into stardom by producing their own reality show, *Keeping Up with the Kardashians*. Of things that have redefined "reality," I believe so-called reality TV is at the top of the list.

Writing in *The Washington Times* about why we should care, Jessica Chasmar penned an article, "Kardashian culture is killing America," and stated:

"The Kardashian saga illustrates our nation's moral, spiritual, and cultural decay like few other media stories do. America of 50 years ago would regard Ms. Kardashian with a mixture of disdain and pity, embarrassed by the very idea of a young lady's most private moments being broadcast for all the world to see. America of 25 years ago would stop and think before promoting through business channels a figure with such sordid background and negligible public relations attributes."[68]

Kim Kardashian and family's addiction to self-worship has further polluted the soul of a nation that has forgotten its roots. With so much of today's entertainment falling under the category of soul pollution – most of it promoting what the Bible considers to be sin – it's no surprise American culture has gone into the gutter. But this is where Kardashian and other celebrity gods have taken us. This stuff wouldn't be on TV if people didn't watch it and if advertisers didn't make a profit. That also goes for the most popular, raunchy movies in the theater, as well as television shows with top actors and actresses. We support them by watching.

That's the sad part: they keep getting rewarded. Kim Kardashian, rapper husband Kanye West, and Caitlyn Jenner were named among *Time Magazine*'s thirty most influential people on the Internet last year. Beyond the stunning popularity of a show like *Keeping Up with the Kardashians*, think of its negative influence on young people (especially girls) today: offensive language, disrespect for authority, promotion of promiscuity, greed, hypersensuality, showing cleavage almost constantly, inappropriate dress; glorifying shopping, partying, leisure, adultery, selfishness, and an extreme emphasis on sex. Talk about fantasy.

I know very little about video games and iPhone apps, but apparently Kardashian has a game app worth over $200 million. (Her cut was a mere $71.8 million last year alone.) The game invites players to pursue a fantasy life of digital fame. Fans and players have downloaded the mobile game "Kim Kardashian: Hollywood" over 45 million times.

---

68   Jessica Chasmar, "Kardashian culture is killing America," 1/3/2013, *www.washingtontimes.com/news/2013/jan/ 3/kardashian-culture-is-killing-america/.*

According to *Wired* magazine (6/30/16), that equates to nearly 16 billion minutes playing an idiotic game and wasting about 30,342 years.

The Kardashians have succeeded at taking advantage of a dumbed-down and bored generation of people with misplaced priorities, and the show is in its twelfth season. Twelve. On Instagram alone, Kim Kardashian has 84 million followers. How does she keep them enthralled? With endless posts featuring celebrity friends, Kanye West, her travels, and her scantily clad self, of course. Like it or not, parents, she is a role model for today's teen girls.

Sometimes I hate what America has become. Then I remember that I was once just as lost. We can't expect the godless to act as if they know God and are saved. These people may think they have it all in life and don't need anything, but you and I know they need Jesus Christ. Let's pray they come to the truth before it's too late.

Our society probably deserves Kim Kardashian, and God's judgment. Lord, have mercy.

WHATEVER HAPPENED TO BRUCE JENNER?

Another famous member of the Kardashian clan is Caitlyn Jenner. His fame began much differently as a man known as Bruce Jenner – a great athlete who competed in the 1976 Olympics and won the gold medal in the decathlon. You've got to be quite the athlete to win this competition, as you are up against the best of the best in the world in ten separate events.

I still remember Jenner on the cover of Wheaties cereal and on magazine covers, draped in the American flag. He then became an entrepreneur, a product spokesman, and a motivational speaker. In 1991, Bruce Jenner met Kris Kardashian and they soon married. The couple had two daughters together and Jenner became the stepfather of Kim and three other children.

Jenner participated on the family show *Keeping Up with the Kardashians*, but eventually divorced his wife, Kris, in 2014. He grew out his hair and in 2015 announced to the world he had been living a double life. He had been cross-dressing for years, so the effusive media stepped in immediately to bring his story to the world. The cover of

People Magazine proclaimed Bruce was "Living as a woman every day – and feeling elated." Jenner's second wife, Linda Thompson, described her ex-husband as "a champion for those who share the struggle to just be who they are."

Jenner said things such as "My brain is much more female than it is male. That's what my soul is." And though he has the support of his extended family, they may be feeding his disease. After his interview with Diane Sawyer, Kim Kardashian tweeted, "Love is the courage to live the truest, best version of yourself. Bruce is love." But the Bible says, "God is love." Which one is your truth? So, we have not only seen reality be redefined, but now "courage" as well. Kourtney Kardashian said she couldn't be a prouder daughter, and "With courage and bravery, let's change the world."

Sports are games and for the athlete, a form of competition. For the rest of the world, they are a form of amusement and entertainment. And make no mistake, the liberal sports media in America does have a political agenda and they will use whomever serves their purposes. Jenner legally changed his name to "Caitlyn," and in 2015 he received ESPN's Arthur Ashe Courage Award due to "his brave journey." I agree it must have been hard to come out publicly and do what he did, but if his is a documented mental illness, all the cheerleaders, promoters, media, and fans are encouraging the wrong thing.

The same month the award was announced was the anniversary of D-Day when brave men in the military stormed the beaches of Normandy knowing it was a deadly mission during which thousands gave their lives serving this country. That's courage. Today's veterans who come back to society after having served and who push through PTSD or permanent injuries including lost limbs – they are courageous.

True courage is a child fighting a terminal disease and parents enduring the process. It is being a caregiver for the disabled or elderly. Courage is choosing to have the baby. It is the single mom or single dad raising children after a spouse dies. Courage is a couple fighting to save their marriage or giving up everything to become missionaries. It is protecting and serving citizens as a police officer despite the lies and propaganda against them. Courage is Christians around the world in hostile nations refusing to deny their faith in the midst of severe persecution knowing it could cost them their lives – and often does.

Caitlyn Jenner needs help, and we should continue to pray for him and others following the same path – such as Jazz Jennings.

In February 2017, toy company Tonner announced the first transgender doll on the market, made in the likeness of sixteen-year-old transgender activist, Jazz Jennings. Jennings appeared on a Barbara Walters *20/20* special back in 2007 at the age of six. Jazz was named one of *Time Magazine*'s Most Influential Teens for 2014 and 2015, during which Jennings co-wrote a children's picture book, *I Am Jazz*.

Tonner company founder Robert Tonner designed the doll and said Jazz stands for everything he respects from a human nature point of view, and that "she's incredibly brave, intelligent, warm-hearted, and creative." One rule liberals and activists must follow is always present whatever goes against God and Scripture in the most positive light possible.

Speaking about Donald Trump's policy rescinding Obama's bathroom order, young Jennings said that growing up he faced discrimination and "I had it really hard because I wasn't allowed to use the girl's restroom," adding that "I didn't understand why I was being treated differently." Less than two weeks earlier, in an Instagram post about the doll, Jazz Jennings said though the doll is based on an individual who is transgender, "Of course, it is still just a regular girl doll because that's exactly what I am: a regular girl!"[69]

Tell me, in the Bible, biology, or science, is a person who is born male just "a regular girl"? Of course not, but people are buying it! Whether it is Caitlyn Jenner or Jazz Jennings, deep down there must have been a measure of torment in their soul, but these and many other activists have become the new faces of change and *reality*. I feel sorry for them, angry at their enablers, and disappointed by the accommodating public. I hope God gets through to them before it's too late.

Most of us understand that no human-made modification can remedy our sin problem and only through the forgiveness of Jesus Christ can any of us be saved. Sure, we can change our names, our physical

69   Katie Reilly, "First Transgender Doll Modeled After Teen Advocate Jazz Jennings," 2/24/2017, *fortune.com/2017/ 02/24/transgender-doll-jazz-jennings/*.

features, take testosterone or add implants, and put on makeup, but we can never truly *reassign* what God designed. It's interesting that Jenner identifies as female, claims he is still heterosexual in his attractions, but looks like a masculine woman and goes by "Caitlyn." Children of this generation are confused as they watch the cultural circus known as "anything goes except God."

Ours is an ABC culture: **A**nything **B**ut **C**hrist. There are answers in Scripture for every possible human question, concern, and problem, and this one certainly is no different. One key question is, who or what is your final authority? It's quite simple, really.

> *A woman shall not wear man's clothing, nor shall a man put on a woman's clothing; for whoever does these things is an abomination to the LORD your God.* (Deuteronomy 22:5)

Finally, Jenner says he is really excited about the future and what good he can do in the world, saying, "My whole life has been getting me ready for this." He explained how he told his children God was looking down and made "little Bruce," and "gave me all these wonderful qualities."

His theology is correct about creation up to this point, and then, apparently God second-guesses Himself and, in Jenner's words, God thought, "Wait a second, we've got to give him something in his life to struggle with." Still not a complete departure from Scripture until he said, "Let's give him the soul of a female."

We saw the support from his family. Many celebrities who entertain us also made statements about the news at the time. Ellen DeGeneres called "Bruce Jenner" a beautiful, brave human being, and said, "He's saving lives and opening minds tonight." Of course. Lady Gaga stated, "Now that is bravery," and encouraged others to empower transgenders all over the world and make history together. And Miley Cyrus tweeted: "I LOOOOVE LOOOVE LOOOVE Bruce Jenner!!!!!!!"

Loving him is one thing. Cheering someone on to pursue a path of sin, which will likely lead to serious health issues, is another. Only God can heal the human heart. We can love and have compassion toward Caitlyn Jenner and still speak the truth. Every one of us will stand before the Maker of all hearts. Mine goes out to those who are truly suffering.

MILEY CYRUS WARNED US

A few years ago, it was reported that the management for Miley Cyrus received complaints from parents because her tour was like a "porn show." Cyrus defiantly took to Twitter to respond, "You can't say I didn't warn you . . . Save your complaints for the McDonald's drive thru." Around that same time she used her Instagram account to talk about Jesus. But not the way most Christians would talk about Him. Get ready for some theology according to Miley Cyrus! Here are the words from a picture she posted:

> "Jesus was a radical, nonviolent revolutionary who hung around with lepers, hookers, and crooks; wasn't American and never spoke English; was anti-wealth, anti-death penalty, anti-public prayer (M 6:5); but was never anti-gay, never mentioned abortion or birth control, never called the poor lazy, never justified torture, who never fought for tax cuts for the wealthiest Nazarenes, never asked a Leper for copay; and was a long-haired brown-skinned homeless community-organizing anti-slut-shaming middle eastern Jew."

You read that right. Like many in the entertainment industry who claim to know it all, Cyrus is redefining truth by creating a god in her own image. There are too many problems with this to address every alleged claim, but for one thing, Jesus Christ was not at all against wealth. The Bible does teach that the *love* of money is a heart issue (1 Timothy 6:10). Also, a man is worthy of his wages (Romans 4:4), and we are supposed to honor the Lord with our wealth (Proverbs 3:9), in part by setting aside a portion of our income for God's work (1 Corinthians 16:2).

Good Fight Ministries is an excellent resource on demonic influences in entertainment. Contributor Chad Davidson shared some thoughts on the Jesus that Miley Cyrus is describing, and addressed the claim that Jesus was against praying in public when in fact He spoke out against praying to please men:

> He was calling out those who would draw near with their lips, while their hearts were far from Him. He was looking for a people who would truly seek Him, be it in public

or not. The picture then attempts to use an argument from silence on issues such as [homosexuality], abortion and birth control. But with this logic, one would have to assume that Jesus wasn't anti-pedophilia, -rape, -incest, nor -bestiality because He never spoke about those things, either.

What many people want to do is separate the person of Jesus from the God of the Old Testament. The problem with this is: Jesus IS the God of the Old Testament. . . . Christ not only referred to Himself as "the Truth" but as the entire Old Testament as well. . . . While the civil and ceremonial laws of the Israelites may have been negated and fulfilled, the very nature of God in His holiness will never change.[70]

It is a good reminder for us that the moral laws of Scripture are laws that will never change since Jesus is eternal and remains the same. His laws are written on our hearts.

Cyrus, on the other hand, will apparently say or do whatever will keep her in the news, perhaps in an effort to shock the public. How bizarre or graphic or outrageous does she need to get before people claiming to love her finally show some concern about her well-being? Instead, they encourage her behavior, including her destructive and unhealthy views on the purpose of sex.

In June of 2015, "Wrecking Ball" Miley posed nude with a pig and shared her views on sexuality in an interview: "I am literally open to every single thing that is consenting and doesn't involve an animal and everyone is of age. Everything that's legal, I'm down with. . . . I don't relate to being boy or girl, and I don't have to have my partner relate to boy or girl."[71]

Miley said she told her mother at the age of fourteen that she considered herself bisexual. Evidently, her mother responded with support but concern that Miley would be judged. She didn't want her daughter

---

70   Chad Davidson, "Miley Cyrus' Jesus," *www.goodfight.org/miley-cyrus-jesus/*.

71   Guardian music, "Miley Cyrus: 'I don't relate to being boy or girl,'" 6/10/2015, *www.the-guardian.com/music/ 2015/jun/10/miley-cyrus-i-dont-relate-to-being-boy-or-girl*.

to go to hell. Cyrus claimed that her mother "believes in me more than she believes in any god," which is pretty concerning. Reassuring herself, she stated, "The Universe has always given me the power to know I'll be okay."

She insists her parents are "conservative a-- m------f---ers," and while declaring herself nonjudgmental, Cyrus showed her contempt for Christian and conservative lawmakers who are not progressive, saying, "Those people shouldn't get to make our laws." For those of us who believe Noah's Ark is real, her response was classic rebellion: "That's f---ing insane. We've outgrown that fairy tale, like we've outgrown f---ing Santa and the tooth fairy."

I've read that Miley Cyrus was raised Christian, attended a Southern Baptist church, and even wore a purity ring as a young teen. This begs the question: what happened to Miley Cyrus? Is she a victim of culture, Hollywood, a weak foundation of faith growing up, or herself? When she moved to L.A. from Tennessee in 2005, it took less than five years for her mind and heart to become polluted and corrupt. Her image and her music drastically changed.

Cyrus lost her innocence, inhibitions, integrity, and self-respect, but she is not going down alone! She's taking millions of young, mostly female fans with her. Just like Lady Gaga and Madonna (although both are more talented), Cyrus has chosen the path paved by outrageous visuals and sex-charged stage antics to get attention. In October 2016, she made another statement about her sexuality, saying that she has always hated the word "bisexual" because even that is putting her in a box. Claiming she "didn't understand my own gender and my own sexuality" all her life, she now identifies as "pansexual." After going to the LGBTQ center in L.A., she said, "Once I understood **my gender** more, **which was unassigned**, then I understood my sexuality more. I was like, 'Oh – that's why I don't feel straight and I don't feel gay. It's because I'm not'" (emphasis added).[72]

Between her Instagram and Twitter accounts alone she has over 100 million followers, and a quick scan of her posts proves one goal is

---

72   Ramin Setoodeh, "Miley Cyrus on The Voice, Donald Trump, and Coming Out," 10/16/2016, *variety.com/2016/ music/features/miley-cyrus-the-voice-donald-trump-vmas-woody-allen-coming-out-pansexual-1201884281/.*

to use her celebrity status to further the progressive agenda through the Democratic Party and to criticize President Trump, Republicans, Christians, and whoever else disagrees with her worldview. And she now says she's "genderless."

But let's step back and imagine being in her shoes for a moment, hearing for most of your life that you're the greatest. Every picture you post and every comment or tweet gets thousands of approving, fawning responses or shares. In her mind, perhaps she can do no wrong. Fame can be seductive and destructive to some, and the lure toward the demonic is often too strong to resist.

Some may look at Cyrus and see a desperate cry for help. And yet, she is another who is convinced she doesn't need God. Just like Whitney Houston, Michael Jackson, Anna Nicole Smith, Heath Ledger, Amy Winehouse, River Phoenix, and too many others who fought the darkness and emptiness of fame, wealth, worldly success – and lost – I pray she is not too far gone.

God had a plan and purpose for her life, and she could have been a beautiful, positive influence on young people. So much for being a good, responsible role model.

A blogger mom wrote to her daughter about one particular performance and said Cyrus lacked self-respect, acted like an "overheated hound dog" with her tongue hanging out, and is simply screaming for attention because Miley hasn't heard the word "no" very often. She concluded, "Dear daughter, I am going to fight or die trying to keep you from becoming like the Miley Cyruses of the world. You can thank me later."

Ask God to intervene in the lives of influential celebrities in bondage to sin. He can bring them back, remind them of His enduring love, and save them by changing their hearts like He changed ours. When we address these issues in our culture, let's ask the Lord to give us a proper balance of disgust with the sin, but love for the one caught in its web.

KATY PERRY

Like Cyrus, pop star Katy Perry grew up in a Christian home, but that didn't last long. On March 18 of this year, Perry accepted an award for her activism from the anti-Christian Human Rights Campaign, a prominent homosexual advocacy organization, at their annual gala in Los Angeles. *Time Magazine* called it an "impassioned speech calling for LGBTQ equality."

While accepting their National Equality Award, Perry said, "I have to stand for what I know is true and that is equality and justice for all people – period." Here goes another celebrity using the word *true*. (I do not think it means what she thinks it means.) She also mocked God by taking plenty of jabs at Christianity, saying, "most of my unconscious adolescence, I prayed the gay away at my Jesus camps."

> *Do not be deceived, God is not mocked; for whatever a man*
> *sows, that he will also reap. For he who sows to his flesh will*
> *of the flesh reap corruption.* (Galatians 6:7-8a NKJV)

I get it that her Christian upbringing conflicted with her sexual curiosity because she was taught homosexuality was a sin. What seems to go with the flow of relativism, however, is her comment about sexuality not being black and white. She said:

> "But how was I going to reconcile that with the gospel-
> singing girl raised in youth groups that were pro-conver-
> sion camps? What I did know was I was curious, and even
> then I knew sexuality was not as black and white as this
> dress. But in 2008, when that song came out, ["I Kissed a
> Girl"], I knew that I started a conversation, and a lot of the
> world seemed curious enough to sing along, too."[73]

Perry almost seems boastful about being a worldwide catalyst for sexual openness and experimentation. As Christians, we know this is not something to be taken lightly. She practically admitted that her music led people to sin.

We forget the fact that many people, Christians included, battle temptation and struggle with same-sex *attractions*, though they refuse to act on them or be defined by them. Writing about this, Peter Heck complimented those faithful Christians who didn't choose their desires,

---

73   Daniel Nussbaum, "Katy Perry: 'I Did More' Than Just Kiss a Girl During
      Christian Upbringing," 3/19/2017, *www.breitbart.com/big-hollywood/2017/03/19/*
      katy-perry-just-kiss-girl-conservative-christian-upbringing/.

but "they do choose to surrender their urges to the will of Christ" and deny themselves gratification.

Calling Perry's remarks "flippant," Heck says she was "rudely dismissive" to Christians who have overcome their sexual temptations by the power of the Holy Spirit, and writes:

Youth groups and church camps that preach the power of the gospel to change lives aren't "anti-gay." They are professing the truth that human beings do not have to become slaves to their sins, and that real freedom is found not in self-gratification, but in sacrificing our personal lusts – sexual or otherwise – to the greater cause of obeying Christ.

The only "conversion" that we promote is the life-changing one that involves making the incredibly difficult choice to sacrifice our existence to Christ. Many can't do that because they lack the strength of character it requires. Like Katy, they choose the easier path – one that conforms to the world, revels in shallow superficiality, and calibrates its moral compass on the fads of culture. As Perry admits herself, "I speak my truths and I speak my fantasies." Katy has crowned herself god of her own private universe.[74]

This is why I write about influential female singers and elites in Hollywood. They seem to believe they have the only truth, but if they do, the Bible is wrong and so is God.

In her speech, she mentioned her early days in the secular music business and that her Christian "bubble started to burst" when she was introduced to those who identified as homosexual. Calling them the most "free, strong, kind, and inclusive people" she ever met, Perry continued: "They stimulated my mind and they filled my heart with joy, and they freaking danced all the while doing it. These people are actually magic, and **they are magic because they are living their truth**" (emphasis added).

First, in Scripture, the Lord is the One who fills our hearts with genuine joy. Second, don't ignore her use of the word *magic*. And third,

---

74   Peter Heck, "Katy Perry Attacks Christianity Because She's Weak," 3/27/2017, *peterheck.com/ peterheck/ commentaries/view/39754/katy_perry_attacks_christianity_because_s_weak.*

since they refuse God's truth, they claim to live their own *truth*. But few seem to take the time to think this through. If there are two truth claims, both cannot be right.

There is a statement she made that is somewhat haunting in terms of eternal repercussions and the reality of heaven and hell – both of which Perry says she does not believe in. To score even more points with the LGBTQ crowd, she almost apologized for her Christian roots and perhaps the faith itself when she stated, "I hope I stand here as evidence for all that no matter where you came from, it's about where you are going."

Now, to you and I this would appear to be a biblical statement if we didn't know who said it and in what context. She seems to imply she needed rehab to overcome and trash her Christian upbringing. My heartfelt question to you, Katy Perry, is where exactly are you going when you die? I pray you ask yourself the question, what if I'm wrong?

Both of her parents have had mixed feelings about their daughter Katy and have gone back and forth from warning her to supporting her. As Christians, can they do both?

According to *ChristianNews.net*, Katy's mother, Mary Hudson, wrote a book proposal in 2011 that included some concerns about her daughter. Apparently, following one of Katy's concerts, Hudson reportedly stated, "I recognized the psalmist gift in her performance. Yet she sang out, 'I kissed a girl, and I liked it,' while thousands joined her," she wrote. "One part of my heart soared . . . [but] the other part broke for the thousands of hungry souls being fed something that didn't nourish their spirit, but fed their flesh."

I wonder what her parents thought of her Grammy Awards performance in 2014. Katy Perry revealed her dark, occultic side to the public that night, after years of luring young, impressionable music fans with her bright, colorful, bubble-gum image she spent years crafting. In her song "E.T.," she sings about having sexual relations with a demonic entity, which may be the devil himself. We could go on and on, but one thing we do know is her music is being used to draw her fans into witchcraft, humanism, and sexual perversion.

Who knows for sure if she was joking or serious when she said in an interview years ago that her Christian music career "didn't work out so I sold my soul to the devil." Think about this: Katy Perry denies Jesus Christ and glorifies witchcraft – a very serious sin to God. She stands with the abortion industry, advocates for the LGBTQ movement, mocks Christianity, and promotes moral relativism. Tell me again how you think secular music or entertainment is *harmless* and that these celebrities are *not really hurting anyone*.

BEYONCÉ, GAGA, AND THE LIBERAL WOMEN'S MARCH

Since I wrote about Beyoncé in my previous book in a chapter on witchcraft, and since several Christian sites have detailed her occult influences, her offensive and graphic song lyrics, and her sexually charged gyrating performances, I will just add that it is so disappointing to see millions still following her – including some professing Christians.

"It's just entertainment," right? There is no way a practicing, Bible-believing Christian can in good conscience support and defend Beyoncé and most others. If you love and believe a singer, actor, or other celebrity more than the Word of God, let me be straightforward here: you are either not a Christian or you're dealing with the sins of idolatry and disobedience.

She is another singer who admits to being possessed, and in her case, even named the entity that enters into her during performances: "Sasha Fierce." Do your own research if this sounds crazy. Look up her satanic Super Bowl half-time show performance from a few years back, note Beyoncé's lyrics, her moves, the costumes, symbols, and imagery. (Do a search for "Beyoncé," "Hindu goddess Kali," "the devil's triangle," "Super Bowl," and "Sasha Fierce.")

Beyoncé and her hubby, Jay Z, both influence tens of millions of fans. Here's an excerpt from *The Cost of Our Silence*:

> "Jay Z has also been linked to the Illuminati and Aleister Crowley's OTO (Ordo Templi Orientis) so it's worth noting that Crowley, who was born into an upper-class British family in 1875, styled himself as 'the Great Beast 666.' Jay Z has worn a hooded sweatshirt with, 'Do What Thou Wilt,' on the front, which is known as the law of Thelema that

Crowley developed. Jay Z's 'Roca Wear' apparel features
shirt designs with the Satanic all-seeing eye (the Eye of
Horus, an Egyptian solar god) and a 'Masters of the Craft'
shirt displaying occult symbols."[75]

It is not just entertainment or a game to many of the "entertainers," as
they are attracting an army of deceived fans to play their part in the
rebellion. In many elitist celebrity lives, they are on the throne and
there is no room for God.

We sometimes get discouraged trying to live according to the Bible,
when the world thinks we have nothing and are missing out on all the
fun. But the truth is we have everything we could possibly need if we
have Christ, and it's just a matter of time before they will learn the hard
way that *they* are the ones who missed out.

If it's any indication of what kind of world we live in, these are some
of the wealthiest women according to *Forbes*. They are also the most
raunchy, spiritually impoverished, and rebellious toward God. Believe it
or not, Madonna's net worth is estimated to be nearly $1 billion thanks
to branded merchandise, clothes, books, and fragrances, in addition
to her music and tours.

Beyoncé has raked in over $500 million as a solo artist, this apart
from hubby, Jay-Z, and their many business and endorsement deals.
Katy Perry pulled in $135 million in 2015 alone, even beating out Lady
Gaga who made about $60 million and is growing her net worth as well.

But these are just numbers. God cares about hearts and about who
or what we worship. Some of us covet the lifestyles and wealth of celebrities while other believers deal with different temptations regarding
entertainment. The following Scriptures may be helpful in knowing
Jesus can relate to being tempted in this area.

> *Then the devil, taking Him up on a high mountain, showed*
> *Him all the kingdoms of the world in a moment of time.*
> *And the devil said to Him, "All this authority I will give*
> *You, and their glory; for this has been delivered to me, and*
> *I give it to whomever I wish. Therefore, if You will worship*
> *before me, all will be Yours." And Jesus answered and said*

---

75   David Fiorazo, *The Cost of Our Silence* (Aneko Press, 2015), 270.

> *to him, "Get behind Me, Satan! For it is written, 'You shall*
> *worship the LORD your God, and Him only you shall serve.'"*
> (Luke 4:5-8 NKJV)

An important question for the rich and famous is this: who do you worship? Are you worshipping Satan, self, or the Lord your God? These are good questions for us as well.

THE WORD OF GOD OR THE WORD OF GAGA?

Lady Gaga may not have thought twice about wearing a bizarre Nazi-like uniform to Hillary Clinton's campaign rally a day before the 2016 presidential election. She grew up idolizing pop artist David Bowie, whom Gaga says is one of her greatest influences. Bowie was known to give the Nazi salute and once said, "Adolf Hitler was one of the first rock stars."

As for the Hillary rally, Gaga was there to help draw more youth to the progressive movement of big government, more federal control and regulation, less religious freedom for Christians, and more abortion on demand.

In "Lady Gaga, Hillary, and Militant Satanism," Pastor Joe Schimmel wrote:

> Both Hillary and Gaga have more in common than one might think. They both not only promote the right to kill innocent children by the millions, but they both are guided by demonic entities. Hillary claims that she receives messages from a spirit entity that she would have us believe is Eleanor Roosevelt. Bill Clinton had claimed that Hillary received a special new communication from Eleanor for the audience he was addressing at Franklin D. Roosevelt Four Freedoms Park in October 2012.
>
> Gaga also claims to have a spirit guide. Gaga named her new album *Joanne*, because she believes she is possessed by her dead aunt, whose name is . . . you guessed it, Joanne! Let's keep in mind, God's word teaches that the spirits of the dead are either in Hades or in heaven (Luke 16; 2

Corinthians 5:8), and that the only kinds of spirits that possess people are Satan and demonic entities that serve in Satan's kingdom (Mark 5:1-9; Ephesians 6:10-18).[76]

We could detail plenty of her song lyrics, but I am confident you already have a good idea of what fills Lady Gaga's music. In a German song she wrote after a night of debauchery and partying in Berlin, the lyrics reduce feminism to the idea that a woman should be able to be as sleazy as she wants and shouldn't have to ask permission.

Through her demonic spirit guide, which she says helps her with her "art," Gaga indoctrinates her impressionable young audiences with lyrics such as:

> Rejoice and love yourself today
>   'Cause baby, you were born this way
> No matter gay, straight or bi
>   Lesbian transgendered life
> I'm on the right track, baby

This is "her truth." Though unusually bizarre, the following story is relevant since it involves two of the most powerful, influential women in the world (Hillary Clinton and Lady Gaga).

It was revealed through emails, thanks to Wikileaks, that Hillary Clinton's 2016 presidential campaign chairman, John Podesta, was invited to a special dinner at the home of Marina Abramović, a friend and satanist. Apparently, Lady Gaga is also friends with Abramović, and had attended what they refer to as "Spirit Cooking" dinners.

What on earth is Spirit Cooking? Also called "Cake of Light" by disciples of Aleister Crowley, it is basically a satanic ritual and mockery of the Christian communion service. In an interview, Lady Gaga lavishes endless praise on Marina Abramović and, being so in awe of her and wanting to emulate her work "on a domestic level," repeatedly proclaims that Abramović is "limitless."

Limitless is an interesting word in reference to any human being.

---

76   Joe Schimmel, "Lady Gaga, Hillary, and Militant Satanism," *www.goodfight.org/lady-gaga-hillary-militant-satanism/*.

To be fair, an article was written at CatholicLink about celebrities who profess their faith publicly but do not live appropriate lifestyles. In the past, Gaga admitted in an interview with Larry King she is confused about religion and is Catholic. (In 2017, a New York Catholic parish's gay group hosted a gay dance party for Gaga's LGBT charity.) She posted a photograph with a priest after receiving communion and, taking offense to being mentioned in the article, responded on Instagram:

> "Dear Becky Roach, Mary Magdalene washed the feet of
> Christ and was protected and loved by him. A prostitute.
> Someone society shames as if she and her body are a man's
> trash can. He loved her and did not judge. He let her cry
> over him and dry his feet with the hair of a harlot. We are
> not just 'celebrities' we are humans and sinners, children,
> and our lives are not void of values because we struggle.
> We are as equally forgiven as our neighbor. God is never a
> trend no matter who the believer."

She made a few good points, but got a few things wrong. Not everyone is forgiven. For example, we must repent, receive forgiveness, and also change our behavior. If we fail to examine ourselves and we take communion "in an unworthy manner" without repenting, and then go right back to our sinful behavior, we bring judgment on ourselves, not forgiveness (1 Corinthians 11:27-31). Also, though Jesus did not condemn Mary Magdalene, He made a judgment on her past sinful lifestyle and said to her, *Go and sin no more* (John 8:11 KJV).

The rich and famous need to return to God if they once trusted Him, they need to be reminded about truth, and they need to understand they will be held accountable for how they influence people. Having performed during the 2017 Super Bowl half-time show, Lady Gaga is at the top of her game, but she is just one of the many pawns being used to promote immorality to millions and millions of fans. Just like Beyoncé. Just like Katy Perry. Just like Miley Cyrus. Just like Kim Kardashian.

Before we expose the hypocrisy, political ideology, and moral relativism regarding the radical "Women's March" that took place in January, it may be helpful to point out:

The spirituality behind contemporary feminism often comes in the form of goddess worship. The more radical feminists seem to believe in an internal god, if any, which is contrary to the God of the Bible, and they have a desire to overthrow the patriarchal structure in society. Some New Age proponents teach that Wicca, goddess worship, paganism, and witchcraft are all centered on a religion involving the mystery and sexuality of the female. The idea is for women to regain their natural power and to have authority over men. In order to accomplish this dominance, they must invoke certain spirits to help destroy the Judeo-Christian religion. God can no longer be "Father."[77]

NASTY WOMEN UNITED?

And just like Madonna, who told the crowd of pro-abortion, anti-Trump feminists at the so-called "Women's March": "Welcome to the revolution of love . . . to the rebellion. To our refusal as women to accept this new age of tyranny. Yes, I am outraged. Yes, I have thought an awful lot about blowing up the White House . . . but I choose love."

To critics whom she called "detractors" of the march (those who oppose the leftist, progressive, communist agenda), she said simply, "f—k you!" Several more f-bombs escaped uncensored so all the kids could hear it.

Madonna and actress-turned-activist Ashley Judd abandoned "inclusivity and tolerance" and demanded respect as they heaped personal attacks on Trump and his family, including Ivanka. Judd took the stage and, referring to herself as a nasty woman over and over, nearly turned blue as she growled into the microphone (apparently attributing parts of her speech to a teenager):

> My name is Ashley Judd and I am a feminist. . . . I am a
> nasty woman. [But] I am not as nasty as a swastika painted
> on a pride flag. . . . I didn't know devils could be resur-
> rected, but I feel Hitler in these streets, a mustache traded

---

77   Joe Schimmel, "Lady Gaga, Hillary, and Militant Satanism," *www.goodfight.org/ lady-gaga-hillary-militant-satanism/*.

for a toupee, Nazi's renamed the cabinet . . . the new gas
chambers shaming the gay out of America turning rain-
bows into suicide notes.

I am not as nasty as racism, fraud, conflict of interest,
homophobia, sexual assault, transphobia, white supremacy,
misogyny, ignorance, white privilege. . . . I'm a loud, vulgar,
proud woman. I'm not nasty like the combo of Trump and
Pence being served up to me in my voting booth! . . . We
are here to be respected.

News flash to Judd and other condescending, liberal elites: if you want
respect, show some respect to fellow Americans who disagree with your
politics, and go about protesting another way instead of insulting more
than half of the country. If you saw her speech, you'd know how evil is
brewing on a whole new level in Hollywood.

They feed off of each other's anger, narcissism, and entitlement.
These are the people we support by going to their movies and buying
their music. If more people boycotted their products, maybe they'd
get the message because money talks. Judd concluded: "So if you're a
nasty woman or love one who is, let me hear you say, 'Hell, yea!' Hell,
yea . . . hell yea!"

Radicals aren't upset over women's rights (in America, really?),
they're throwing a George Soros-funded temper tantrum because
their candidate lost and they didn't get their way. Their partners in the
media helped promote the March and broadcast it around the world
as if all 152 million women in America were unified and on their side.
They claimed to be the majority, but I'm confident most women would
not subscribe to the display of immorality, the nonsensical speeches,
and the public vulgarity, including feminists dressed up as vaginas or
carrying graphic signs.

Nasty is right. What some of them apparently don't understand is
that having female body parts has to do with basic biology; it is not a
political argument. In many interviews, especially with millennials,
they couldn't even explain exactly why they were marching.

Actress America Ferrera kicked things off by saying they were marching "for the moral core of this nation, against which our president is

waging war." Moral core? She said women were under attack and that "our safety and freedom are on the chopping block." Dramatic, but that's closer to how millions of us felt during the Obama administration. She continued:

> "We reject the demonization of our Muslim brothers and sisters, we demand an end to the systematic murder and incarceration of our black brothers and sisters, we will not give our rights to safe and legal abortions, we will not ask our LGBTQ families to go backwards, we will not go from being a nation of immigrants to a nation of ignorance."

Sadly, the event was one of the most infantile displays of a collective temper tantrum I've seen over election results. An election, I might add, in which millions of women (42 percent) of all races and nationalities did in fact vote for Donald Trump. Did you hear that from the liberal media? Some believe the Women's March backfired and only served to further divide and polarize America. I agree. The dishonest pundits, however, built up the event like no other, purposely failing to inform the public about where the well-organized march funding came from.

Writing for *The New American*, William F. Jasper stated that very few mentioned radical billionaire George Soros and major tax-exempt foundations that were underwriting the "grassroots" anti-Trump, anti-Republican demonstrations. Jasper pointed to an investigative article:

> Apparently in the interest of appearing "balanced," the *New York Times* allowed journalist Asra Q. Nomani a small corner of print to expose the money behind the celebrated rent-a-mob demonstrations in the nation's capital and other major cities. Nomani, a feminist Muslim from India, is a former instructor in journalism at Georgetown University . . . .

> Her . . . piece . . . is titled "Billionaire George Soros has ties to more than 50 'partners' of the Women's March on Washington." Her subtitle to the article reads: "What is the link between one of Hillary Clinton's largest donors and the Women's March? Turns out, it's quite significant."

Soros has funded, or has close relationships with, at least 56 of the march's 'partners,' including 'key partners' Planned Parenthood, which opposes Trump's anti-abortion policy, and the National Resource Defense Council, which opposes Trump's environmental policies. The other Soros ties with 'Women's March' organizations include the partisan MoveOn.org (which was fiercely pro-Clinton), the National Action Network (which has a former executive director lauded by Obama senior advisor Valerie Jarrett as 'a leader of tomorrow' as a march co-chair and another official as 'the head of logistics'). Other Soros grantees . . . are the American Civil Liberties Union, Center for Constitutional Rights, Amnesty International and Human Rights Watch.[78]

Particularly among the rich celebs, they may well have been upset and marching because they wasted so much money donating to Hillary Clinton's campaign. According to *Politico*, at least one reliable source estimated that Hollywood liberals raised about $60 million for Clinton, only to be left out in the cold, literally, if they attended the anger march in Washington.

There were coordinating marches in several locations in the country for those who couldn't make it to D.C. Who else was at these women's marches? Cher, Julia Roberts, Scarlet Johansson, Alicia Keys, Yoko Ono, Rosie Perez, Emma Watson, Amy Schumer, Chelsea Handler, Charlize Theron, Whoopi Goldberg, Gloria Steinem, Gloria Allred, Elizabeth Warren, Janelle Monae, John Kerry, John Legend, Jake Gyllenhaal, and after having eight years off during the Obama presidency, Code Pink is back as well.

Other Hillary backers who didn't march but were just as disappointed included celebrities such as Rob Reiner, Tom Hanks, Magic Johnson, Seth MacFarlane, Robert De Niro, Lionel Richie, and George Clooney; bigger wigs Jeffrey Katzenberg, Disney's Robert Iger, Haim Saban, Barry Diller, and Michael Eisner, many of whom held fundraisers for

---

78   William F. Jasper, "Anti-Trump 'Women's March' – Celebrity Profanity, Media Duplicity," 1/23/2017,
      www.thenewamerican.com/usnews/politics/item/25219-anti-trump-women-s-march-celebrity-profanity-media-duplicity.

Clinton, or entertained for free to support her. Other heavy contributors include Steven Spielberg, Matt Damon, Ben Affleck, Meryl Streep, and Sally Fields.

Joss Whedon's "Clinton Save the Day" super-PAC video featured stars like Robert Downey Jr., Don Cheadle, Scarlett Johansson, Martin Sheen, Mark Ruffalo, Julianne Moore, James Franco, Neil Patrick Harris, and Stanley Tucci.

A liberal advocacy group founded by Norman Lear, People for the American Way, cancelled a hotel ballroom it had reserved for a Hillary inauguration party. That's right. Another thing they were upset about is Trump and millions of Americans spoiled their celebrations! Imagine the thousands of party cancellations. Members of this leftist group include Alec Baldwin, Kathleen Turner, and Jane Lynch. The lists could go on and on and include 80 percent of Hollywood.

A convincing and overwhelming majority of rich celebrities in the entertainment industry don't care about us or about what we think or value. We shouldn't expect them to care. Many of them hate what you and I stand for and believe. In fact, *The View*'s Joy Behar and Whoopi Goldberg again referred to Christians as worse than the Taliban. Feminists have an extremely different vision for the country as well as the world. And, as Lady Gaga correctly stated, they have values too; it's just that theirs go against the Bible.

Entertainers need Christ like we all do. Maybe some do know Jesus, used to know Him, or think they know Him, but by the sins they celebrate and support, it would seem they are quite lost and most likely do not even realize it.

As for the rest of us, one glaring problem Christians in America have is that we *don't* have a problem with much of the entertainment we consume. If we have become desensitized to evil and its influences, how are we going to obey God's commands and keep an eternal perspective?

We must repent of celebrity worship, discern false gods, practices, and teachings, and stay committed to the gospel of repentance, which will lead others to a knowledge of the only truth.

> *[That] they may come to their senses and escape from the snare of the devil, having been held captive by him to do his will.* (2 Timothy 2:26)

Chapter 12

Seduced by Scientology

O Timothy, guard what has been entrusted to you, avoiding worldly and empty chatter and the opposing arguments of what is falsely called "knowledge"—which some have professed and thus gone astray from the faith.
(1 Timothy 6:20-21)

"In a time of universal deceit, telling the truth becomes a revolutionary act." – George Orwell

I can count on two hands the television programs I've watched somewhat regularly in the last ten years or so. Though our standards are not perfect, my wife and I try avoiding shows that glorify sin including adultery, idolatry, homosexuality, and pornography, or shows containing harsh, profane language, nudity, graphic violence, blatant political correctness, or other anti-Christian themes.

This certainly limits our television viewing, but one of the shows my wife and I used to watch on occasion was a sitcom called *King of Queens*, starring Kevin James and Leah Remini. In November 2015, Remini coauthored a number-one *New York Times* best seller, *Troublemaker: Surviving Hollywood and Scientology*. The book is described as an "eye-opening, no-holds-barred memoir about life in the Church of Scientology," and has led to her own A&E docuseries, *Leah Remini: Scientology and the Aftermath*.

This heartbreaking series further exposing the inside secrets of

Scientology is what drew me to the outspoken actress's story. Many interviews were filmed featuring tearful and heartbroken participants who had left Scientology and were trying to pick up the pieces of their lives, often estranged from family members who remained in the church.

In July of 2013, Remini left the church after thirty years as a devout scientologist, upset about the church's alleged control, corruption, harassment, and abuse of "parishoners." Knowing her outgoing personality, it is not surprising that she didn't go quietly. Though her disappointment had been building for years, things intensified when Leah Remini began questioning the practice of the church excommunicating people. Cults generally do such things to protect their leaders and to cover up lies and questionable practices.

Excommunication is when individuals who have been declared "Suppressive Persons" (SPs) by Scientology leadership are kicked out. Church members then, if they want to remain in good standing, are forced to disassociate and "disconnect" from the person or risk being disciplined or excommunicated themselves. Due to brain washing and extreme loyalty to Scientology, families can be and have been permanently split up.

From what I've researched about Scientology leader David Miscavige's abusive, authoritarian behavior, his reported mistreatment of people within the church, as well as his untouchable and unaccountable God-like position, much could be written about him. I only bring him up here because Leah Remini was a friend of his wife, Shelly Miscavige, who some believed to have mysteriously disappeared as she had only been seen once since 2007, according to reports.

Out of concern, Remini spoke up about the whereabouts of Shelly Miscavige and reportedly threatened to call the police regarding her missing friend. As a result, Leah was put through what is called "Security Checking" by the church, as was her family and circle of friends who were members of Scientology. In 2013, Remini filed a Missing Persons Report with the LAPD.

Apparently, when you question Scientology leadership you are immediately brought in and interrogated. They reportedly demanded, "Why are you asking [about Shelly], who are you connected to, are you going on the internet?" Tony Ortega, a Scientology blogger, said Miscavige was last seen at her father's funeral in the presence of Scientology "handlers" back in 2007.

That was until December 2016 when, according to Ortega, a source claims to have spotted a woman resembling Shelly Miscavige in the small town of Crestline, California, near the Church of Spiritual Technology (CST). She was allegedly seen in public looking "thin," "frail," and "almost like she was homeless" after she had not been seen publicly for nearly a decade.[79]

According to PageSix, a source explained Leah Remini was already put through Scientology's "thought modification" for five years, but when they tried it again in 2013, she said, "Enough." After leaving the church, news got out and Remini expressed appreciation for the "overwhelming positive response I have received from the media, my colleagues, and fans." She also declared that she and her family "stand united" in the decision to leave Scientology. In an interview with *People Magazine*, Remini defended her decision, saying, "I believe that people should be able to question things. I believe that people should value family, and value friendships, and hold those things sacrosanct. That for me, that's what I'm about. It wouldn't matter what it was, simply because no one is going to tell me how I need to think, no one is going to tell me who I can, and cannot, talk to."[80]

Naturally, Church of Scientology reps deny any and all allegations against them. It is interesting that the niece of Scientology leader David Miscavige left the church back in 2005 and has publicly stated she is "happy for Leah" and that "it took a lot of courage to do this so publicly." Jenna Miscavige praised Remini for getting out for the sake of her younger daughter.

Jenna once called her uncle, David Miscavige, "evil" and says she has no idea what happened to her aunt, Shelly Miscavige. Commenting on

---

79   Tony Ortega, "CLAIM: 'Frail' looking Shelly Miscavige spotted near Scientology compound in California,"
     tonyortega.org/2016/12/15/claim-frail-looking-shelly-miscavige-spotted-near-scientology-compound-in-california/.

80   Ragan Alexander, "Leah Remini on Scientology: 'No One is Going to Tell Me How I Need to Think,'"
     7/29/2013, *people.com/celebrity/leah-remini-on-scientology-no-one-is-going-to-tell-me-how-i-need-to-think/.*

the church's reaction to the parting of such a public figure as Remini, she said in an interview it was definitely not good PR for the organization, since "PR for the most part is all they care about."

Regarding the manipulation of Scientology leadership, Jenna Miscavige stated, "Scientology definitely does use families in order to get people to do what they want them to do, they know people care and love their families. So if they have to use the threat of possibly losing them in order to get them to [toe] the line, they'll do it."[81]

Miscavige also said she felt "completely brainwashed" and, sadly, had to permanently part with the friends she grew up with. Starting at age six until she was twelve, the Church of Scientology forced her to do manual labor for several hours a day such as hauling rocks and digging trench holes for irrigation. According to an interview with the *Daily Mail*, Jenna was admitted to the church's "Sea Organization," a branch of the most dedicated followers, and was forced to sign a billion-year contract that bound her immortal spirit (known as the "Thetan") to a life of dedication. Sadly, between the ages of twelve and eighteen, Jenna saw her mother only twice and her father, four times.

Scientology claims it alone "brings man to total freedom and truth," which we know is a lie. In fact, Scientology's founder Lafayette Ron Hubbard's (LRH) writings and lectures (tapes) are considered to be infallible "Scripture." He is known as the exclusive "Source" of the only truth to lead man to all the answers. Any false teaching in conflict with the Bible is an attempt to redefine the truth of God and Jesus Himself.

Hubbard has no successor, he made himself into a god, and the cult has followed suit. According to the book *World Religions and Cults Volume 3*, Scientology was meant to be a moneymaker, and Hubbard once openly stated in a 1952 lecture in *Journal of Scientology*, "The only way you can control people is to lie to them. You can write that down in your book in great big letters."[82]

Hubbard taught that "all men have inalienable rights to their own

---

81   Sara Nathan, "Exclusive: "…Scientology Leader David Miscavige's Outspoken Niece hails Leah Remini as 'fantastic and brave,'" 7/12/2013, *www.dailymail.co.uk/tvshowbiz/ article-2362113/Scientology-leader-David-Miscaviges-outspoken-niece-hails-Leah-Remini-fantastic-brave.html*.

82   Bodie Hodge and Roger Patterson, *World Religions and Cults Volume 3* (Green Forest, AR: Master Books, 2016), 97.

religious practices and their performance." This religion might as well be called "Hubbardism." Christians are instructed to pull down strongholds, demolish arguments, and destroy *speculations and every lofty thing raised up against the knowledge of God*, and take *every thought captive to the obedience of Christ* (2 Corinthians 10:5). We have the right and responsibility to respond to that which challenges biblical Christianity. Scientology is dangerous, deceptive at its core, and blasphemous.

WHAT EXACTLY IS SCIENTOLOGY AND WHAT IS ITS HISTORY?

Scientology is a religious system of beliefs and practices based on the seeking of self-knowledge and spiritual fulfillment through graded courses of study and training. A variation of religious humanism, the Church of Scientology was founded in 1954 by American science fiction writer L. Ron Hubbard (1911 – 1986). He initially developed a program of ideas called Dianetics and wrote a book about it in 1950.

One tenet of Scientology holds that matter, energy, space, and time (MEST) were created by thetans beyond a quadrillion years ago, including alien life on other planets. Scientologists also have a pluralistic belief system that allows the individual to progress toward living a better life in his own estimation. After Hubbard died in 1986, his former assistant, David Miscavige, shrewdly and forcefully took over the helm and has been leader of the organization ever since.

The Church of Scientology's base is a five-hundred-acre compound in southern California about 100 miles from Los Angeles known as the "Gold Base." The desert site was bought by the church in 1978 and at least $30 million has been spent redeveloping it. Its Hollywood location or Pacific Area Command Base (PAC Base) is known as "Big Blue." Scientology also has a sixty-acre United Kingdom base – the former home of Hubbard – called Saint Hill Manor, in East Grinstead, Sussex.

The church has practically purchased the city of Clearwater, Florida. Hubbard came to Clearwater in 1975 to begin "Project Normandy," the code name for a top-secret Church of Scientology operation to take over the city. Local politicians, police, and residents have long given up fighting Scientology and most residents are too afraid to say anything critical, as they fear repercussions.

Scientology owns sixty-seven buildings and over ten square miles of property worth more than half a billion dollars, including hotels, training centers, offices for "Special Affairs" and religious retreats. Two examples in downtown Clearwater include the Super Powers Building, Scientology headquarters and location of advanced church courses (real estate value is over $30 million), and the Fort Harrison Hotel which boasts 220 rooms and suites for visiting Scientology members, the Crystal Ballroom, Flag Building, and Convention Center (worth over $13 million).

According to the *St. Petersburg Times* and the *Daily Mail*, visiting scientologists often pay upwards of $100,000 for what they refer to as "services." Members are charged thousands of dollars for special required courses held in the Super Powers Building and are promised they will gain super-human powers. Of course, the church has denied there are fixed fees, saying, "Donations requested for courses at the Church of Scientology begin at $50 and could never possibly reach the amount suggested."[83]

Mike Rinder, a former high-level scientologist who worked with David Miscavige, said every scientologist around the world has to go to the Clearwater, Florida, location for required courses, and some members extend their visit for years, paying up to $1.5 million each. "Hundreds of millions of dollars go through Clearwater each year," said Rinder, "at least $2 million a week." The church's total assets are worth billions of dollars.

There are no scientific reasons to think Scientology will work as advertised, and no studies proving the effectiveness of Dianetics, which has been classified as a pseudoscience. One thing the organization is profoundly good at, however, is generating revenue. Their impressive holdings have been gained through business dealings and real estate. Then there are the fees accumulated through required auditing sessions.

83   Chris White, "Exclusive: Inside the Town Scientology Built," 3/31/2015, *www.dailymail.co.uk/news/article-3015144/Inside-town-Scientology-built-Clearwater-Florida-Tom-Cruise-John-Travolta-Kirstie-Alley-rule-palatial-estates-Sea-Org-members-live-six-room-pay-100-000-learn-super-human-powers.html*.

Because these costs are extremely pricey, rich celebrities are over-represented in Scientology. The church has also received hundreds of millions in donations from its elite, wealthiest members.

According to their official literature: "Scientology is a religion that offers a precise path leading to a complete and certain understanding of one's true spiritual nature and one's relationship to self, family, groups, mankind, all life forms, the material universe, the spiritual universe and the Supreme Being." Critics – and there are many – claim Scientology is not a typical "religion," but a system "built chiefly as a cover for exploitive commercial operations" based on financial exploitation, and is "a multi-national racket masquerading as a religion."[84]

The foundational beliefs of Scientology start with the concept that man is "basically good, and that his spiritual salvation depends upon himself, his fellows, and his attainment of brotherhood with the universe." Core principles include the belief that man is an immortal spiritual being, his experience extends well beyond a single lifetime, and his capabilities are unlimited even if they are not presently realized. The word *scientology* is focused on attaining knowledge: "the study of knowing," or "knowing how to know." Scientologists have a concept of a God but their performance-based system is all about works and self-empowerment.

Here's a spoiler for those who may be wondering and who have not looked into this before: Scientology is not at all comparable to Christianity, as the two have very little if anything in common. Scientology is based on humanism, and its teachings lead away from the authority of God and the truth of Scripture. It is not remotely Christian. If any confusion or uncertainty exists between Christianity and Scientology, it may be due to some of the language and wording used by scientologists perhaps in an effort to disguise their actual beliefs.

Since Hubbard based Scientology on his own study and writings on Dianetics, let's take a look at these teachings from his book that launched a movement, later to be defined as a religion.

---

84   Craig Branch, "Church of Scientology: A Religious Mafia," *www.watchman.org/articles/scientology/church-of-scientology-a-religious-mafia/*.

DIANETICS

Dianetics: The Modern Science of Mental Health, is a book by L. Ron Hubbard about a system of psychotherapy he developed from a combination of personal experience, basic principles of Eastern philosophy, and the work of psychoanalysts such as Freud.

Christian leaders, medical professionals, and scientists have generally criticized the book, and most reviews of *Dianetics* have been negative. An early review in *The New Republic* summed up the book as "a bold and immodest mixture of complete nonsense and perfectly reasonable common sense, taken from long-acknowledged findings, disguised and distorted by a crazy, newly invented terminology," and warned of medical risks: "it may prove fatal to have put too much trust in the promises of this dangerous book."[85]

On the cover of Hubbard's book, he uses an image of an exploding volcano, referring to the story of "Xenu," an ancient dictator of a "Galactic Confederacy." According to Hubbard, seventy-five million years ago, Xenu brought billions of people to the earth and placed them around volcanoes, killing them by blowing them up with hydrogen bombs. Scientology therefore believes that the "thetans" (immortal spirits) of these aliens attach themselves to human beings, causing spiritual harm.[86]

"Dianetics" is basically the generic term for the underlying beliefs of Scientology.

> Dianetics is the claim that each person's painful past experiences create a lasting impression, termed an "engram," on that person's "reactive" (subconscious) mind. According to Dianetics, these engrams are the root cause of various diseases, conditions, neuroses, and injuries. According to Scientology, the list of maladies caused by engrams includes deficient vision, sexual problems, allergies, joint pain, headaches, and so forth. Engrams are also blamed for psychological disorders from depression to violence.

> Biblically, the claims of Dianetics are completely false.

---

85   Wikipedia, "Dianetics: The Modern Science of Mental Health," *en.wikipedia.org/wiki/ Dianetics:_ The_Modern_Science_of_Mental_Health.*

86   Wikipedia, "Xenu," *en.wikipedia.org/wiki/Xenu.*

There are no prior lives from which to remember pain and trauma (Hebrews 9:27). A person's primary moral problem is not the memory of pain but his own in-born sin (Romans 3:23; 5:12). Dianetics claims that a person can, through force of will, make himself a better and more moral person. The Bible teaches that true change only happens when a person is reformed by Christ (1 Corinthians 6:10-11). As a mishmash of pseudoscience, Eastern spirituality, and New Age concepts, Dianetics is not only factually false but also incompatible with the worldview of the Bible (Colossians 2:8).[87]

The origins of Scientology include claims of having roots in the beliefs of all great religions in order to suggest a religious heritage thousands of years old, but the fact is it is a creation of one man in the 1940s and '50s. And yet, Hubbard went so far as to claim that if dianetic therapy were applied worldwide, there would no longer be any crime, war, or insanity. Prior to the publishing of *Dianetics*, Scientology had its first exposure to the public in a science fiction article Hubbard wrote, "Dianetics: The Evolution of a Science," published in the May 1950 issue of *Astounding Science Fiction Magazine*. Scientology has been around for less than seventy years.

SCIENTOLOGY VS. CHRISTIANITY

Tom Cruise was introduced to Scientology in the late 1980s by his first ex-wife, Mimi Rogers, and is believed to be second in command today, and yet lost his cool in a 2014 interview with Matt Lauer on *Today*. Since that interview, he refuses to discuss Scientology, perhaps because it showed a lack of progress or his human nature. Arguably the most famous scientologist, Tom Cruise said at one point to Lauer, "You could be a Christian and be a scientologist."

Actor Will Smith is not a scientologist, but reportedly donated $125,000 to the church and once stated Scientology and Christianity are almost identical: "I was raised in a Baptist household and went to a Catholic school, but the ideas of the Bible are ninety-eight percent

---

87   Got Questions, "What is Dianetics?" *www.gotquestions.org/Dianetics.html.*

the same ideas as Scientology." Many claims (lies?) have been made by proponents of Scientology that it is compatible with Christianity and that "there is no attempt to change a person's beliefs or to persuade him away from any religion to which he already belongs," which we know is completely false.

Hubbard stated there were other messiahs prior to Jesus Christ. He also stated that early Christianity is not the same as Christianity today, the New Testament contains legends, and judgment day is a superstition. *But the Spirit explicitly says that in later times some will fall away from the faith, paying attention to deceitful spirits and doctrines of demons* (1 Timothy 4:1).

Writing for Watchman Fellowship, an independent Christian research ministry, Craig Branch stated that Scientology's own bizarre doctrines can literally be regarded as "doctrines of demons," and adds:

> Claiming to be compatible with Christianity and respect-
> ful of Jesus Christ, they write, "Scientologists hold the Bible
> as a holy work, and have no argument with the Christian
> belief that Jesus Christ was the Savior of Mankind and the
> Son of God. . . . *There are probably many types of redemp-
> tion.*" All of this is subterfuge; none of it is true. In real-
> ity, Scientology is very alien and hostile to Christianity.
> Hubbard's many taped lectures, thousands of policy letters
> and directives, and the so-called secret or hidden teach-
> ings contained in upper level courses, provide ample evi-
> dence of Scientology's duplicity and its true beliefs about
> Christianity [emphasis added][88].

Scientology denies the existence of the Creator God of the Bible as well as heaven and hell being actual places. Scientologists believe in multiple gods and that some gods are above others. Hubbard's teachings clearly deny the deity of Jesus Christ and His resurrection, so they think Jesus was just a good teacher or a prophet who was killed. Members are taught it is detestable to tell others the heart of mankind is wicked and that we must repent of our sins. Moreover, Scientology supports the idea of reincarnation or at least, past lives for each person, and that personal

---

88   Craig Branch, "Hubbard's Religion," *www.watchman.org/articles/scientology/hubbards-religion/*.

salvation in one's lifetime is to be freed from the cycle of birth and death associated with reincarnation.

Scientology teaches that thetans continue to enter into our bodies after we die. One cannot progress unless the engrams mentioned earlier, "aberrations" from past lives, are dealt with. Some people might veer toward Scientology because of its alleged scientific approach, its religion of works – not to better society, but to improve and exalt self – and the claim that science alone does not provide the answers to life.

The Church of Scientology suggests they have the right applications and best methods to make it possible for man to reach "the ancient goal he has been striving toward for thousands of years: to know himself and, in knowing himself, to know and understand other people and, ultimately, life itself." With this man-centered focus in mind, it is interesting that reportedly, L. Ron Hubbard once declared, "We do more good in any ten minutes of this planet's time than the combined efforts of all social ministries on Earth to better mankind."

The "scriptures" taught in Scientology are limited solely to the writings and teachings of Hubbard. It is also a very expensive religion to pursue. Practically every aspect of Scientology has some sort of fee associated with it. One of the "defectors" mentioned earlier, Mike Rinder, was high up in the church and left in 2007 after being raised in Scientology. He confirmed that the words of Hubbard are not treated as allegorical or taken merely as suggestions by church leaders. They are given the weight of "absolute unalterable truth." He said the expected attitude of a scientologist is to understand and apply Hubbard's words with extreme focus and dedication.

We deal with sin and stress and trauma according to the Word of God. We confess, repent, and trust in Christ and the truth of the Bible so we can be forgiven, restored, and healed. But how does a scientologist deal with bad behavior or actions in their past, everyday stresses, tragedy, or trauma? By fixing the mind.

THE PROCESS OF "AUDITING"

Scientology teaches that the human mind is made up of two parts: the reactive mind and the analytical mind. The reactive mind may be similar to the subconscious. Past negative or painful experiences (engrams) are stored in the reactive mind which may include those of past lives, are the source of irrational behavior, and things that aggravate us or cause our mind and body to be ill. Since engrams are the source of man's problems according to Scientology, the solution is to free yourself from them by taking expensive courses and being "audited."

Side note: apparently, there is little if any hope in Scientology for poor or impoverished people or for those living in third-world countries. Most wouldn't make enough money in their lifetime to pay a fraction of the required fees.

The process of auditing involves a device called an "electropsychometer" or E-meter, which is somewhat like a lie detector. A member of Scientology is hooked to the meter and asked a series of structured questions, supposedly revealing some "buried" past experiences. Scientologists say the E-meter measures the body's electric flow during questioning and reveals sources of trauma. The goal is to eliminate the effects of engrams and refile them in the analytical part of the mind.

Scientology's goal is for the auditing to result in a person having no reactive mind at all, a state they refer to as being "clear." They claim a person who is *clear* is free from psychosomatic illness, and is then "able to perceive, recall, imagine, create, and compute at a level high above the norm." Not only would memory improve, but they are told that the person's IQ will also "increase rapidly."[89] Auditing is supposed to help identify spiritual distress from a person's current life as well as from past lives.

Scientologists believe each person is an immortal being, and you advance levels or move up "The Bridge" to total freedom by working toward being an "Operating Thetan" (OT) by a series of steps to spiritual enlightenment. Laid out by Hubbard, these are progressive upper levels that vary in number and reveal "deeper" philosophies. Members are taught they are actually inhabited with clusters of "body thetans." A mass of these spirits have attached themselves to every person and are influencing their thoughts, feelings, and behavior with their own engrams and "implants."

---

89   Craig Branch, "Hubbard's Religion," *www.watchman.org/articles/scientology/hubbards-religion/*.

An implant is "a painful and forceful means of overwhelming a being with false concepts in a malicious attempt to control and suppress him" (*Dianetics and Scientology Technical Dictionary*, p. 206). Of course, this is also a handy explanation for why some scientologists, despite working for years to be designated "clear," may still be depressed at times, lose their tempers, or not have the promised high IQ and perfect memory.

So after questioning leadership, Leah Remini had to go through another expensive, lengthy, and tedious auditing process that former scientologists refer to as "the confessional."

CRIMES, DEFECTORS, AND SCIENTOLOGY SCANDALS

He who speaks truth declares righteousness, But a false witness, deceit. Lying lips are an abomination to the LORD, *But those who deal truthfully are His delight.*
(Proverbs 12:17, 22 NKJV)

Many have left Scientology, several of whom were quite famous, but those still within the church may never learn the truth because it is strictly frowned upon for members to read or watch anything critical of Scientology. They have been convinced the "attackers" are not only criminals, but are also always wrong regardless of the claim or accusation against the church. David Miscavige's own father, Ron, left the church and ended up publishing a book called *Ruthless*, in May 2016, which detailed his relationship with Scientology's "ruthless" leader.

Defending criticism of her church in 2008, actress Jenna Elfman (*Dharma and Greg*) actually compared scientologists to Christians who were once persecuted in the Roman Age. She also said she just ignores people who talk negatively about "something they've never actually studied" because they don't have integrity. She said she will not listen to hearsay and gossip. But what if people are trying to present evidence and facts to help? I understand how some say they have no tolerance for those who talk negatively about someone else's religion, but if what is being said is true, is it still considered "hearsay" or "gossip"?

According to reports, Katie Holmes, ex-wife of Tom Cruise, divorced him to protect their daughter Suri from Scientology. Cruise admitted this and Suri is no longer a member. On the Howard Stern radio show, actress and scientologist Kirstie Alley slammed Leah Remini as a "bigot" when she left the church. Alley then sent profanity-laced tweets to her fans. According to *Us Magazine* in December 2013, Alley downplayed a few of Remini's claims: "First of all, I just want everyone to know I have hundreds of friends and people that I know that have come into Scientology and left Scientology," the actress said. "It is not true that you cannot [depart the church] . . . You're not shunned, you're not chased. All that stuff's bulls--t."

Scientology, however, strongly warns members about staying in contact with *anyone* who has left. The good news is it appears more "defectors" are speaking up or at least reaching out to others who have left.

In fact, one former scientologist went on record to boldly state that women who are part of the Sea Organization are forced to obtain an abortion should they become pregnant. In tears, Claire Headley recounted the fact she was told by Scientology leaders to kill her unborn child. After leaving the church in 2005, her and her husband had three beautiful children. In an interview for one of the A&E series episodes, however, Headley stated, "If a woman got pregnant, she would instantly be scheduled to get an abortion. If she refused in any manner, she would be segregated, not allowed to speak with her husband; put under security watch, put on heavy manual labor and interrogated for her crimes."[90]

Mike Rinder confirms the policy and said it is considered a "mortal sin" to become pregnant while serving in the Sea Organization. Since leaving and speaking out, Rinder is reportedly receiving hundreds of emails a day from other defectors (former Scientology members). Another California woman has been fighting for the last seven years to have her case heard by the courts and was finally granted her request this year. In the lawsuit, Laura Ann DeCrescenzo claims to suffer from trauma after being forced at seventeen to have an abortion while involved with Scientology.

When she was twelve years old, DeCrescenzo moved out of her parents' house and into the organization's Pac Base in Hollywood and signed a billion-year contract with the elite Sea Organization. She worked from

---

90   Heather Clark, "Former Scientologist Claims Women in Sea Org Who Become Pregnant Forced to Obtain Abortion," 12/30/2016, *christiannews.net/2016/12/30/former-scientologist-claims-women-in-sea-org-who-become-pregnant-forced-to-obtain-abortion/*.

8:30 a.m. to 10:30 p.m. She said she suffers trauma since she was forced to have an abortion even though she was already married.

"I wasn't allowed to speak with my family. You're not allowed to have more than twenty dollars on you at any given time," DeCrescenzo told reporters at a 2010 press conference. "You're not allowed to go anywhere without another person. You're watched 24/7."[91]

Defense attorney for Scientology, Bert Deixler, said that under the First Amendment, churches may encourage a minister to "forego child rearing so she or he may continue a religious life" and added that the courts "may not interfere."

According to DeCrescenzo's lawsuit, "Defendants forced Plaintiff to have an abortion by threatening Plaintiff with losing her job, housing, and losing her husband if she did not have an abortion."

As a result of the abortion, Laura Ann DeCrescenzo says she "suffers from severe emotional stress, including anxiety, embarrassment, humiliation, shame, depression, feelings of powerlessness, and anguish." She was also told it was "only tissue," not a baby.

"I never agreed to have an abortion," she told reporters. "Did I concede? Yes, I did. Does it kill me every day? Yes, it does."

Another defector, Elvis Presley's daughter, Lisa Marie Presley, left the Church of Scientology in 2012. A few years before that, film director and screenwriter Paul Haggis left in 2009 and in 2011, *The New Yorker* published a 25,000-word story on his career and life within Scientology, which Haggis said horrified him. He was extremely bothered by a report in the *St. Petersburg Times* on physical abuse committed by church leaders, particularly on some very young members.

Haggis stated, "I was in a cult for 34 years. Everyone else [outside Scientology] could see it. I don't know why I couldn't."[92]

In March of 2015, a documentary that aired on the HBO television network was highly critical of the church and its practices. The program

91   Heather Clark, "Court Rules Woman's Lawsuit Against 'Church of Scientology' for Forced Abortion May Proceed," 5/2/2016, *christiannews.net/2016/05/02/court-rules-womans-lawsuit-against-church-of-scientology-for-forced-abortion-may-proceed/*.

92   MSN Entertainment, "13 celebrities who left Scientology," *www.msn.com/en-nz/entertainment/celebrity/13-celebrities-who-left-scientology/ar-AAaCWvn#page=3*.

was titled "Going Clear: Scientology and the Prison of Belief." The church responded by attacking those interviewed with harsh personal insults. Based on the book *Going Clear: Scientology and the Prison of Belief*, which preceded the documentary, here are some of the key points made in the 2015 exposé:

- L. Ron Hubbard's life was built on a series of lies and bullying.

- Hubbard sent letters about Dianetics to the American Psychological Association.

- Scientology's "clergy" formed as a response to investigations.

- The church essentially went to war with the IRS over tax exemption.

- Scientology blackmails its members with private auditing sessions.

- The church broke up Tom Cruise's marriage to Nicole Kidman.

Later that same year, Leah Remini published her memoir, *Troublemaker: Surviving Hollywood and Scientology* (Nov. 2015). In the book, among other problems with the church, she accuses David Miscavige of being controlling and oppressive. Even before leaving Scientology, an organization she had defended and which she invested heavily in for decades, she became a target just because she was asking questions about the church's actions.

Other than issuing a public statement denying all charges and accusations, how else does a billion-dollar entity respond to critics? Remini would eventually be declared by the church to be a threat and therefore a Suppressive Person. Sadly, all of her fellow parishioners – including members of her own family – were told to "disconnect" from her. Forever.

Leah Remini admitted that she spent close to $2 million on Scientology courses, auditing, and training, and donated roughly $3 million to church causes. She said the average person probably spends upwards of $500,000 to get to the highest levels, which often takes more than twenty years. During that time, they are required to purchase about

300 books, 3,000 lectures, and 100 courses. It's not surprising that when members leave for whatever reason, the church makes them out to be enemies, partly to discourage others from doing the same. But their tactics are not your basic methods of retaliation; theirs are big-brother or mafia-like.

According to researcher Craig Branch, Scientology has a very twisted view of ethics and morality, believing anything is permissible if it advances the goals of the church. Goals include doing whatever it takes "to bring the government and hostile philosophies or societies into a state of complete compliance with the goals of Scientology."

Scientology's history of terror and abuse appears to be the result of its founder's delusion and paranoia. Evidence of L. Ron Hubbard's delusional character was well documented in court where the trial judge concluded, "The organization [Scientology] clearly is schizophrenic and paranoid, and this bizarre combination seems to be a reflection of its founder, LRH. The evidence portrays a man who has been virtually a pathological liar when it comes to his history, background and achievements" (*Church of Scientology v. Armstrong, No. C420153*, California Supreme Court, 1984).

A 1977 FBI raid on Scientology headquarters produced comprehensive evidence of stolen government documents, spies planted in the IRS and Justice Department, planted bugging devices, and 48,000 documents detailing smear campaigns orchestrated against critics of the church. Hubbard's wife, Mary Sue, and ten other scientologists were convicted and received prison terms. One of the more egregious clandestine attacks uncovered in evidence obtained in the raid was carried out against Paulette Cooper, author of the 1972 book *The Scandal of Scientology.* Following Hubbard's directive of "If possible, of course, ruin him utterly," scientologists smeared Cooper's reputation, then framed her for a felony.

Using stationary she had touched, which therefore

contained her fingerprints, they forged a bomb threat
against the church. Upon discovering the plot, called
Operation Freakout, the prosecutors dropped all charges
against Cooper. Besides the emotional anguish and disrup-
tion of her life, Scientology's outrageous, fraudulent persecution of her cost Cooper $26,000 in legal and psychiatric
fees (*Los Angeles Times*, June 24, 1990, A39).

Punishing people who dare leave the church is sad enough, but the ruthless tactics sound closer to what the Mafia employs, not a non-profit
"religious organization." The truth is, Scientology has caused people
losses of marriage, babies, possessions, life savings, family relationships,
and sanity. But even more tragic is the potential loss of a future with
the Lord in heaven and a relationship with Jesus Christ today.

In the introduction of her book *Troublemaker: Surviving Hollywood
and Scientology*, Remini lets loose:

Let me start with this: I am an apostate. I have lied. I have
cheated. I have done things in my life I am not proud of,
including but not limited to:

Falling in love with a married man nineteen years ago,
being selfish and self-centered, fighting with virtually
everyone I have ever known (via hateful emails, texts, and
spoken words), physically threatening people (from park-
ing ticket meter maids to parents who hit their kids in public), not showing up at funerals of people I loved (because
I don't deal well with death), being, on occasion, a horrible
daughter, mother, sister, aunt, stepmother, wife (this list
goes on and on).

The same goes for every single person in my family . . . .

Why am I revealing all this? Because after the Church of
Scientology gets hold of this book, it may well spend an
obscene amount of money running ads, creating websites,
and trotting out celebrities to make public statements that
their religious beliefs are being attacked – all in an attempt

to discredit me by disparaging my reputation and that of anyone close to me. So let me save them some money.[93]

As a spinoff to the book, a docuseries, *Leah Remini: Scientology and the Aftermath,* aired last year and had a very successful first season on A&E. They are now working on a second season. Also appearing in the series as co-star and a consultant to the program, Mike Rinder expects the church to put out more "outrageous smear sites, vitriolic videos and ridiculous statements to the press" about Remini, himself, and others who have been interviewed in the series.

Rinder confirms that many of the Saul Alinsky-like tactics are right out of Hubbard's instructions to the church, and says scientologists are blind to everyone else's view of the world and "believe anyone who disagrees with them is evil. But this is just how cults operate." On his blog, Rinder explains what are known as "High Crimes," the worst transgressions one can commit, such as departing from Scientology. Acts of SPs also fall under this category according to Hubbard's writings. Rinder states:

HIGH CRIMES . . . Any of these will cause you to be named an enemy of Scientology. This list of "High Crimes" includes the following:

- Writing anti-Scientology letters to the press or giving anti-Scientology or anti-Scientologist evidence to the press

- Public disavowal of Scientology or Scientologists in good standing

- Public statements against Scientology or Scientologists

- Testifying as a hostile witness against Scientology in public

- Testifying hostilely before state or public inquiries into Scientology to suppress it

- Reporting or threatening to report Scientology or Scientologists to civil authorities

---

93   Leah Remini, *Troublemaker: Surviving Hollywood and Scientology* (New York: Ballantine Books, 2015), ix-x.

- Demanding the return of any or all fees paid for standard training or processing actually received or received in part and still available but undelivered only because of departure of the person demanding

- Continued adherence to a person or group pronounced a Suppressive Person or Group by HCO

- Failure to handle or disavow and disconnect from a person demonstrably guilty of Suppressive Acts

Rinder has a wealth of evidence and information on his website, and he is not kidding when he says Hubbard reserves special treatment for his enemies. Writings tell scientologists that when it comes to SPs – in this case, Leah Remini as well as Rinder – "they may be deprived of property or injured by any means, tricked, sued, or lied to or destroyed."

To summarize the scripture of scientology regarding church attackers or enemies:

- Everyone who speaks publicly about Scientology without authorization from the church is deemed an enemy (Suppressive Person).

- Scientology is at war with its enemies/critics and they are to be obliterated and destroyed.

- All critics are enemies and all critics have crimes.

- No expense should be spared to stop a critic – they must be muzzled and shuddered into silence.

- Any action is "fair game" when it comes to stopping critics/enemies.

- This includes use of Private Investigators and covert operations and agents.

- It also includes creating fake "complainants," threats and smears, even discussing "unknown" crimes as if they were real.

- If they cannot find enough threat, they will manufacture it.

It would be easy, and somewhat understandable, to dismiss these as "over-the-top" exaggerations – to believe that even if all these statements are accurate, they are simply allegorical. But the real-world examples of Scientology in action, on display for the world to see, say otherwise.[94]

The church claims this is all "religious scripture" (because it is part of the infallible writings of L. Ron Hubbard), while cloaking themselves in a mantle of "we are victims of bigotry and hatred." To Miscavige and church leaders, the ends always justify the means. Critics of Scientology beware. But thanks to Remini, one of the most high-profile scientologists to bail and be able to talk about it, more people are hearing the truth. Some are even searching for facts and information about the church (business) including testimonies of former members.

According to the UK's *Telegraph*, there are numerous reports involving Scientology, allegations of human trafficking, and holding people against their will. Church leaders respond to these types of reports by declaring such attacks are from the uninformed and that any alleged controversy involving Scientology is "merely the bitter old resisting the ambitious new."

Apparently, the church also has a cruise ship called the MV Freewinds, based in Curacao, used for the wealthiest and most committed members of Scientology. Another former member from Australia, Valeska Paris, claims she was held against her will on board the ship for twelve years and forced to perform hard labor. She made it clear she did not want to be there and claims she could only leave the ship with an escort. According to the article, Paris's mother left the church and denounced it on French television after the suicide of her father. The church denied that Valeska Paris had been mistreated in any way.[95]

One Australian senator reportedly called Scientology a "criminal organization," accusing the church of blackmail and embezzlement. If a fraction of the charges and accusations detailed in this chapter (and there are many more) were against a Christian ministry or pastor, how

---

94 Mike Rinder, "Dealing with Critics of Scientology – the L. Ron Hubbard Playbook," 11/5/2016, *www.mikerindersblog.org/dealing-with-critics-of-scientology-the-l-ron-hubbard-playbook/*.

95 Jonathan Pearlman, "Former Scientology member held against will aboard cruise ship," 11/29/2011, *www.telegraph.co.uk/news/worldnews/australiaandthepacific/australia/8923123/Former-scientology-member-held-against-will-aboard-cruise-ship.html*.

would the media report the story and what do you think would happen? They'd probably be heavily fined, lose their non-profit status, and the pastor and church leadership would all be forced to resign if not convicted and sent to prison.

Scientology is no small business and yet somehow it achieved a non-profit status from the U.S. government. For twenty-five years, the IRS labeled the church a commercial enterprise and the government's refusal to give Scientology a tax-exempt status was upheld in every related court case. Even a 1984 Tax Court ruling found the church "made a business out of selling religion" and that Hubbard and his family diverted millions of dollars to their personal accounts.

But in October 1993, thousands of Scientology church members filled the L.A. Sports Arena to celebrate a most important milestone in the cult's history: victory over the IRS and recognition as a religious enterprise. Saving the church tens of millions of dollars in taxes, leader David Miscavige declared, "The war is over!" It took *New York Times* reporter Douglas Frantz four years of investigating to find that the church used its power, force, and a covert operation (called "Snow White") to personally intimidate IRS officials, leading to a meeting with Miscavige and IRS Commissioner Fred Goldberg Jr. in 1991. The church was awarded its 501(c)(3) status two years later.[96]

Former Scientology members have written books and have done interviews, which are valuable because eyewitness testimony is significant. Also available are transcripts of court proceedings related to Scientology as well as federal investigations and reports. Reviews and criticism from other related fields include psychology, philosophy, medicine, science, sociology, and theology. On a mission to reveal the truth, Remini said she is hearing from people who haven't spoken up before. She said they have been "brainwashed into believing they couldn't do anything," and they were told there would be repercussions if they went to the police or the FBI.

A serious and obvious question must be asked: with all we know now, how in the world do intelligent people fall for the lies of Scientology? It

---

96 Douglas Frantz, "Scientology's Puzzling Journey from Tax Rebel to Tax Exempt," 3/9/1997, *www.nytimes.com/1997/03/09/us/scientology-s-puzzling-journey-from-tax-rebel-to-tax-exempt.html.*

is a deceptive and seductive movement filled with sugarcoated teachings, super-human claims, and lofty promises. Another draw is the church's celebrity members and its massive public relations machine. Remini said some are raised in the organization, others came to it after a falling out with their own religion or family, but "the central tenet of Scientology is incredibly alluring." She added that it offers people a "scientific process that helps you overcome limitations and realize your full potential for greatness."

Hubbard wrote that the aims of Scientology are "a civilization without insanity, without criminals and without war, where the able can prosper and honest beings can have rights, and where Man is free to rise to greater heights." Remini found this to be "empowering" and admits the promises of higher living and a higher level of thinking "drew me in, along with thousands of others who were looking for an alternative to therapy or more traditional self-help."

The point is anyone is susceptible to the Enemy's deception. Christian friend, be warned again how alluring the world and its philosophies can be.

Why would a legitimate religion need celebrities to endorse it? Hollywood is known by many to be generally fake, the neurotic center of the universe. One of its nicknames is "tinsel town" because of its insincerity, the unreal nature of the entertainment industry, and the superficially glamorous world it represents. Leah Remini appears to be on the right track, but pray for her and Mike Rinder. Pray God will reach them with His truth, that they will know He is real and trustworthy, and that salvation is attainable through faith in Christ alone. Let's pray also for *all* those who have been badly hurt by a church or cult.

One thing I disagree with Remini on is a simple statement she made saying she wanted to be clear that "I'm not trying to turn people. We don't need to get people out." Seriously? After all we've learned, I'm not completely sure what she meant by this. If your friend or loved one were in a burning building, wouldn't you want to do everything in your power to save them? They are in need of rescue. Their eternal security is at risk and they do not have the assurance of everlasting life in the presence of the God. What if they're wrong about following L.

Ron Hubbard? They are. What if Christianity is true? It is. Can you know that you're saved? You can.

> But what does it say? "The word is near you, in your mouth and in your heart"—that is, the word of faith which we are preaching, that if you confess with your mouth Jesus as Lord, and believe in your heart that God raised Him from the dead, you will be saved; for with the heart a person believes, resulting in righteousness, and with the mouth he confesses, resulting in salvation. (Romans 10:8-10)

Among other things, the Los Angeles Superior Court deemed Hubbard "a pathological liar" driven by "egotism, greed, avarice, lust for power and vindictiveness and aggressiveness against persons perceived by him to be disloyal or hostile." I completely agree with Watchman Fellowship, the Christian Research Institute,[97] and others who conclude that Scientology is a controversial modern movement developed by one man as an extension of his earlier psychological theories of Dianetics.

By the time this book is published, *Leah Remini: Scientology and the Aftermath* will be airing its second season on A&E, exposing lies and sharing more heartbreaking stories. I hope you believe those who have escaped this cult and have been badly damaged, who have poured their lives into what they thought was a religion with the answers only to find out they were lied to, manipulated, and ended up feeling empty and disillusioned.

Remini did not originally plan to speak out against the church when she first left Scientology, but she has been encouraged by the overall response to the book and TV series. She recently said she hopes to inspire more people to take action, to help get the truth out there.

> "People are doing what they can, and that's a great thing. If you can write a letter, do it! If you can simply call a congressman, do it! In this climate, often people feel they don't have a voice or power to do something, whether it's [in response to] a cult, an abusive relationship, or politics. A

---

97   John Weldon, CRI, "Scientology," *www.equip.org/article/scientology/.*

docuseries like this makes people feel that there's hope that
anyone can do something to effect change."[98]

I agree with researchers, journalists, and former church members
who have chronicled the origin, development, beliefs, and practices
of Scientology and view it as an abusive, totalitarian, business cult,
wrapping itself in the cloak of religion for reasons of opportunism and
expediency. Its teachings are dangerous, and whenever we have a chance
to warn others, we should do so. Hubbard himself once declared truth
is so strange one cannot actually distinguish between science *fiction*
and science *fact*.

With a solid foundation on the Holy Bible, our pursuit of truth continues with other man-made deceptions, fads, and religions promising
to fill our needs and satisfy our souls. Only one thing can truly satisfy
us in this life and prepare us for the next: the Christian faith. Only one
Person can provide eternal life and through His Holy Spirit – clarity,
guidance, wisdom, joy, peace, hope, healing, and restoration: Jesus
Christ. He is the only living God, and there's so much more awaiting
us when this life is done.

*In a statement, the church claims all "allegations are false and are tired
rumors stemming from the same small group of anti-Scientologists."*

---

98   Joey Nolfi, "Leah Remini roars back with Scientology and the Aftermath season 2 preview,"
      3/27/2017, *ew.com/tv/2017/03/27/leah-remini-interview-scientology-aftermath-season-2/.*

Chapter 13

Atheism, Gnosticism, New Age, and Wicca

See to it that no one takes you captive through philosophy and empty deception, according to the tradition of men, according to the elementary principles of the world, rather than according to Christ. (Colossians 2:8)

O n my way to work today, the car in front of me had a bunch of bumper stickers on it. "World Peace," a rainbow flag; you've seen them, I'm sure. But one of the trendier ones is the cleverly spelled-out "COEXIST" sticker using symbols for major religions and ending with a "T" representing the cross of Jesus. Why is this concept naive, and is it possible to "coexist"?

The purpose of COEXIST is to promote all gods and religions as acceptable, and a moral relativistic tolerance as the highest of all virtues. Therefore, Christianity is supposedly intolerant because it exclusively teaches Jesus is the only Way to God the Father, to an abundant life, and to eternal salvation. COEXIST is meant to silence the truth and criticize Christianity.

Why are people so reluctant to follow the narrow path? Jesus did say few would find it, but the truth is man generally doesn't want a higher authority or accountability. Someone has said even if there were 100 ways to God, it wouldn't be enough because we would then want 101.

Most of us who are committed disciples and Bible-believing

Christians will not fall for these deceptions and lies, but that doesn't mean we *cannot* fall for them or at least be tempted to believe a false teaching. Understanding what others believe will challenge us to know our Bibles better so we can immediately recognize counterfeits and be confident in discussions about faith and spiritual things. Remember, we have the truth. Charles Spurgeon stated, "If there be any difficulties in the faith of Christ, they are not one-tenth as great as the absurdities in any system of unbelief which seeks to take its place."

ATHEISM

Let's begin with the letter "a," but first it must be stated it takes much more faith to be an atheist than to be a Christian. The word *atheism* comes from the negative *a* which means "no," and *theos* which means "god." Atheism, in the most basic terms, means "no god" or "without God." It is the lack of belief in any god and/or the belief that there is no god. By contrast, theism is the belief that there is a God, He is knowable and sovereign, and He is involved in the world. Most atheists do not consider themselves anti-theists but merely non-theists.

Psalm 14:1a states, *The fool has said in his heart, "There is no God."*

Atheism is an attempt to maintain a belief system without any notion of God. Though atheists only make up about 3 percent of the U.S. population, it is a gradually growing movement. Generally supported by the major institutions in our culture, proponents are becoming more demanding and less tolerant of others' beliefs, especially the Christian faith.

According to Ken Ham and Bodie Hodge, variations of atheism include classical atheism, new atheism, non-theism, anti-theist, Church of Satan, and Epicureanism. A few religions that are atheistic in their outlook or practice are agnosticism and Buddhism, which we'll soon address. In the book *World Religions and Cults Volume 3*, Ham and Hodge also add:

> "The atheist holds that all things consist of matter and
> energy (nature and matter only). They argue with the
> loudest voice that there is no immaterial, spiritual, or

ideal realm. Their position relies on strict materialism. . . . Atheists argue against the existence of an immaterial realm. If they left open the idea that the immaterial exists, then God, who is not material, could exist and atheism would be wrong."[99]

Not all atheists believe every one of the following presuppositions, but these are basic tenets held by many atheists: there is no God or devil, there is no supernatural realm, miracles cannot occur, there is no such thing as sin or a violation of God's will, the universe is materialistic and measurable, man is material, evolution is considered a scientific fact, and ethics and morals are relative.

Atheism and secularism are being promoted together with more intensity these days. When it comes to new atheism, think about the Freedom *From* Religion Foundation, which features some of the most hostile atheists who are intolerant toward Christianity and yet hypocritically silent on other religious views. New atheism supports the idea that blind, natural forces are responsible for all reality, and they do not restrict themselves from a passive disbelief.

Many new atheists are God-denying or God-hating evangelists. They actively engage others to denounce their faith in God and to follow them in working to eradicate Christianity in both practice and belief. They are in the minority, but have very loud voices and monetary support. Tragically, what these folks do not have, however, is faith in the only One who can save them.

> And without faith it is impossible to please Him, for **he who comes to God must believe that He is** and that He is a rewarder of those who seek Him. (Hebrews 11:6, emphasis added)

GNOSTICISM

The goal in this chapter is not to explain every nuance of the teachings of Gnosticism and other religions, but to provide an informative overview. Christianity and Gnosticism are mutually exclusive belief

---

99   Bodie Hodge and Roger Patterson, *World Religions and Cults Volume 3* (Green Forest, AR: Master Books, 2016), 39.

systems, as principles of Gnosticism contradict the true meaning of Christianity. Because Gnosticism denies the incarnation of God as Jesus, the Son, it also denies the atonement of Christ.

The word *Gnosticism* comes from the Greek word *gnosis*, which means "to know" or "knowledge." The adjective *gnostikos* means "leading to or pertaining to knowledge, intellectual." Gnosticism teaches that salvation can be achieved through special or divine knowledge. It is a heretical movement of the second century that derived from independent teachings of Christians and Jews of that time. Gnosticism can also be traced to the writings of Irenaeus, Hippolytus, Tertullian, Origen, and some later manuscripts discovered in the eighteenth century.

**This is not to be confused with someone claiming to be "agnostic." Very briefly described, AGNOSTICISM is the view that the existence of God or the supernatural are not only unknown, but cannot possibly be known (unknowable). An agnostic is someone who believes nothing is known about the nature of God or anything beyond the tangible, material realm. An agnostic claims neither faith nor disbelief in God. *Gnosis* means "knowledge"; *a-gnosis* means "without knowledge."

In his famous Acts 17 sermon on Mars Hill, the apostle Paul observed all the idols and gods in Athens, and the altar they erected just in case they missed one.

> *Then Paul stood in the midst of the Areopagus and said, "Men of Athens, I perceive that in all things you are very religious; for as I was passing through and considering the objects of your worship, I even found an altar with this inscription:*
>
> *TO THE UNKNOWN GOD.*
>
> *Therefore, the One whom you worship without knowing, Him I proclaim to you: "God, who made the world and everything in it, since He is Lord of heaven and earth, does not dwell in temples made with hands. Nor is He worshiped with men's hands, as though He needed anything, since He gives to all life, breath, and all things." (Acts 17:22-25 NKJV)*

Who is the *Agnosto Theo* – the "Unknown God"?

> *If you had known Me, you would have known My Father*
> *also; from now on you know Him, and have seen Him.* –
> Jesus Christ (John 14:7)

So then, Gnosticism is a modern name for a variety of ancient religious ideas (anything with an "-ism" is typically considered a belief system) having Jewish origins. To the gnostic, freedom comes through knowledge.

You may have heard of early heretical writings known as the gnostic gospels, which teach that the physical world (matter) is actually evil. These writings are a collection of forgeries that contain false teachings about Jesus, God the Father, and other erroneous ideas. Gnostics, as well as some atheists, claim these gnostic gospels are actually "lost books of the Bible," but the early church leaders recognized the scrolls were fraudulent and inconsistent with the rest of God's Word.

Gnostic doctrine holds that the world was created and ruled by a lesser and perhaps even evil deity. Gnosticism also teaches that salvation is understood as a revelation that awakens knowledge to the human race's divine identity. Gnostics may claim to admire or even to follow the teachings of Jesus Christ, but their beliefs and practices contradict Him.

According to *GotQuestions.org*, Gnosticism is based on two false premises:

> First, it espouses a dualism regarding spirit and matter.
> Gnostics assert that matter is inherently evil and spirit is
> good. As a result of this presupposition, Gnostics believe
> anything done in the body, even the grossest sin, has no
> meaning because real life exists in the spirit realm only.

> Second, Gnostics claim to possess an elevated knowledge,
> a "higher truth" known only to a certain few. . . . a higher
> knowledge, not from the Bible, but acquired on some mys-
> tical higher plane of existence. Gnostics see themselves as

a privileged class elevated above everybody else by their
higher, deeper knowledge of God.[100]

Most Gnostics also believe Jesus Christ's body only *seemed* to be a physical body, and that His spirit descended upon Him at His baptism but left Him just before the crucifixion.

There is another theological view of Gnosticism that teaches the idea that the *unknowable God* was too perfect and far removed from the evil, material universe, so He generated lesser deities. Because one of these emanations, "Wisdom," had an erroneous desire to know God, an evil god or *demiurge* was formed and it was this god that actually created the universe.[101]

After we die, this god prevents human spirit souls from ascending back to god, and deliverance is only possible through special knowledge attained through gnostic teachers. To gnostics, Jesus Christ was a human, but also a divine redeemer who came down from the spiritual realm to reveal the knowledge necessary for redemption. Thus, the One who is, in reality, the Way is seen as only a revealer of the way to salvation.

At the risk of being redundant, we can either trust man with his reason and intellect, or we can trust God and His flawless, infinite wisdom. It shouldn't be a difficult choice for most of us.

"To be or not to be?" – Shakespeare

"I think, therefore I am." – Descartes

"I AM WHO I AM" – YHWH, GOD

THE NEW AGE

Embarking on the daunting task to write a condensed section on the New Age movement, I went to the Lord and spent time in prayer. The New Age Movement is a seductive and oppressive religious and social movement. It is a worldview alien and hostile to Christianity. It is multifaceted in varying degrees of the Far Eastern mystical religions (mainly Hinduism, Buddhism, Taoism, and Western Occultism), adapted to a Western, materialistic culture.

100   Got Questions, "What is Christian Gnosticism," *www.gotquestions.org/Christian-gnosticism. html.*

101   Matt Slick, C.A.R.M., "Gnosticism," *carm.org/gnosticism.*

New Age influence appears at times in secularized forms. It is comprised of hundreds of groups and individuals who have gained significant influence, affecting almost every area of the culture – sociology, psychology, medicine, the government, ecology, science, arts, education, the business community, the media, entertainment, sports, and even the church. The movement expresses itself in widely divergent and various mutated forms, from the blatantly obvious to the subtle.[102]

It is expressed in organized religious forms such as Christian Science, Unity, and even forms of witchcraft (Wicca). Yet it shows up in secular forms as well, in various human-potential seminars, music, transcendental meditation, some alternative holistic health practices, and certain curriculum in public (and private) schools. I've also heard the New Age described as a potpourri of occult and metaphysical ideas.

The number of people involved in New Age is nearly impossible to estimate due to the fact that this movement does not fall under the umbrella of a specific organization or extension of a church, but consists of a varied set of beliefs. The New Age has no particular holy book, church, leader, or list of members. However, the massive amount of people worldwide who have accepted some form of New Age belief, philosophy, practice, or teaching, is sobering.

It is no surprise a majority of people believe in an afterlife, with over 80 percent of Americans still believing in heaven, and about 30 percent believing there is a literal hell. But what about reincarnation ("entering the flesh again"), one of the central tenets of the New Age movement? Considering various polls, an estimated average of 28 percent of Americans including nearly one in four "professing" Catholics (24 percent) believe in reincarnation.

The New Age movement is like a smorgasbord for spirituality and religion, and can be traced back to the 1860s, and seems to have catapulted out of the American counterculture rebellion of the 1960s and '70s. One might also describe it as a sponge, in that a person with New Age beliefs soaks up and attempts to combine various religious ideas, cultural practices, and philosophies. Many adherents blend a form of Christianity with Universalism, Hinduism, and other beliefs such as

---

102   Craig Branch, "The New Age Movement," *www.watchman.org/profiles/pdf/newageprofile.pdf.*

astrology, necromancy, and fascination with the supernatural as well as spiritual energy.

It is interesting that many practitioners and proponents of New Age ideas deny they are *religious* (they prefer *spiritual*), and yet they religiously pursue many methods of meditation and also seem to align with moving toward a New World Order, global socialism, or a One World Religion. Think "Coexist" and the concept of a world without biblical Christianity, a world in which moral relativism reigns and man is supreme. New Age thinking has its roots in Eastern Mysticism, which attempts to bypass the mind, and allows for individuals to choose their own "door," "path," group, or guru.

Author, missionary, and world religion expert William Honsberger writes:

> "A New Age person might be a Hindu, Buddhist, Wiccan, or an astrologer, channeler, or parapsychologist. His or her cause might be "deep ecology," animal rights, holistic healing, or UFOs. The surface belief, expression, or practice is not that important. What is important is that underneath all the groups and practices lies a unifying philosophy that binds the movement together."[103]

The term *New Age* refers to the coming *Aquarian Age*, a phrase taken from astrology, an age of knowledge and bliss which is in the process of replacing the old Age of Pisces. According to astrologers, every 2,160 years constitutes an "age." The New Age idea is that humanity has taken a great step forward in consciousness and spiritual discovery and it is said to be a time of utopia, and some believe it has already dawned. This is supposed to be an age of enlightenment, harmony, peace, and one in which humanity is reunited with (their concepts of) God.

I'm about to embarrass some of you over forty years old. (Don't feel bad, I sang along with this song too and completely missed its meaning and misunderstood the New Age celebration.) Here are the song lyrics from the big 1969 hit "Aquarius/Let the Sunshine In" by The 5th Dimension:

---

103 Dean C. Halverson, *The Compact Guide to World Religions* (Bloomington, MN: Bethany House Publishers, 1996). 161.

When the moon is in the Seventh House, And Jupiter aligns with Mars
Then peace will guide the planets, And love will steer the stars
This is the dawning of the age of Aquarius, Age of Aquarius
Aquarius, Aquarius

Harmony and understanding, Sympathy and trust abounding
No more falsehoods or derisions, Golden living dreams of visions
Mystic crystal revelation, And the mind's true liberation
Aquarius, Aquarius

Little explanation is needed for these lyrics which then went into a repeating chorus of "Let the Sunshine In." One of the album covers featured the five group members within an astrological circle with the twelve signs of the zodiac listed around the outside circle. One meaning of the Age of Aquarius is to finally do away with Christianity and religion in order to live free from absolute truth, without accountability, in a perceived utopia. Since the group did not write the song and it was used for the Broadway musical *Hair*, I wonder if they knew what it meant.

Other than its anti-war message, the story of *Hair* was about how a group of young adults sought to balance their lives, relationships, and the whole sexual revolution with their rebellion against God, their conservative parents, and American society. One cannot deny the occultic influences in songs from that period supporting the "true liberation" of the mind as well as planets aligning, and cosmic awareness mixed with mystery. Drugs became a big part of the rebellion and opened people up to the realm of demonic spirits. The momentum of New Age philosophy grew rapidly during the hippy movement that exploded in the sixties.

When a New Ager speaks of God, they are not referring to the Judeo-Christian understanding of God – the personal, holy Creator who existed before all things and is separate from all things. God, to them, is an impersonal energy force that can be referred to as he or she, mother or father, god or goddess. In the New Age movement,

God can be defined as a being, a dimension, a divinity, an expression, a presence, a principle, a power, a quality, etc.

They believe that since everything supposedly flows from the divine Oneness, then it is all divine to some extent. This is Pantheism, the belief that "all is God" or divine, which describes the very Oprah-like New Age concept of Ultimate Reality. This force is a Cosmic Mind or Consciousness, often called the Universal Self. To some, the movement is a way to think and understand reality without relying on traditional religion or Western rationalism. The New Age is very attractive and alluring to those wanting to practice spirituality with no higher authority so they don't have to deal with moral issues or give up their selfish lifestyle including materialism.

Before we look at some of the religious and cultural influences of the New Age movement, I want to provide a very condensed timeline of its progression. (Much more research is available from Watchman Fellowship at Watchman.org.)

In the 1860s, the New Thought movement emphasizing the power of the mind expanded after being initiated by Phineas Parkhurst Quimby in the 1840s. Quimby was a student of hypnotist and physician Franz Anton Mesmer. (The word *mesmerize* even comes from his name.) Mesmer had an electro-magnetic theory of "animal magnetism," which is basically hypnotism, and combined that with the Hindu and Buddhist beliefs that matter is only an illusion and physical maladies can be overcome by the power of the mind. A woman named Mary Baker Patterson began her own "New Thought" studies teaching metaphysical healing and that human beings are divine.

In the 1870s, Patterson became Mary Baker Eddy and underwent hypnosis by Phineas Parkhurst Quimby and, soon after, founded the Christian Scientist Association (later, Church of Christ, Scientist). In Eddy's new religion, rooted in this New Thought, she taught that the early Christian church believed the mind is the only reality.

In 1874, occultist Helena Petrovna Blavatsky came to the United States and founded the Theosophical Society to expound her teachings that within each person is the divine spark of the Universal Mind. She was first introduced to Eastern Spiritualism in London where she met her "Master" in 1851.

> "And now it stands proven that Satan, or the Red Fiery Dragon . . . Lucifer, or 'Light-Bearer,' is in us: it is our Mind – our tempter and Redeemer, our intelligent liberator and Saviour from pure animalism. . . . It is Satan who is the God of our planet and the only God" (Helena Petrovna Blavatsky, *The Secret Doctrine, Volume 2*, Theosophical University Press, 1988, p. 513).

In the 1880s, Charles Fillmore and his wife, Myrtle, started the Unity School of Christianity after Myrtle read the book by Mary Baker Eddy, *Science and Health*. Myrtle's affirmation that she was a child of God and she did not "inherit sickness" alludes to Unity's belief that sickness is an illusion. The couple also added belief in reincarnation to the New Thought movement.

In the 1900s, Earnest and Fenwicke Holmes founded the United Church of Religious Science or the Metaphysical Institute of Los Angeles, which teaches the Science of Mind and wrote a book of the same name. The idea is that freedom is attained through the "scientific" (knowledge) study of God through meditation and affirmations.

In 1906, Alice Baily proclaimed a young boy named Krishnamurti the Messiah, and in 1923, she started the Arcane School which was part of the Lucis Trust. Baily was a student of Helena Blavatsky. Krishnamurti denied being the Messiah in 1929 and founded the Order of the Star, focusing on Hinduism and mystical experiences.

In the late 1950s, Maharishi Mahesh Yogi developed Transcendental Meditation (TM) as the Spiritual Regeneration Movement Foundation, which took off after the Beatles' trip to India in 1967 to study under Maharishi. He devised a "World Plan" in 1972 to promote TM and purchased a college in Iowa, renaming it Maharishi International University. Transcendental Meditation revolves around the repetition of, and meditation upon, certain *mantras* (sounds or words) which enable practitioners to enter states of higher consciousness.

In the 1960s, Church Universal and Triumphant was established, and Swami Prabhupada founded ISKCON in America (The

International Society for Krishna Consciousness). Commonly known as Hare Krishnas, it can be traced back to sixteenth-century India, but was brought to America in 1965 by Abhay Charan De Bhaktivedanta Swami Prabhupada (full name). The next year he began publishing *Back to Godhead* magazine and the Society grew in popularity following the release of the song *My Sweet Lord* by former Beatle George Harrison. It featured the mantra "Hare Krishna" which was repeated at the end of the song.

"An Aquarian Exhibition: 3 Days of Peace and Music" known as Woodstock took place in 1969 in New York attracting nearly five hundred thousand and marking the peak of the hippie movement. Complete with sex, drugs, rock music, and New Age influence, Woodstock is considered one of the top fifty events that changed history.

In the 1980s, famous New Age actress Shirley MacLaine published her autobiography (1983), *Out on a Limb,* detailing her experiences with astral projection and UFO encounters, and displayed her theology in a 1986 TV miniseries based on her book. In one scene, MacLaine's guru convinces her to stand on the beach and shout toward the ocean, "I am God!" Also during this decade, Deepak Chopra met the Maharishi and joined TM.

In the 1990s, TM staff member Deepak Chopra had a conflict with the Maharishi, left TM, and in 1993, published his book, *Ageless Body, Timeless Mind: The Quantum Alternative to Growing Old.* After an appearance on *The Oprah Winfrey Show,* Chopra sold 130,000 copies of the book in one day. Chopra teaches Ayurveda, a form of Indian folk medicine which holds that humans can be healed from all problems by opening themselves up to the flow of the single source of universal energy. His 1995 book *The Seven Spiritual Laws of Success* claims that opening oneself to this energy flow will enable you to create unlimited wealth and material success.

Winfrey also boosted the career of author and New Age priestess Marianne Williamson, an advocate of the occult program *A Course in Miracles.* Also in the '90s, James Redfield published *The Celestine Prophecy,* and self-help guru Anthony Robbins authored *Awaken the Giant Within* and *Unlimited Power.* Bill and Hillary Clinton hosted

Marianne Williamson and other New Age leaders at a Camp David retreat, and Hillary engaged in sessions with the psychic Jean Houston.

In her early days before Oprah skyrocketed to fame and success, people were under the impression she was a Christian because she grew up in a Baptist church, but that idea came to a halt as the years progressed. Endorsing many controversial guests on her programs teaching things that the Bible clearly warns about, Oprah once stated, "I center myself each morning by trying to touch the God light I believe is in all of us. Some people call it prayer, and some call it meditation. I call it centering up. I get boundless energy from that. . . . It is because of this God-centeredness that I am where I am."[104]

Oprah helped promote German mystic Eckhart Tolle, whose influences include Zen Buddhism, Sufism, and Hindu mysticism including bizarre teachings on the use of human sexuality. Oprah's shows and topics included Universalism, The Law of Attraction, as well as "past life regression." Has she been able to reconcile such anti-Christian teachings with her past understanding of faith? Oprah said she was able to "open my mind about the . . . indescribable hugeness of that which we call 'God.' I took God out of the box." When she heard a minister say, 'The Lord thy God is a jealous God,' she said, "Something about that didn't feel right because . . . God is love, God is in all things." She said that was when her "search for something more than doctrine began to stir" within her.

Why is doctrine so important? Because the Scriptures are God breathed, inspired, perfect, and without error. Read Psalm 119. Notice that when someone doesn't like something taught in the Bible, they so easily look to practically anything else. Talking about how we should be concerned about credulity, Malcolm Muggeridge stated, "It has been said that when human beings stop believing in God they believe in nothing. The truth is much worse: they believe in anything."

What exactly does the New Age movement believe about Jesus Christ? Many would consider Him an angelic messenger, messiah, and reincarnated avatar, and believe that one greater than Jesus will soon appear to usher in the ultimate age. (Christians who know Scripture

---

104 Virginia Smith, "Oprah reveals secret of her incredible success" (Examiner, 7/14/1987), 29.

understand this New Age "Christ" to be the Antichrist.) Their cosmic evolutionary belief in a coming new world order is a counterfeit kingdom led by Satan.

It is another belief system in which you can create your own reality because it is all about human potential, just like the self-help gurus teach. Moral boundaries have been erased and there are no absolutes. To a New Ager, God is not a "He" but an "it." They suggest our problem is we don't realize we are God so we must change our consciousness. They see history not as humanity's fall into sin but as a fall into ignorance. Therefore, rather than redemption and restoration by grace through faith in Christ, they believe in mankind's efforts to ascend into enlightenment.

In the Bible, we are instructed to meditate. The difference between New Age and biblical Christianity is not only how we meditate, but on whom or what do we meditate. God told the people of Israel to meditate on the laws of God, obey what is written, and they would have good success (Joshua 1:8). Some forms of New Age meditation encourage one to shut off the mind or put it in neutral, so to speak, but this idea is not supported in the Bible.

Do our methods of meditation align with biblical standards or are we adding things of the world? Are we chanting, twisting, focusing on our own breathing, "emptying our mind," or are we setting our hearts on things above and filling our minds with the Word of God? Many religions pursue knowledge for the sake of attaining a higher level or just knowledge for the sake of gaining information. The Bible contains over a thousand verses featuring words like *know*, *knowing*, and *knowledge*. Most of these Scriptures, however, emphasize knowing the truth of God and Jesus Christ – not knowing oneself or the universe, etc.

The mind is a battlefield and we are not unaware of the schemes of the Enemy. The thought of leaving our mind and body open to being invaded by demonic spirits is bewildering. Worst-case scenario is you actually allow spirits to enter your life or you connect with the kingdom of darkness, a world of which Satan is ruler and is opposed to God and His children (true believers). Biblical meditation is focused on Christ and His presence, and can be a sweet time of communion and fellowship with our Creator.

YOGA

It is important to briefly address the practice of yoga, which many see as a form of exercise as well as meditation. Some Christians are concerned about yoga, some are committed to it, and others are confused about it. I do not believe in judging Christians for doing yoga, but at the same time, I recommend you be discerning and understand the spirituality behind it, and even avoid yoga. It's common for Christians to take yoga classes, sometimes even at a church, but because meditation is central to yoga, it is not simply an innocent exercise or relaxation method.

Why should you care? Yoga is an ancient practice derived from India, believed to be the path to spiritual growth, self-realization, and enlightenment. The word *yoga* means "union," and the goal is to unite one's (temporary) self with the infinite Atman or Brahman, the Hindu concept of God. This god is an impersonal spiritual substance that is one with nature and the cosmos. The *Yoga Journal* tells people who practice yoga not to label or judge inner thought patterns as right or wrong but to connect "the mind, body, and breath."

The Yoga of the West is known as Hatha yoga and focuses on the physical body through special postures, breathing exercises, and concentration or meditation. It is a means to prepare the body for the spiritual exercises, with fewer obstacles, in order to achieve enlightenment. The practice of yoga is based on the belief that man and God are one. It is little more than self-worship disguised as high-level spirituality.[105]

Is it possible for a Christian to isolate the physical aspects of yoga as simply a method of exercise, without incorporating the spirituality behind it? Yoga teaches you to focus on yourself instead of on the one true God. It encourages its participants to seek the answers to life's difficult questions within their own consciousness, and it may also leave one open to deception. According to a former astrologer, Christian yoga is an oxymoron.

The average person may not realize the poses in Hatha yoga are often

---

105 Got Questions, "What is the Christian view of yoga?" *www.gotquestions.org/Christian-yoga.html.*

depictions of Hindu deities, and the hand positions mimic the hand positions seen on statues of Hindu gods. Many gurus promise that yoga will completely alter "consciousness" and reform reality. Some yoga teachers skip the first two steps and, drawing on "tantric" practices, they offer instructions on the seven "chakras" (spiritual centers) in the body and the techniques for raising the "kundalini" (coiled serpent power) that allegedly lies dormant at the base of the spine.

One swami spoke of the importance of kundalini, claiming the power is awakened through the practice of spiritual disciplines, rises through the spinal column, passes through the various centers, and at last reaches the brain, whereupon the yogi experiences "Samadhi," or total absorption in the Godhead. The eight limbs of yoga represent the stages or steps leading to this end.

In the hands of modern gurus, the definition of yoga undergoes a good deal of adjustment. Depending on the angle of approach, Atman and Brahman, for example, may be replaced by Krishna, Shiva-Shakti, Divine Mother, Mother-Father God, the Goddess, True Self, Higher Self, Higher Power, the All, the One, the God Within, Cosmic Consciousness, and in some circles Christ-Consciousness.[106]

Here are some characteristic New Age words or ideas: Aquarius, astrology, aura, awakening, chakras, channeling, chi energy, Christ-consciousness, contemplative, crystal powers, divination, divine, energy, evolve, globalism, goddess, harmony, holistic, holographic, human potential, kundalini, psychic forces, mantras, masters, mystery, networking, numerology, oneness, personal growth, reiki, reincarnation, self-realization, signs and wonders, spirit guides, synergistic, tarot cards, trance states, transformation, unity, universalism, visualization, yin-yang, yoga, Zen.

The influence of Eastern Mysticism in America cannot be understated and it goes back further than most of us realize. It has penetrated every area of society including everything from children's cartoons and comics to YMCAs and public universities. A recent news story, "Meditation Comes to the Classroom," was about a grammar school,

---

106   Brad Scott, "Yoga – Exercise or Religious Practice?" *www.watchman.org/articles/new-age/ yoga--exercise-or-religious-practice/.*

while another article reported about prison inmates doing yoga for stress management.

Even at places such as Harvard Divinity School, there's no mention of Palm Sunday or Passover, but the school paper reminds students to "listen to the Buddha and meditate." One columnist wrote, "Will the last graduating Christian please collect the Bibles and turn out the lights?"

> "One of the biggest advantages we have as New Agers is, once the occult terminology is removed, we have concepts and techniques . . . acceptable to the general public. So we can change the names and . . . open the New Age door to millions who normally would not be receptive." – Dick Sutphen, New Age leader

INFLUENCE CHANGES EVERYTHING

We cannot blame it all on the hippies. The church in America has been biblically illiterate and vulnerable as a result. Television show hosts such as Merv Griffin promoted Maharishi Mahesh Yogi and TM in the 1970s, and the drug movement in the '60s and '70s really opened the West up to the teachings of invading Eastern gurus. We had no idea these men were Hindu missionaries pushing a mystic gospel.

In his nearly 650-page book, *Occult Invasion*, author Dave Hunt discusses the influence of the New Age. He points out that people claim religious freedom and tolerance for all religions, and yet Christianity is being banned while Hinduism and Buddhism infiltrate our society, government, and public schools under the guise of science or world history. Hunt also explained that no guru has done more damage to the West by establishing the credibility of Eastern mysticism than Tenzin Gyatso, the Dalai Lama or spiritual leader of Tibet's Yellow sect of Mahayana Buddhism.

> He claims to be the fourteenth reincarnation of the original Dalai Lama, a god on earth with the power to initiate others into their own godhood. Here we have again the persistent occult theme of human deification echoing the serpent's lie in the garden of Eden.

In 1996, Hollywood elites such as actor Richard Gere and MGM President Mike Marcus honored the Dalai Lama at a fund-raising dinner for the American Himalayan Foundation. One thousand guests contributed about $650,000. Harrison Ford introduced the self-proclaimed god. Shirley MacLaine was on hand along with Leonard Nimoy, and other well-knowns. [Soon] two major films were in production about the Dalai Lama's life.[107]

Oprah will answer to the true God one day as she may have sold millions on the "all religions lead to God" lie. Many other celebrities joined her embrace of the occult in various forms through the years, including Robert Stack, Della Reese, Demi Moore, Dionne Warwick, George Harrison, John Denver, Elizabeth Taylor, and those mentioned earlier.

Some New Agers believe humanity's goal is the perfection of our ability to love, and New Agers encourage people to get in touch with their spirit guides to help them evolve and achieve harmony. These are, in fact, spirits, but since they are not of God, they are evil, demonic spirits. A New Ager can also contact beings such as "Ascended Masters," disembodied spirits who no longer live in physical bodies, and are UFOs, the spirits of animals, or angels. *Contacting* or *getting in touch* are other words for "channeling," which is an activity that may fill the void left by an impersonal, Ultimate Reality.

How does a New Ager approach or warm up to such a being or force? In her book *Going Within*, Shirley MacLaine wrote, "When I go within, I look for communication and guidance . . . and in general have a friendly exchange with someone or something which I perceive to be more advanced than I perceive myself." Therefore, we fill the void left between us and this abstract form of Ultimate Reality with spirit beings who can be channeled and who guide us along our paths.[108]

Even though it is a perversion to revere nature and created things over the Creator, New Age philosophy logically includes earth worship since all things are part of God. These counterfeit ideas have attracted scientists as well as those in the environmental movement, which we do

---

107   Dave Hunt, *Occult Invasion* (Eugene, OR: Harvest House, 1998), 219-220.

108   William Honsberger, *The Compact Guide to World Religions* (Bloomington, MN: Bethany House Publishers, 1996), 166.

not have time or space to cover here. Their theory is that since mankind is the product of evolutionary forces within the universe, we must get back in tune with nature, our Mother.

Many have adopted the shamanistic view that Mother Earth is a goddess named Gaia, and as you've probably guessed, she is extremely appealing to feminists. New Agers believe the Eastern mystical view that the universe is a living entity and we are all somehow connected. What we need to do, therefore, is recognize our "essential oneness" with the Universal Mind and experience higher states of consciousness.

It is necessary to touch on one more element of the New Age – Global Unity. We already discussed humanity being united to one another and man being one with nature, but in addition to this hoped-for age is economic unity. Much anticipation exists for a New Age world leader who will bring the world together economically and spiritually into a one-world religion. As stated earlier, this New Age hope sounds just like the coming Antichrist prophesied about in the Bible.

Human beings are fallen, limited, and not divine; every person is *destined to die once and after that to face judgment* (Hebrews 9:27 NIV). True morality is revealed in God's Word, and anything beyond this is works-based from the sinful mind of man. We need forgiveness, a hope, and a Savior. New Age teachings are in opposition to the Bible, which teaches history is linear, having a distinct beginning and an end. God is the Creator and Sustainer of all things and is sovereign over time. Genesis describes the beginning, and Revelation, the end. Moral relativism is irrational and it all comes down to what a person does with the source of truth; His name is Jesus.

WICCA (THE CRAFT)

There shall not be found among you anyone who makes his son or his daughter pass through the fire, one who uses divination, one who practices witchcraft, or one who interprets omens, or a sorcerer, or one who casts a spell, or a medium, or a spiritist, or one who calls up the dead. For whoever does these things is detestable to the Lord; and because of these detestable things the Lord your God will drive them out before you. You shall be blameless before the LORD *your God.* (Deuteronomy 18:10-13)

You might be surprised to know Wicca (Church of Wicca, or Wiccan Interfaith Council) holds a 501(c)(3) non-profit status with the federal government as a "non-profit religious, educational, and charitable organization." Wicca is a growing trend in New Age spirituality. It is closely related to goddess worship and neo-paganism. These groups hold to the divinity of nature and to the idea that spiritual power can be attained by manipulating these natural forces. Some suggest Wicca is mainly a twentieth-century manifestation of ancient nature worship systems that existed thousands of years ago. At first, Wicca attracted older adherents, but it is now a major attraction for young people.

Witchcraft promises power, mystery, and self-gratification (and rebellion against Christianity). It didn't take long for interest in witchcraft to accelerate, particularly among teenagers, after J. K. Rowling's *Harry Potter* book series (1997 – 2007) was turned into successful Hollywood feature films. The eight *Harry Potter* movies were released starting in 2001 with the final film in 2011. The books sold millions, the movies each made millions at the box office alone, and the *Harry Potter* brand is now worth billions. That is a whole lot of occult influence!

Today, though the Bible and Christianity have been long banned from public schools in America, millions of children have learned about witchcraft and occult practices, not just from movies, but also in the comfort of the classroom. On the NEA website there are *Harry Potter* teacher lesson plans for classes starting as young as third grade, and sixth through eighth graders can learn about "Making Magic," pop culture mythology, urban legend, and archetypes. Grades nine through eleven can study the science behind Harry Potter including "the basics of acid/base chemistry, genetics and trait prediction, and force and projectile motion."[109]

In the midst of Potter madness, reports came out around 2008 that Wicca was one of the fastest-growing religions in the United States. I'm sure it has tapered off quite a bit, but the damage was done. And it

---

109 NEA.org, "Teaching Harry Potter," *www.nea.org/tools/lessons/teaching-harry-potter.html.*

didn't start with the fictional character Harry. Would you believe the entertainment industry is a main culprit once again?

Witchcraft was endorsed and glamorized in *The Craft* (1996) with Neve Campbell, *Sabrina the Teenage Witch* (1996 - 2003) with Melissa Joan Hart, *Practical Magic* (1998) with Sandra Bullock and Nicole Kidman, and *Charmed* (1998 - 2006) with Alyssa Milano and Shannen Doherty, just to mention a few. Skipping back several decades, following the television series *Bewitched* (1964 - 1969), many fans admitted they had looked into or even practiced some form of witchcraft due to the Samantha Stephens (Elizabeth Montgomery) character. And who can forget Glinda, "the Good Witch of the North," or the "Wicked Witch of the West" in the 1939 classic, *The Wizard of Oz*?

Some trace witchcraft back to the time periods of the Inquisition and eventually to early American colonies, but the catalyst to the Wiccan revival began with the fruit of Gerald Gardner from the UK. Initiated into a witchcraft coven in 1939, he met satanist Aleister Crowley in 1946, and wrote *High Magic's Aid* in 1949, followed by *Witchcraft Today* in 1954. Also accelerating the interest and promotion of the occult in 1951, the Witchcraft Act of 1736 was repealed and Gardner was thrilled because for the first time in three hundred years in Britain, witchcraft was no longer a crime.

Wicca, as it is known and practiced today, is only about seventy-five years old, but its Celtic, New Age, and Eastern mysticism influences make it a contemporary pagan religious movement. Also referred to as Pagan Witchcraft, there is no central authority or consensus among followers as to a definition or mission, but this neo-pagan system draws from a diverse set of ancient and modernized rituals that may include meditation, chanting, nature, nudity, the use of herbs, incense, idols, various knives, and even swords. Wicca is a diverse religion that has grown and evolved over time into a number of sects, denominations, or traditions with each having its own organizational structure.

As with most groups that fall under the wide umbrella term of occultism, the theology of Wicca varies from group to group and even from coven to coven. It is explained in *Buckland's Complete Book of Witchcraft* that, generally, witches are very open-minded people,

especially where religion is concerned, because they do not have cat-
echisms or commandments set in stone. Also,

> "By creating our own divinities we create mental steps
> for ourselves, up which we can mount toward realizing
> ourselves as divine. . . . The lack of dogma in the Craft, the
> fact that one can worship the Goddess without believing
> in Her, . . . these are precisely the things that have caused
> the Craft to survive, to revive, and to be re-created in this
> century."[110]

Having been initiated into the Craft in 1953 by Gardner, English poet
and Wiccan Doreen Valiente practiced witchcraft as a teen and later
published five books documenting the early religious ceremonies and
rituals of Wicca. Published by Aquarian in 1962, her first book was
called *Where Witchcraft Lives*. Many secret and oral teachings were
part of the traditions though not all were written down. Also incorporated into this belief system were Freemason rituals and the idea
of reincarnation. Some Wiccans pick and choose parts of Christian
teachings while others totally reject the Bible; some are polytheistic
while others worship a single god or goddess.

Doreen Valiente has been credited with increasing the awareness and
worship of the goddess. On the "Goddess Guide" website, for example,
there were over seventy goddesses listed just for fertility, pregnancy, and
childbirth, so a woman could call upon a specific goddess regarding
her situation. A mother goddess is one who represents nature, moth-
erhood, fertility, creation, destruction, or who embodies the bounty
of the Earth. One historian said Wicca is basically a fertility cult with
many holy days or festivals geared to the months and seasons.

Believing that women once ruled the world and society, some goddess movements have turned political in order to lobby for change. The
thinking is the current male-dominated society must return to the
matriarchy of earlier, ancient times. With this mindset, it is easier to
understand why modern feminists support goddess worship through
various channels or concepts, and are even drawn to the Craft. Women

---

110   Raymond Buckland, *Buckland's Complete Book of Witchcraft* (Woodbury, MN: Llewellyn
      Publications, 1986), 99.

do not have to be evil or Wiccan to find joy in certain rituals, and most groups and covens say they don't believe in or practice evil. In fact, in the Principals of Wiccan Beliefs it is stated, "We do not accept the concept of absolute evil, nor do we worship any entity known as 'Satan' or 'The Devil,' as identified by the Christian traditions."[111]

Founder of the Church of Satan, Anton LaVey, however, viewed Satan as a real entity and deceived many people who began by "innocent" dabbling in witchcraft or the occult. Most Wiccans will vehemently deny that Satan is part of their pantheon, citing major doctrinal differences between themselves and satanists. Wicca has one law or rule, called the Rede: "An' ye harm none, do what ye will." At first blush, the Rede seems like complete, uninhibited personal license. You can do whatever you want, as long as no one gets hurt; however, Wiccans are quick to point out that the ripple effect of one's actions can carry far-reaching consequences. They articulate this principle in the Three-fold Law, which says, "All good that a person does to another returns three-fold in this life; harm is also returned three-fold."

Former Church of Satan leader, Nikolas Schreck (married Anton LaVey's daughter, Zeena) said witches in the 1960s admitted they were satanists. In his 2001 book, *The Satanic Screen: An Illustrated Guide to the Devil in Cinema*, Schreck stated, "the dark aesthetic of the '60s witch must be emphasized" because the word "Wicca" was hijacked by the "sweetness-and-light Wiccans" who influenced people's understanding of the Craft: "Seeing themselves as sisters of Satan, the majority of that era's witches were a far cry from the current Wiccan movement. . . . the witchcraft movement of the sixties reveled in its romantically diabolical associations."

According to occult expert and pastor, Joe Schimmel, of Good Fight Ministries:

> Many Wiccans are unaware of the fact that much of
> their teachings, ceremonial magic and "scriptures" are
> based on the teachings of Satanist, Aleister Crowley.
> Many of Crowley's ceremonies and teachings were simply

---

111   Rick Branch, "Witchcraft/Wicca," *www.watchman.org/profiles/pdf/wiccaprofile.pdf.*

reformulated by Gerald Gardner, who . . . was a member of Crowley's satanic organization, known as the OTO.

Even the Wiccan Rede (aka "counsel" or "advice"), "An' Ye Harm None, Do What Ye Will" was influenced by Crowley's maxim, "Do What Thou Wilt Shall be the Whole of the Law." While many Wiccans seek to disassociate from Satanists for understandable reasons, they have been deceived into believing that there is a difference between good and bad demons and so-called "white" and "black" magic.[112]

One major factor that contributes to the abiding fascination with Wicca is the purported use of spells and magick (a deliberate misspelling intended to separate Wiccans from magicians and illusionists). Curiosity seekers, as well as spiritual neophytes, are most eager to delve into these mysteries. Not all Wiccans practice witchcraft, but those who do so claim magick is to them what prayer is to a Christian.

So, Wiccans claim magick is simply using their minds to control matter, or they are appealing to their favorite deity to do them a favor. In contrast, Christians call upon an omnipotent, omnipresent God to heal people, to intervene, and to work in their lives. Because the Rede disallows witches from hurting others and the Three-fold Law spells out the consequences for Rede-breakers, witches who practice magick prefer to call themselves "nature witches" or "white witches" to further distance themselves from satanists.[113]

Since the theology behind Wicca is not from God, it must be authored by Satan. This includes all the "goddess" worship, which in reality is an offering to the devil. This does not mean every single person involved in some form of witchcraft is wicked or demonic. From a biblical perspective, however, even though most Wiccans are not knowingly or purposefully worshipping a being known as Satan, they are, in fact, tragically doing just that.

This information is condensed, but hopefully, there is enough here

---

112 Joe Schimmel, "Twilight, Harry Potter, The Wizard of Oz and the Wiccan Revival," *www.goodfight.org/twilight-harry-potter-wizard-oz-wiccan-revival/*.
113 Got Questions, "What is Wicca? Is Wicca witchcraft?" *www.gotquestions.org/Wicca.html*.

to give you a basic background and history to equip you with some facts. Does this stuff come from the mind of God or the ideas of man? Unfortunately, we need to warn Christians to be more discerning, and educate others who may be entertaining practices that they think are harmless or innocent. Ideas do have consequences.

And how you turned to God from idols to serve a living and true God. (1 Thessalonians 1:9)

Chapter 14

Islam, Jehovah's Witnesses, and More Truth about False Religions

(Buddhism, Christian Science, Freemasonry, Hinduism, Islam, and Jehovah's Witnesses)

For even if there are so-called gods whether in heaven or on earth, as indeed there are many gods and many lords, yet for us there is but one God, the Father, from whom are all things and we exist for Him; and one Lord, Jesus Christ, by whom are all things, and we exist through Him. (1 Corinthians 8:5-6)

Assuming the average reader of this book is well versed in Scripture and the essential doctrines of the Christian faith, my goal here is to provide a brief overview of some of the more common world religions and cults for your reference. As we continue to grow in discernment and evaluate man's claims and teachings, here are some questions to ask about each one:

How did the religion or philosophy originate? (history)

Do its followers agree or disagree with the teachings in the Bible? (compatibility)

What do they believe about Jesus Christ? (deity)

Is their holy book or leader higher than the Lord Jesus and His Word? (authority)

How do they attain enlightenment or reach heaven? (salvation)

We need to be able to explain how they differ from the truth of Christianity in at least a few main areas. If even the elect can be deceived, then less-discerning people are easy prey for false teachings. Spurgeon once said discernment is *not* knowing the difference between right and wrong, "It is knowing the difference between right and almost right." There are many ways to attempt to redefine truth, and it often begins with something subtle that sounds good.

Most of the following religious systems are variations of humanism, as they are based on man's ideas and words, which Satan uses to lure people away from the truth of Jesus. Simply stated, Christianity is Christ, and our entire faith rests securely upon the truth of His resurrection.

Man-made secular-progressive religions, however, have crept in and dominate America's education system, entertainment industry, government, media, museums, and universities. We now have, sadly, anti-Christ systems.

> *Beloved, do not believe every spirit, but test the spirits to see whether they are from God, because many false prophets have gone out into the world. By this you know the Spirit of God: every spirit that confesses Jesus Christ has come in the flesh is from God; and every spirit that does not confess Jesus is not from God; this is the spirit of the antichrist, of which you have heard that it is coming, and now it is already in the world. (1 John 4:1-3)*

Our job is to trust and obey the Bible as the final authority, know and proclaim the truth, and shine the light of Christ into the darkness. We need not know all the details, so these chapters are provided to give you an idea of what others believe. First, some words from Ravi Zacharias:

> "Naturalism settles for the theory of chaos; Jesus offers coherence. Islam talks about Allah, the Compassionate; but it is Jesus who went to the cross. You see, Compassion

literally means 'to suffer with.' There is no place like the
cross. Hinduism talks of 'karma' and the debt of morality;
but it is Jesus who offers forgiveness and paid the price of
sin. Buddhism talks of the eradication of desire; Jesus offers
to fill those who hunger and thirst after righteousness."

BUDDHISM

Born in southern Nepal, Siddhartha Gautama (563 - 483 BC) created Buddhism during the sixth century BC, which coincides with
the time the people of Judah were exiled in Babylon. There are three
forms of Buddhism: Theravada Buddhism (Cambodia, Laos, Thailand),
Mahayana Buddhism (China, Hong Kong, Japan), and Vajrayana, or
Tantric Buddhism (Bhutan, Mongolia, and Tibet). Some estimates
suggest Buddhists make up about 6 percent of the world population.

Siddhartha Gautama's father was a king in India. He tried keeping
his son inside the palace to shelter him from the suffering in the world.
Tradition holds that one day the prince ventured away from the palace
and encountered four kinds of suffering: sickness, old age, poverty,
and death (he saw a corpse). This experience was said to have had a
profound impact on him.

As a result, Gautama left his family, including his wife and child,
and his life of luxury to search for peace, as well as the source of and
solution to mankind's suffering. The story holds that he tried living in
poverty and self-denial for six years, but realized it wasn't the answer
to what he was seeking. He walked to a city named Bodh Gaya and sat
under a fig tree by the edge of the river.

It was during Gautama's meditation there that he became the Buddha
("the enlightened one") and Bodh Gaya is now the site of the holiest
Buddhist shrine, the Mahabodhi Temple. He called his path to enlightenment the Middle Way because it avoided the extremes of affluence
and asceticism. Buddha's life can be divided into three periods: enjoy-
ment, enquiry, and enlightenment.

Do not put your trust in princes, in human beings, who
cannot save. When their spirit departs, they return to

the ground; on that very day their plans come to nothing.
(Psalm 146:3-4 NIV)

He traveled to Benares and preached his first sermon. He eventually gained thousands of followers, spending forty years teaching what he learned in his deep meditation. The most common of Buddhist teachings include the "Four Noble Truths" and the "Eightfold Path." There are quite-extreme variations of Buddhism, but most Buddhists share some common beliefs.

The First Noble Truth is that life consists of suffering, which includes pain, misery, sorrow, and unfulfillment. The Second Noble Truth is that everything is temporary and ever changing, and we suffer because we desire temporal things. The Third Noble Truth is that the way to eliminate all suffering is by eliminating all craving or desire. We must stop craving that which is temporary. The Fourth Noble Truth states that desire can be eliminated by following the Eightfold Path. These eight points on this path can be categorized into three major sections:

WISDOM (*Panna*) 1. Right Understanding 2. Right Thought (or intention)

ETHICAL CONDUCT (*Sila*) 3. Right Speech 4. Right Action 5. Right Livelihood

MENTAL DISCIPLINE (*Samadhi*) 6. Right Effort 7. Right Awareness 8. Right Meditation

Apparently, these do not have to be done in order, they are attitudes and actions to be developed simultaneously. The first two points, however, understanding and thought, are foundational. Dr. Dean Halverson explains:

When one has Right Understanding, for instance, he or she sees the universe as impermanent and illusory and is aware that the "I" does not, in reality, exist. [Such a concept is known as the doctrine of *anatta* ("no self").] At the basis of the concept of ethical conduct are the *sila*, or moral precepts. These precepts include commands to refrain from:

1. The taking of life (all forms, not just human), 2. stealing,

3. immoral sexual behavior (monks must be celibate), 4. lying, 5. the taking of intoxicants.

Buddha's immediate goal was to eliminate the cause of suffering. His ultimate goal, though, was to become liberated from the cycle of death and rebirth (*samsara*) by teaching how we can cease craving and thereby eliminate our attachment to . . . the illusory self. As we are successful in eliminating such attachment, then the effects of karma will have nothing to attach themselves to, which releases the individual from the realm of illusion. At that moment of enlightenment, the person achieves the state of *nirvana* – the ultimate goal for the Buddhist, and Buddhism's equivalent of salvation.[114]

There is no Supreme Being or Ruler, and no sin, so of course, no savior. The Buddhist view of Nirvana is an abstract Void and enlightened state, the end of consciousness where the ego is extinguished.

According to Buddha, human beings are an impermanent collection of five "aggregates." These "skandhas" include the physical body, emotions, perception, volition, and consciousness. Death causes these to be dismantled. Buddhism has been referred to as an "atheistic religion" because Buddha rejected all the gods of Hinduism which surrounded him. While Buddhism teaches human effort and self-reliance, Christianity teaches faith and reliance upon God. Many Buddhists consider Jesus an enlightened master or spiritual example, not divine and not the Son of God. But only Jesus, the true Prince of Peace, has power over life and death.

One form of Buddhism at the heart of the Japanese culture is known as Zen Buddhism. Meditation is at the core of this quest for spiritual awakening and self-discovery, as is the practice of *zazen* ("sitting meditation"), living moment to moment. The emphasis is on practical experience, and it is said that Zen is not an idea, belief, theory, or religion. When you go to the website for Zen, this is the first thing you read:

---

114   Dean C. Halverson, *The Compact Guide to World Religions* (Bloomington, MN: Bethany House Publishers, 1996), 58-59.

"To study Buddhism is to study the self, to study the self is to forget the self." – Dogen Zenji

According to the website, people cannot fully grasp Zen because "human intelligence and wisdom is too limited." Also from the website (*zen-buddhism.net*): "Trying to explain or define Zen Buddhism, by reducing it to a book, to a few definitions, or to a website is impossible. Instead, it freezes Zen in time and space, thereby weakening its meaning."

Apparently, this also helps sum up Zen: you are encouraged to "let your ego and unconscious mind melt away and merge with the universe." Zen Buddhism focuses on "the freeing of the will." Think about this concept and goal for a moment. Our world in reality is filled with trials, injustice, disease, hunger, poverty, suffering, persecution, and all forms of evil, and rather than love others and help people in need, Zen encourages you to work on yourself in the hopes of detaching from truth until "one's real self calmly floats over the world's confusion."

It is clear to see some major differences between this and Christianity. While Zen seeks enlightenment, Christians seek God's help and wisdom. Zen looks inward for guidance and inspiration; Christians meditate on God's Word for truth and direction.

Another philosophy or sect of Buddhism is Tibetan Buddhism, perhaps the most complicated but also the most well known due to the popularity of its leader, the Dalai Lama, who has lived in India since fleeing the Chinese occupation of Tibet in 1959. The current Dalai Lama's given name is Tenzin Gyatso and he is the fourteenth Dalai Lama. He won the Nobel Peace Prize in 1989. In an interview with *Christianity Today*, the Dalai Lama said Jesus actually lived previous lives and His purpose was to teach a message of tolerance and compassion.

> And this is the primary problem with the Dalai Lama and all of Buddhism. While some aspects of the Dalai Lama's message are undeniably positive, and while most Buddhists are indeed kindhearted and "good" human beings, their denial of the biblical Jesus infinitely outweighs any positive aspects of Buddhism.[115]

The idea of Tibetan Buddhism is to try freeing oneself from the

115 Got Questions, "Who is the Dalai Lama," *www.gotquestions.org/Dalai-Lama.html.*

attachment of worldly things, but this sect focuses more on its monks, or "lamas." It also recognizes a multitude of Bodhisattvas, beings who have attained ultimate enlightenment *having gone through numerous lifetimes*, but have chosen to remain in this world to help others. This concept could be remotely comparable to the compassionate sacrifice of Jesus Christ as well, and placing others above ourselves, but the theology is much different.

Many other points and variables could be addressed, but at its core, Buddhism is a very religious, works-based philosophy that places much emphasis on the love of self, and little is said about a person's relationship with others or responsibility to God and society. Jesus Christ promises us there will be a day when suffering will be no more (Revelation 21:3-4) because He endured the cross and overcame death by His resurrection. The causes of human pain and suffering have been dealt with (Isaiah 53:4-6, Philippians 2:8-10), and will be done away with forever. He provided the way to salvation – and every other alleged way is no way at all.

CHRISTIAN SCIENTISM

Formally named the Church of Christ, Scientist, Christian Science was incorporated in Boston in 1879 by Mary Baker Eddy (1821 - 1910), who claimed her teachings were "the final revelation of God for mankind." With about three thousand churches in fifty-six countries, Christian Science holds that the Bible should only be interpreted in a metaphorical or spiritual sense, not literally, and instead of God the Father, the Son, and the Holy Spirit, its trinity consists of "Life, Truth, and Love."

Christian Science teachings are found in the book by Eddy, *Science and Health with Key to the Scriptures*, a book which is revered as the Bible's equal or companion. A few of the teachings of Christian Science include God is the Father-Mother, Jesus did not die, the Holy Spirit is divine science, there is no devil, God cannot indwell a person, and "Matter, sin, and sickness are not real, but only illusions."

Apparently, as a result of her own personal healing of a spinal problem in 1866, Mary Baker Eddy began researching healing information and methods, and spent years trying to understand the mind-body connection and its relation to the spiritual. Several years after starting a church, Baker Eddy renamed her Boston church The Mother Church in 1892, the first church she established.

One statement revealing a large part of Christian Science philosophy is "So the sick through their beliefs have induced their own diseased conditions." This idea promotes the avoiding of doctors (they go to *practitioners*) and modern medicine, and has proven to be dangerous and even fatal in some cases. Baker Eddy did not produce any convincing medical evidence about any of her claimed healings. Local Christian Science "churches" hold weekly testimonial meetings where members share experiences of healing and regeneration.

World religion expert and author Mark Water stated the main purpose of Christian Science is universal salvation from every phase of evil – including sin and death, that you are as much a Son of God as Jesus is, and you are reincarnated until you become perfect. Its distinctive doctrine is the healing of disease by spiritual purposes alone. After reading about Jesus healing the paralyzed man in Matthew 9, Baker Eddy claimed to heal people who had incurable ailments through prayer-based healing. Water adds:

> As a result of her "glimpse of the great fact" that life is in
> and of God, which she called her great discovery, Mary
> Baker Eddy went on to found the Science of Christianity
> which . . . claims to be the science of healing but on close
> inspection it becomes clear that it is anti-Christian, anti-sci-
> ence, anti-healing, and not a church. Christian Science does
> not believe in the most basic scientific thought that the uni-
> verse is physical and subject to natural laws. . . . Christian
> Scientism teaches . . . God is an impersonal Principle of life,
> truth, love, intelligence, and spirit; Jesus Christ . . . could
> not suffer for sins, did not die on the cross, and He did not
> rise physically [and] will not literally come back.[116]

Christian Science does not have what most of us know as "church services." Bible lessons are read during the week so there is an appearance of Christianity. They have lectures in halls and the Bible is read

---

116   Mark Water, *World Religions Made Easy* (Peabody, MA: Hendrickson Publishers, 1999), 55-56.

on Sunday by two elected lay members of a particular congregation, but there are no pastors or ministers and no sermon. There are selected readings from the book, *Science and Health with Key to the Scriptures*, which Baker Eddy claimed was co-authored by God.

According to one former Christian Science follower, Mary Baker Eddy was the revealer of truth while Jesus Christ was simply a human being who demonstrated the "Christ Truth," just as you and I can when we become as spiritually advanced as He was. Baker Eddy's ideas (there is no sin, death, judgment day, or hell) are attractive but permeated with error.

> "Your dual and impersonal pastor, the *Bible*, and '*Science
> and Health with Key to the Scriptures*,' is with you; and
> the Life these give, the Truth they illustrate, the Love
> they demonstrate, is the great Shepherd that feedeth
> my flock, and leadeth them 'beside the still waters.'"
> – Mary Baker Eddy[117]

Baker Eddy was the only American woman to found a worldwide religion and was elected to the National Women's Hall of Fame in 1995. In addition to founding the Massachusetts Metaphysical College in Boston, she founded a publishing enterprise that includes two magazines and the respected newspaper, *The Christian Science Monitor*.

Christian Science denies the core, essential truths of what makes a system "Christian." Moreover, it is not only opposed to science, but it is also more of a mystical new-age spirituality particularly in its quest for physical and spiritual healing. Remember, just because something is called "Christian," even a church, does not make it true or biblical.

FREEMASONRY

Freemasonry *is* a religion and is not Christian. Some argue Freemasonry is not a religion; others claim it is Christian. With its beginnings sometime in the 1700s in Western Europe, Freemasonry, Freemasons, or simply, "the masons" are a very religious, secretive organization that goes beyond simply having fraternal characteristics to an elaborate

---

117   Ibid., 57.

235

religion surrounded by mystery. However, the "Craft," as some call it, can be very alluring.

Much has been written about Freemasonry from various perspectives, causing ongoing speculation and debate. Public perception of Freemasonry ranges from thinking it is harmless, suspicious, to flat-out dangerous. I hope to clarify some basic points about this fascinating organization. One of the clearest definitions of Freemasonry is that it is a very peculiar system of morality veiled in allegory, illustrated by symbols, and expressed through rituals.

One apparent requirement of Freemasons is that members must believe in the existence of a Supreme Being, not necessarily the true God and Creator of the universe. This may give an outward appearance of similarities with Christianity, but the core beliefs and practices of Freemasonry are unbiblical. Freemasonry teaches that God or the Supreme Being is known as G.A.O.T.U. or the "Great Architect of the Universe." As with most every other world religion that is not Christian, salvation is gained by a man's good works and self-improvement. Consider this quote from a book titled *The Meaning of Masonry*:

> "[I]t is clear, therefore, that from grade to grade the candidate is being led from an old to an entirely new quality of life. He begins his Masonic career as the natural man; he ends it by becoming through its discipline, a regenerated perfected man. To attain this transmutation, this metamorphosis of himself, he is taught first to purify and subdue his sensual nature; then to purify and develop his mental nature; and finally, by utter surrender of his old life and losing his soul to save it, he rises from the dead a Master, a just man made perfect."[118]

There are many and varied beliefs of Freemasonry, but faith in Jesus Christ is not one of them. In fact, I have read in multiple sources that although other gods are encouraged, the name of Jesus is prohibited in the formal ceremonies of the lodges. It is considered "un-Masonic" to invoke Jesus's name when praying. Lodges do not represent physical buildings necessarily, but regional groups of Freemasons are similar

---

118   W. L. Wilmshurst, *The Meaning of Masonry* (New York City, NJ: Gramercy Books, 1980), 46.

to a local Christian congregation. Technically, Freemasons meet as a lodge, not in a lodge. Masonic premises have also been referred to as Masonic temples, halls, or centers.

Freemasons have structure, member roles, and levels of authority. Lodges are governed by national or state authorities known as Grand Lodges, and under their published constitutions they appoint officers from their senior masons. The highest position is known as the Worshipful Master. Lodge leadership manages the affairs of each lodge and is key in the advancement of its members. Through instruction, Freemasons progress through a series known as *degrees*, which determine a member's rights and standing. These degrees can also be referred to as *rites*. Degrees go from 4th up to 33rd and higher. Another well-known group is the Shriners. Female-oriented Freemason groups are known as The Order of the Eastern Star and the Rainbow Girls.

One former Freemason explained that he had to swear to keep its rituals secret and had to swear certain required blood oaths. He learned secret handshakes and received instruction at each degree. The Order is supposedly inspired by the legend of an ancient character named Hiram Abiff and the building of Solomon's temple. Though not mentioned in the Old Testament, this extra-biblical legend is espoused to deceive and to give Masonry some legitimacy to attract religious men.

But Christians do not take oaths, and we swear allegiance to the only mighty God, the reigning and returning King of Kings. All the rest are wannabes and counterfeits.

But let your 'Yes' be 'Yes,' and your 'No,' 'No.' For whatever is more than these is from the evil one. (Matthew 5:37 NKJV)

Though they do not have a main holy book or primary scriptural authority, Freemasons consider the Bible to be one of many religious sourcebooks, a good guide for morality. Looking at the lodge concept spiritually and its mystical quest to achieve perfection however, there is little room to accept the sacrifice of Jesus.

Albert Pike (1809 – 1891) was a 33rd-degree mason and the Sovereign Grand Commander of the Southern Masonic organizations for thirty-two years. He was in favor of slavery and, believing southern states should secede from the Union, he and other southern delegates walked out of the Southern Convention in 1854.[119] Pike wrote *Morals and Dogma* of Freemasonry in 1871, and in it, he explained that Masonry conceals its secrets from people and uses false interpretations of its symbols to lead them away from the Light in order "to mislead those who deserve only to be misled."

On a website called Ex-Masons for Jesus (www.emfj.org), former Freemasons who have left and now embrace the truth of Christ answer questions people have about the actual beliefs and practices of Freemasons. They clearly state that "Freemasonry is a pagan religion," and these were people who were actively involved. From the "Honest Answers" page of their website, it reads:

> "While we were Masons, we sometimes were asked questions about Freemasonry by other church members who were not Masons. Because we had taken an oath to ever conceal and never reveal the secret teaching of Freemasonry, under the penalty of having our throats cut from ear to ear, we were reluctant to respond truthfully. We beg the forgiveness of our brothers and sisters in Christ for the less than honest answers we provided while we were Masons. Since we have repented . . . we have been released from the oaths."[120]

World religion expert Texe Marrs has written about many prominent Freemasons, including another Grand Master, Henry Clausen, who authored *Emergence of the Mystical*, and seemed to confirm the New Age underpinnings of Freemasonry and talked about using "the insight and wisdom of the ancient mystics . . . and the mysticism of Eastern religions." Marrs then turned to another high-ranking Freemason, Foster Bailey (founder of the Lucifer Publishing Company in 1923) of the Lucis Trust, who taught in his book *Things to Come* that those who don't live up to "New Age standards" will end up as "irreconcilable outcasts" (p. 39).

Foster is also the husband of well-known New Age author and proponent of occultism, Alice Ann Bailey. In Foster Bailey's book *The Spirit*

119 Wikipedia, *Albert Pike*, en.wikipedia.org/wiki/Albert_Pike.
120 Ex-Masons for Jesus, "Honest Answers to Important Questions," *www.emfj.org/answers.htm*.

of Masonry, which was touted in the book review section of the *Scottish Rite Journal* in August 1990 (pages 24 and 58), Baily, also an occultist, explained what the masons believe about the concept of a holy trinity:

> "The Temple in the Heavens is therefore presided over
> by the Triune Deity, . . . the Three Persons of the divine
> Trinity. This Trinity of Persons, . . . are well known in
> all the world religions. . . . known under various names,
> of which the most familiar to us are Sheva, Vishnu and
> Brahma. . . . In Masonry, this same Triplicity is known as
> the Most High, the Grand Geometrician, and the Great
> Architect of the Universe."[121]

Whether you consider Freemasonry a cult, a religion, or a systematic fraternity, it is quite possibly one of the furthest things from biblical Christianity. The problem is there are approximately four million Freemason participants worldwide, with the strongest presence being in the United States. Not all members know about all practices or the true history of some of its former leaders.

In fact, because of some of its philanthropic work, good people can be drawn to Freemasonry, and that includes Christians. If a person is a Bible-believing Christian, however, they won't last very long as a Freemason once they learn their beliefs. Some suggest Freemasonry is a form of deistic humanism. Due to the extreme diversity of teachings and rituals, it is not surprising their practices can extend beyond simple self-improvement or self-worship all the way to the worship of nature and satanism.

Once again, we see the lie being promoted that any one of these *paths* could wind around a mountain, so to speak, and end up at (God) the same point on the top. My advice is to avoid that mountain and its dangerous paths, and choose the One who declared He is the only Way.

In a book revealing the spiritual aspect of Freemasonry, author Carl Teichrib sums it up well:

> The man, therefore, who joins Freemasonry under the
> pretense that "we make good men better" places himself in

---

121 Texe Marrs, *Texe Marrs Book of New Age Cults & Religions* (Austin, TX: Living Truth Publishers, 1990), 199-200.

a most difficult position where man is ascribed to be God
and thereby able to perfect himself through his own efforts.
We have, in effect, another gospel that excludes the Cross
and leaves man to seek after his own devices. Hence, the
souls of all involved may be imperiled by a human method
that cannot save. . . . Scripture runs counter to the ideas of
the Lodge and Freemasonry, which seeks mystical perfection through its own works, making it an avenue that delivers the antithesis of the Gospel message of Jesus Christ.[122]

The only perfection that exists is in God. He made you and me for His
purposes, and when people search for meaning apart from anything
or anyone else except the Lord Jesus, the end result is righteousness by
works. The religion of Freemasonry offers a pseudospirituality through
meaningless rituals, degrees, and oaths. But for those trapped within,
it may not be that clear.

HINDUISM

Having no founder or creator, the origins of Hinduism date back to
around 1500 BC in what is now India, and Hinduism began as a very
ritualistic religion. There are approximately 750 million Hindus in the
world today, but their influence extends far beyond their numbers. The
third-largest religion in the world, there are thirty-three main deities
in Hinduism and most Hindus live in southern Asia.

Obviously, belief in many gods conflicts with the truth of one God.
Forgiveness is not available in the Hindu religion due to the law of
Karma, and humanity's greatest problem is ignorance of our divine
nature. Karma is like the natural law of cause and effect, or the biblical
principle of sowing and reaping. Consequences or effects of a person's
actions supposedly follow him from one lifetime to another.

In my 2012 book, *Eradicate: Blotting Out God in America*, I high-
lighted the rapid increase of immorality as well as some of the things
that caused people to fall for certain religious deceptions. It was the
popularity of the Beatles that influenced many Americans to open their

---

122 Carl Teichrib, "FREEMASONRY: A Revealing Look at the Spiritual Side," *www.lighthouse-
trailsresearch.com/ blog/ ?p=22022*.

hearts and minds to the gods of Hinduism and New Age. In 1968, they travelled to Rishikesh, India, to study yoga and transcendental meditation (TM) with Hindu mystic Maharishi Mahesh Yogi.

> During their retreat, the Beatles, especially Lennon and Harrison, were looking for more "cosmic awareness" and had been experimenting with LSD. Maharishi helped them process the death of their manager, Brian Epstein, who had died of a drug overdose. Joining the Beatles in India were Mick Jagger of the Rolling Stones, Frank Sinatra's wife, Mia Farrow, her sister Prudence Farrow, Yoko Ono, as well as several other celebrities. Prudence Farrow, a UC-Berkeley graduate, went on to teach TM for thirty-seven years.
>
> The 1968 gathering in India, with all its high-powered celebrities, attracted a press following. *The Saturday Evening Post* ran a cover story on the trip in a May 1968 edition, having sent a reporter to go with the Beatles to Rishikesh. Because of this exposure, millions of people in America chose to follow their pop idols by experimenting with drugs, practicing TM, or both, and that trip to India began a process of unraveling that would lead to the group's demise.[123]

Many Hindu gurus and swamis came to the United States in the late '60s and '70s, and between the Beatles and the expansive hippie movement, the influence of Hinduism spread through the New Age community and our nation has never been the same. In 1971, John Lennon wrote one of his most popular songs, "Imagine," which promoted a world of peace, unity, and "living for today" in which there is no heaven, no hell, and "no religion, too." In that fantasy world, who needs God or Jesus Christ? But even a united world could not save the eternal souls of human beings.

The way of salvation for the Hindu is either through knowledge, devotion to a particular deity, good deeds, or ceremonial rituals. The Hindu scriptures or *Vedas* ("knowledge") were originally written to

---

123 David Fiorazo, *Eradicate: Blotting Out God in America* (Abbotsford, WI: Life Sentence Publishing, 2012), 349.

give priests instructions on how to perform the rituals. The Vedas are so interwoven with India's culture that rejecting the Vedas is viewed as rejecting India. This is why any other religious system that does not embrace India's culture is rejected.

According to Dean C. Halverson, there are four Vedas: the Rig Veda, the Sama Veda, the Yajur Veda, and the Atharva Veda, which reveres cows in specific verses. Each Veda divides into four parts: Mantras (the verses or hymns sung during the rituals), Brahmanas (explanations of the verses), Aranyakas (reflections on the meaning of the verses), and the Upanishads (mystical interpretations of the verses). This is also known as Shruti, or "that which is heard." Shruti literature is the Hindu equivalent to revealed Scripture.[124]

The Upanishads were written for the purpose of focusing more on internal meditation rather than on external rituals. Then there are the Mahabharata (most popular of the Hindu scriptures) and the Ramayana (epic stories of India) which include poetry, hymns, philosophies, and rituals from which Hindus base their beliefs. The Upanishads, also called *Vedanta* ("the conclusion of the Vedas") expound on the idea that behind many gods stands one Reality, which is called *Brahman*, an impersonal force.

The highest form of Brahman has no attributes or qualities, but the Hindu concept of God continued to develop in the direction of a more personal God, *saguna Brahman*. *Saguna* means "with attributes," and this personified form of Brahman is called *Ishvara*.

According to Hindu tradition, Ishvara became known to humanity through the *Trimurti* (literally, "three mani-festations") of Brahman. Those manifestations include *Brahma* (the Creator), *Vishnu* (the Preserver), and *Siva* (the Destroyer). Each of these three deities has at least one *devi*, or divine spouse. Ishvara became personified even further through the ten mythical incarnations of Vishnu, called *avatars*.[125]

Forms of these incarnations include animals and people, and a few of

124 Dean C. Halverson, *The Compact Guide to World Religions* (Bloomington, MN: Bethany House Publishers, 1996), 91.
125 Ibid., 88.

the writings mentioned earlier tell the stories of these myths. It is estimated there are over 330 million gods in Hinduism. In the course of its history, Hinduism has birthed other religions including Buddhism. Nearly every Hindu home has a shrine to gods that fills a room or a corner of a room, as Hindu gods are meant to ward off evil spirits.

Again, in Hinduism, Nirvana is considered the final stage where the soul arrives after it is freed from all its rebirths. It is a blissful spiritual state in which the individual is freed from all desire. Yogas are disciplines by which the body and emotions can be controlled, and *Dharma* (Law of Moral Order) must be found by each person who wishes to attain Nirvana.

Hindus consider Brahman as an impersonal oneness that is beyond all personal and moral distinctions, and they see the universe as a continuous extension of Brahman. Most adherents of Hinduism believe they are in their true selves (atman) extended from and one with Brahman.

As mentioned earlier, a person's karma determines the kind of body into which he will be reincarnated in the next life – human, animal, or insect. *Samsara* refers to the revolving wheel of life, death, and rebirth. The solution in Hinduism is to attain liberation (moksha) from this cycle through realizing that the concept of the individual self is an illusion, and then detaching oneself from the desires of the ego.

Three paths to enlightenment include *karma marga* (the way of action and ritual), *jnana marga* (the way of knowledge and meditation), and *bhakti marga* (the way of devotion). Hindus also respect cows and hold them in high esteem, although some say the cow is taboo and off-limits to the Hindu. One reason for this view of cows is they give so much to humans, primarily milk leading to dairy products. But Hindus also believe the supreme god lives in all creatures, human and animal, and to them all life is sacred.

Historically, Hindu societies have operated within a strict form of caste system. In this system, one was born into a specific class that determined one's career and place in society. Members were expected to marry within their caste and work the trades of their caste. This system tied directly to karma. One was born into a specific caste based on karma from previous lives. Ambition to break out of one's given role would bring on a "karmic debt" and perpetuate samsara.

While Buddhism and Jainism have much in common with Hinduism, they denounced the caste system and were not considered Hindu. The caste system has since been legally disbanded in India, and many Hindu scholars today say that what the caste system had become was a corruption of the pure, ancient Hindu teaching. Nevertheless, many of the ideas of the caste system are socially ingrained and have proven difficult to remove.[126]

There are four major classes within the caste system: the elite, linked to the priesthood (the Brahmins), the military and the ruling class (Kshatriyas), farmers and businessmen (Vaisyas), and the peasants (Sudra).

Miraculously, God saved Rabi Maharaj, who came from a line of Hindu priests (Sanyasi) and whose biography can be found in the book, *Death of a Guru*. He is an evangelist to India and founder of East-West Ministries. You may find his words insightful and compelling:

> "I had never heard in Hinduism that God is a God of love or that God loves me. God is impersonal in Hinduism. . . . The fact that God is a God of love really shook me up, and also that God wants to come into my life. That really kind of knocked me over, especially the fact that Jesus died to forgive me all my sins. In Hinduism, you do the dying for the gods, the gods don't die for you."[127]

Hinduism is a vastly diverse religion, but remember that most Hindus have never heard the gospel or are not aware such a God as ours actually exists. They do not know or understand what Jesus did for them. With all the variances, we shouldn't assume every Hindu believes the same as other Hindus or practices the same rituals. There are many gods, many ways, and each Hindu is unique. Though it is helpful to have an idea of other beliefs, the main thing is to know the Bible well enough to be able to share with those who are lost.

---

126 Ryan Turner, CARM, "What are the beliefs of Hinduism?" 3/24/11, *https://carm.org/ hinduism-beliefs*.

127 Texe Marrs, *Texe Marrs Book of New Age Cults and Religions* (Austin, TX: Living Truth Publishers, 1990), 220.

ISLAM

Do Christians and Muslims worship the same God? Does Allah command mercy or jihad? Compassion or conquest? A combination? What is the truth? Millions of Muslims simply want to live in peace, work, and raise their children as they live out some of the moral principles of their faith. Though we must take the threat of violent jihad seriously, Christians are to love our neighbors and this includes Muslim neighbors. We are to surrender suspicion and share the truth of the gospel. We should also be as informed as possible on biblical and world history.

French political scientist and historian Alexis de Tocqueville (1805 – 1859) stated, "The Prophet [Muhammad], though gifted in the arts of persuasion and clearly a considerable military leader, was both doubtfully literate and certainly ill-informed about the contents of the Old Testament . . . I studied the Quran a great deal. . . . by and large there have been few religions in the world as deadly to men as that of Muhammad."

Claiming he ushered in a new era of peace and prosperity for America, one of the most controversial yet influential voices in the world in the last decade has been former U.S. President Barack Hussein Obama. Speaking at the Islamic Society of Baltimore in 2016, a mosque that has deep ties to extremist organizations, he claimed that for more than a thousand years, "people have been drawn to Islam's message of peace."

He also claimed Islam has always been part of America and is rooted in a commitment to compassion, mercy, justice, and charity. I thought one of the more surprising things the former president stated in his speech promoting tolerance was that Islam has a tradition of respect for other faiths. Anyone who even remotely follows the news knows that is not true, so why would Obama make such claims? He knew the media and liberal fact-checkers would protect him, and the uninformed masses would believe him.

As I write this, another terror attack took place at a concert in Manchester, England, in which at least twenty-two were killed and fifty-nine wounded; ISIS claimed responsibility. News headlines seem to shout, "Wake up, America!" Another policeman was gunned down in Paris and two others were wounded as Islamic terrorists have now claimed 238 lives in France alone since 2015. By the time this book is published, who knows how many more will end up as victims of this deadly ideology.

According to Pew Research in 2016, seventy percent of the Islamic countries in the Middle East and Africa have made it a crime to convert to Christianity from Islam, with punishments ranging from incarceration to execution. Every hour, around the world, a Christian is killed for the simple reason of worshiping Jesus. Last year, about 9,000 Christians were killed for practicing their faith. Overall, approximately 21,237 people were killed (and 26,680 injured) due to 2,478 Islamic terror attacks in 59 countries.

Islamic terrorists once killed 5,000 people in one month (November 2014). In March of 2017, over 1,100 people were killed and 1,325 injured by Muslim extremists in 154 attacks and 29 suicide blasts in 23 countries.[128] Where do they get these violent instructions?

> "Slay the idolaters wherever you find them. Arrest them,
> besiege them, and lie in ambush everywhere for them."
> (*Surah* 9:5)

Obviously, not all Muslims are terrorists, but why aren't the moderates speaking out? With the world population consisting of 1.6 billion Muslims, what if just 10 percent are radicalized and believe in taking the teachings in the Quran literally? That equates to 160 million people. From cradle to grave, from the moment of birth to lying on his death bed, a variation of these Arabic words are whispered into every Muslim's ears: "There is no god except Allah, and Muhammad is his messenger [or prophet]."

Why is there so much confusion about whether or not *jihad* ("striving" or "struggle") and conquest are commanded in Islamic holy books? Why do so many, particularly in the media, avoid calling it for what it is: Islamic extremism and terrorism? What is the truth about Islam and how is it different from Christianity? Similarities exist, but just because something is similar does not mean it is the same.

First, in contrast to what President Obama and others espouse, we are not all children of God, nor is the God of the Bible the same as

---

128 Jihad Report, "The Religion of Peace," *www.thereligionofpeace.com/*.

Allah, the god of the Quran. This is a good starting point. Christians and Muslims do not worship the same God. Different names, different doctrines, different deities. Albert Mohler, president of the Southern Baptist Theological Seminary, stated, "The deity we name is the God we believe in. Christians believe in only one God, and He is the Father who sent the Son to save us from our sins. Allah has no son, and, thus, Christians cannot know God as Allah. In this light, Muslims and Christians do not only use different names for God; in reality, these different names refer to different gods."[129]

A few major irreconcilable points: We believe Jesus Christ is God and Lord, Muslims do not. They say Jesus was created. We believe the entire Bible is true, Muslims do not. They believe their Quran is infallible and inspired. They do not believe in the person of the Holy Spirit, which rules out the Bible entirely and particularly the book of Acts. Islam teaches that mankind is inherently good, and Allah does not love sinners (*Surah* 3:140). The Bible includes at least forty authors while the Quran has just one. So how did Islam come about?

More than six hundred years after the resurrection of Jesus Christ, the (now) second-largest world religion, Islam, was birthed in Saudi Arabia in AD 622. The Prophet Muhammad was born in 570 into an influential tribe called the Quraysh who controlled the city of Mecca. His father died before he was born and his mother died six years later. By all accounts, Muhammad lived a normal life as a youth, raised by an uncle and grandparents, eventually marrying a wealthy woman named Khadija who had hired Muhammad to lead a caravan to Syria.

Located in Mecca was the Ka'bah, a cubical structure that contained 360 deities at that time. Tribes handpicked a deity and visited Mecca annually to pay homage to their god, so the city was important for religious reasons. When Muhammad was forty years old, while on a retreat of solitude in the year 610, he supposedly received his first revelation from the angel Gabriel in a cave in Mount Hira. This was the beginning of Islam ("submission to Allah") and of a series of angelic visitations eventually complied in the *Quran* ("recitations").

These revelations continued for about twenty-three years until his

---

129   Albert Mohler, "Do Christians and Muslims Worship the Same God?" 12/1/13, *billygraham. org/decision-magazine/december-2013/do-christians-and-muslims-worship-the-same-god/*.

death, and Muslims believe the angel revealed the words of Allah (the Arabic word for *God*) to Muhammad. It is said that at first, Muhammad thought he was either possessed by demonic spirits or he was delusional, but Khadija insisted the revelations were divine and encouraged him to tell others about them. His preaching about strict monotheism (one deity) was not popular in a polytheistic society, especially due to the income Muhammad's tribe received from all the pilgrimages people made to the Ka'bah in Mecca.

In AD 622, Muhammad and many other families left and traveled about two hundred miles north to a city named Yathrib (now called Medina). This event is known as the *Hijrah* (or *Hegira*), which means "a series of migrations." This is the ideology many adherents of Islam follow as they migrate to new locations around the world, but many do not assimilate to society.

Within just eight years, Muhammad and his followers established a military and after several successful victories against Mecca, his army took control of the city. Within a year of Mecca's surrender and submission to Muhammad, the tribes of the Arabian Peninsula unified under the religion of Islam. To achieve victory, he reportedly killed men in opposing tribes while enslaving the women and children.

Similar to other works-based religions, Islam gives no guarantees of salvation and teaches that Muslims must obey the Five Pillars of Islam. They must confess the *shahada,* pray facing Mecca five times a day, fast for one month (Ramadan) a year during daylight hours, give 2.5 percent of their income to the poor, and visit Mecca at least once. Here are the Five Pillars detailed a bit more:

1. The testimony of faith (shahada): "la ilaha illa allah. Muhammad rasul Allah." This means "There is no deity but Allah. Muhammad is the messenger of Allah." A person can convert to Islam by stating this creed. The shahada shows that a Muslim believes in Allah alone as deity and believes that Muhammad reveals Allah.

2. Prayer (salat): Five ritual prayers must be performed every day.

3. Giving (zakat): This almsgiving is a certain percentage given once a year.

4. Fasting (sawm): Muslims fast during Ramadan in the ninth month of the Islamic calendar. They must not eat or drink from dawn until sunset.

5. Pilgrimage (hajj): If physically and financially possible, a Muslim must make the pilgrimage to Mecca in Saudi Arabia at least once. The hajj is performed in the twelfth month of the Islamic calendar.[130]

Christians are guaranteed salvation, *an inheritance which is imperishable and undefiled and will not fade away, reserved in heaven for you* (1 Peter 1:4). For the Muslim, even if he does his best to follow all these rules, there is still no assurance of entrance into paradise. Allah may still reject him. Even Muhammad wasn't sure Allah would admit him to paradise (*Surah* 46:9; *Hadith* 5.266). Though they do believe in a day of judgment, it involves a person's good deeds weighed against his bad deeds; the standard is not faith, but a person's own actions. (*Surah* 7:8-9; 21:47).

Our works will be judged, but they have no bearing on our everlasting life with God. What else does the Quran teach? Allah directly recited word for word to Muhammad the contents of the Quran, a perfect, holy book divided into 114 chapters (Surahs). In addition, Muslims must follow the example of Muhammad and revere the *Hadith*, which is a collection of his thoughts, sayings, and actions accumulated by those who allegedly knew him best.

Muhammad rose to power as a warrior-prophet and military leader, sanctioning the raiding of caravans in order to seize resources to advance Islam. He literally fought in dozens of battles and prescribed fighting for the cause (*Quran* 2:216) and slaying those who do not believe in Allah or the Last Day (*Quran* 9:29). Muhammad viewed war as a necessary religious undertaking and was notorious for spreading Islam by forced submission and conquest.

Jesus Christ never forced anyone to believe in Him, He defended

---

130 GotQuestions, "What is Islam, and what do Muslims Believe?" *www.gotquestions.org/ Islam.html.*

and honored women, and His law was love God and one another. He never promoted killing, revenge, beating a woman; never enslaved a child, never broke a promise, and never plundered a caravan. On the cross, when Jesus was mocked by those nearby, His response was, "Father, forgive them."

Muhammad had fifteen wives, limited other men to four wives each, and sanctioned the beating of wives (*Surah* 4:34). He also commanded Muslims, "Fight and slay the Pagans wherever you find them" (*Surah* 9:5). He ordered the murder of those who mocked him, he lied, and he broke oaths.

Former Muslim Elijah Abraham is now a born-again Christian who travels the world teaching pastors and churches how to share the gospel with Muslims in part by understanding their ideology and worldview. Born in Baghdad to a Shiite Muslim family who moved to Europe when he was fifteen, he began looking into the Christian faith in his early twenties, and suffered physical harm and threats by Iraqis there. Abraham fled to America in 1987, converted to Christianity in 1995, and eventually formed Living Oasis Ministries.

Abraham describes Islam as "a socio-political and economic system that uses a deity to advance its agenda, which is to be instituted religiously in order to achieve control or conquest." He stated that jihad comes in three stages: first, gain power through migration and increased population, then demand enforcement of Muslim teachings on the community, and finally, if necessary, use force, violence, and upheaval against the *infidels*. In a recent radio interview on *Stand Up For The Truth*, Elijah Abraham explained, "Americans who advocate for open borders do not understand the term *hejira* at all. [To expand Islam] you have to migrate and settle, but don't assimilate to the nation. Plant yourself and create an Islamic state within the borders of the nation [you are migrating to]."[131]

Abraham also stated this migration is part of *stealth jihad*, in which Muslims infiltrate all aspects of a society, including education, business ownership, and political involvement. For many in Islam, the theological (church) and government (state) cannot be separated.

---

131 Elijah Abraham, "The Three Stages of Islamic Jihad," 2/28/17, *standupforthetruth.com/2017/02/the-three-stages-of-islamic-jihad/*.

To Muslims, the Quran is the final authority and since it came later than the Bible, it is the last revelation of Allah which cancels out any previous holy works. However, Christians were warned that false teachers would arise and preach another gospel. A few more instructions written by Muhammad include:

> And fight with them until there is no more fitna (disorder, unbelief) and religion is all for Allah. (*Quran* 8:39)

> It is not for a Prophet that he should have prisoners of war until he had made a great slaughter in the land. (*Quran* 8:67)

Two major sects of Islam, Sunnis and Shiites, were originally divided over religious points, whereas now much of the conflict is political. They differ on who should have succeeded Muhammad as the first caliph after his death in 632. The Sunni Muslims insisted a successor should be elected and they supported Muhammad's friend Abu Bakr. Shiites thought he should come through Muhammad's bloodline and felt the prophet's son-in-law and cousin, Ali Abi Talib, was the rightful successor.

Ali did become the fourth caliph, but was assassinated in 661, and his son was killed in battle, effectively ending the direct line of Muhammad's descendants. Shiites now consider all caliphs to be false. The Sunnis represent over 80 percent of the Muslim population, and they emphasize the authority of the written traditions. Islam is not a united religion and there are even divisions among those divisions.

The Shiites are more consensus oriented, believing God speaks through Imams – Muslim leaders. They await the return of the twelfth Imam, called the *Mahdi*, similar to the way Christians look forward to the return of Christ. There is also a mystical wing of Islam called *Sufism*, whose goal is to renounce worldly attachments and attain assimilation of the self into the vast being of God. Islam has contributed indirectly to the religions of Baha'i and Sikhism.

WHICH HOLY BOOK IS REALLY CORRUPTED?

Biblical manuscript evidence does not support the Muslim claim that "the Bible has been corrupted." Followers of Islam are taught this idea that the early biblical texts were altered by Jews and Christians. Because two specific passages in the Surah suggest this, they say the Bible cannot be trusted. Scholars who dispute the reliability of the Bible have yet to produce verifiable evidence.

This is fascinating for several reasons, one of which being that their own Quran considers revelations contained in "the Book" to be authoritative and actually from God (*Surah* 2:136; 4:163). It also says if you doubt Muhammad's words, ask people of the Book. Isn't it inconsistent of the Quran to advise someone to consult previous Scriptures and believe them, and at the same time teach that those Scriptures are corrupted?

As much as the Quran mentions previous scriptures being revealed by God, it seems a contradiction to suggest Christians and Jews changed any texts when it states the idea: "None can change His words" (*Surah* 6:115; 6:34; 10:64). One just needs to go directly to the abundant manuscript evidence. Where the Old Testament is concerned, the Dead Sea Scrolls (which date from 100 BC) confirm the accuracy of early Hebrew manuscripts. Most significant is the fact that they show the manuscripts that existed after Muslims accused the Bible of being altered are identical to those existing long before Muhammad ever lived![132]

As for the authenticity of the New Testament, biblical scholars have found 3,157 Greek manuscripts that contain either a portion or all of the New Testament and that date from the second century on. As we established in chapter 1, the small number of textual differences were so miniscule, such as a single letter being left out, that the meaning, context, and interpretation would not be affected. Also, no Christian doctrine rests solely on a debatable text.

Back to the Quran. One more point, and this is in response to the argument that because there are verses in the Quran that teach peace, Islam is peaceful overall. However, many verses also call for violence (approximately 149), so how do we reconcile this and what does a Muslim obey when there are contradictions? This word is key to unlocking the answer: "abrogation." You are to apply the more recent command. Abrogation is a recurring theme meaning to cancel, repeal, or officially revoke something. In this situation, the later or more recent verses calling for jihad and for violent measures override earlier verses about peace.

---

132 Dean C. Halverson, *The Compact Guide to World Religions* (Bloomington, MN: Bethany House Publishers, 1996), 112.

Many of America's founders as well as past presidents wrote very honestly about Islam. In 1830, John Quincy Adams wrote:

> In the seventh century of the Christian era, a wandering Arab of the lineage of Hagar, the Egyptian, combining the powers of transcendent genius, with the preternatural energy of a fanatic, and the fraudulent spirit of an impostor, proclaimed himself as a messenger from Heaven, and spread desolation and delusion over an extensive portion of the earth.

> He poisoned the sources of human felicity at the fountain, by degrading the condition of the female sex, and the allowance of polygamy; and he declared undistinguishing and exterminating war, as a part of his religion, against all the rest of mankind. THE ESSENCE OF HIS DOCTRINE WAS VIOLENCE AND LUST: TO EXALT THE BRUTAL OVER THE SPIRITUAL PART OF HUMAN NATURE.[133]

It is clear to see what is happening in Europe, and the building of mosques and the immigration of Muslims into North America has been increasing. We have enjoyed such freedom and prosperity in the United States, but sadly, this nation has been exposed as generally apathetic, biblically illiterate, and uninformed when it comes to world religions and cults.

With the instant 24/7 news cycle and reports of rising Islamic terrorism bringing fear into the hearts of many, the gospel must still be preached. Christians can have faith knowing we have not received a spirit of fear and *he who is in you is greater than he who is in the world* (1 John 4:4 ESV). Matthew recorded Jesus telling His disciples they will be persecuted and hated because of His name (Matthew 10:22-23), and went on to say:

> *Do not fear those who kill the body but are unable to kill the soul; but rather fear Him who is able to destroy both soul and body in hell. "Everyone who confesses Me before men, I will also confess him before My Father who is in heaven. But*

---

133 Dave Miller, "John Quincy Adams on Islam," Apologetics Press, *www.apologeticspress. org/ apcontent.aspx?category=7&article=1142.*

whoever denies Me before men, I will also deny him before
My Father who is in heaven." (Matthew 10:28, 32-33)

JEHOVAH'S WITNESSES (Watchtower Bible and Tract Society)

Christians and Jehovah's Witnesses both believe we are living in the last days, but who is knocking on more doors and handing out more literature? Jehovah's Witnesses (JWs) believe that almost everybody will be resurrected after they die and given a second chance to be saved and inherit paradise. Since there is no heaven and hell then, it is not hard to understand why many find it appealing. Jehovah's Witnesses believe salvation depends on works and on remaining faithful, and *no one* apart from members of Jehovah's Witnesses will receive salvation.

They deny Christ as God, they consider the cross to be a pagan symbol, and they have their own translation of the Bible with dozens of Scriptures edited to fit their religion. Jehovah's Witnesses say Jesus was created by Jehovah as a spirit creature named Michael the arch-angel, and rather than acknowledging the historical evidence for the resurrection, they believe that Jesus's physical body was taken away by the Father. Like Islam, the Watchtower denies the Holy Spirit and the biblical teaching of the triune God (one Being or God existing as three co-equal, co-eternal Persons). They also believe in progressive revela-tion, which allows for their version of the Bible and their doctrines to be modified by their leaders. The God of the Watchtower is not the God of Scripture.

With some of these beliefs being so far removed from traditional Christian doctrines, how do they continue to convert people to their religion? Publishing and marketing. The Watchtower Bible and Tract Society is an international religious organization based in Brooklyn, New York. There are approximately 8.2 million Jehovah's Witnesses worldwide, and every day at their Watchtower publishing complex, they print over 800,000 copies of their two magazines and 100,000 books, published in nearly 200 languages. Every day.

Charles Taze Russell created Jehovah's Witnesses in 1872, and as an eighteen-year-old in Pittsburgh, Pennsylvania, started a Bible class because he didn't like the doctrines of hell, the deity of Christ, the Holy Spirit, and the Trinity. He began writing a series of books called *The Millennial Dawn*, which became six volumes, the bulk of what Jehovah's Witnesses believe. In 1879, Russell published the magazines, *The Watchtower* and *Herald of Christ's Presence*. Two years later he formed Zion's Watch Tower Tract Society, renamed Watchtower Bible and Tract Society in 1884.

As JWs' Governing Body does today, Russell controlled what was written in the *Watchtower* magazine and, typical of religious cult leaders, he claimed the Bible could only be understood according to *his* interpretation, the "New World Translation" (NWT). After Russel's death in 1916, the second president, Joseph Franklin Rutherford, implemented even more controversial doctrinal changes in the Society. The group was known as the *Russellites* until 1931. A split took place over doctrines during which Rutherford changed their name to "Jehovah's Witnesses."

One of those changes was the idea that JWs have replaced Israel, and the 144,000 mentioned in Revelation 14 are *spiritual Jews*. Rutherford also added the requirement that every Witness take part in literature distribution, which they refer to as "publishing." They promote the coming "end of this wicked system of things," and believe they belong to the only group that will survive the last days. Jehovah's Witnesses meet twice a week in Kingdom Halls, which are very plain, but functional, and many can spend up to 100 hours a month at halls and going door to door.

Jehovah's Witnesses do not use the term "church" as it is associated with Christianity, a false religion in their eyes. They also do not have musical instruments and they use their own *Kingdom Song Book*. As mentioned earlier, they do not believe in hell as one of two eternal destinations, a place of punishment and torment. Hell simply means the grave. People go to the grave when they die and at the Last Judgment, they rise out of an unconscious sleep. At that time, each person will either get to live on the new earth or be annihilated entirely. Sadly, according to JWs, no one can know for certain whether or not they are saved until after the Judgment.

The structure of "Jehovah's organization" begins with their Governing

Body, then Branch Committees, Travelling Overseers, Bodies of Elders, Congregations, and then Individual Publishers. No one is allowed to challenge or question the word of the elders, the men who make up the Governing Body, which is perceived as Jehovah God's representative on earth, nor can members disagree with the published literature JWs print. If an individual makes his objections known, he will be disciplined, and the ultimate punishment is to be *disfellowshipped*.

It is explained in the book *World Religions and Cults* that Jehovah's Witnesses claim their authority comes from Jehovah God through Jesus who appointed *them* as His sole channel of communication to the world. And similar to Scientology:

> "A disfellowshipped member is shunned by all Witness friends and family, sometimes resulting in decades of estrangement. Those still in the organization are advised not to have anything to do with shunned individuals: 'Really, what your beloved family member needs to see is your resolute stance to put Jehovah above everything else – including the family bond. . . . Do not look for excuses to associate with a disfellowshipped family member.'"

> The Jehovah's Witnesses maintain a high level of control over what their congregations learn, and independent study is anathema: "All who want to understand the Bible should appreciate that the 'greatly diversified wisdom of God' can become known only through Jehovah's channel of communication, the faithful and discreet slave." Submission to the Governing Body is seen as submission to Christ.[134]

Because the Watchtower sees the entire culture as connected to Satan, they prohibit JWs from serving in the military, celebrating holidays, singing the National Anthem, voting, or saluting the American flag. They have changed their rules on blood transfusions more than once. These men – the Governing Body – insist they are the anointed ones that make up Jehovah's channel of communication to the world and go

---

134   Bodie Hodge and Roger Patterson, *World Religions and Cults Volume 1* (Green Forest, AR: Master Books, 2015), 196-197.

so far as to rule that all "must be ready to obey any instructions" they give whether or not they appear sound.

Let's briefly discuss their instructions and their version of the Bible. In 1961, the Watchtower Bible and Tract Society produced their own translation and interpretation of Scriptures, the *New World Translation*. What should be alarming and eye opening is the fact that this translation is the first intentional, systematic effort to produce a complete version of the Bible edited and changed for the specific purpose of aligning with a religious group's doctrine.

Former professor of New Testament Language at Princeton Theological Seminary and author of several highly acclaimed books on textual criticism, the late Dr. Bruce Metzger stated, "The Jehovah's Witnesses have incorporated in their translations of the New Testament several quite erroneous renderings of the Greek." Dr. Robert Countess, who completed his Ph.D. dissertation in Greek on the *New World Translation*, is on record as saying that the Watchtower's translation "has been sharply unsuccessful in keeping doctrinal considerations from influencing the actual translation. It must be viewed as a radically biased piece of work. At some points, it is actually dishonest."[135]

One subject we haven't touched on is creation and the origin of mankind. Jehovah's Witnesses believe the universe had a beginning. They also claim it is 14 billion years old! Why stop there? Why not a trillion years? They teach the length of each "creative" day in the book of Genesis is seven thousand years long. This is key to their chronology, and because of this, they have predicted various dates for the end of the world, which we will address in a moment.

Jehovah's Witnesses claim to have "the real Bible story of creation," one that contains "a very logical and credible explanation of the beginning of the universe" that, get this, "harmonizes with scientific discovery."[136] So, JWs agree with fallible scientists, most of whom are atheists and refuse to look to the Bible for *any* part of their research on their views of creation and evolution. What ends up happening, particularly with having their own publishing enterprise, is if they disagree with or

---

135 GotQuestions, "What is the Watchtower Bible and Tract Society?" *www.gotquestions.org/ Watchtower-Bible-Tract-Society.html*.

136 *Awake!* March, 2014, "The Untold Story of Creation."

dislike certain Scriptures, then they simply reinterpret those verses into their *New World Translation*. But by doing so, they have created a god in their own image. The Watchtower adds the word *Jehovah* to the New Testament 237 times.

Here is a glaring example of taking a verse and changing it to make it fit their theology. In the original text, after having just declared in Colossians 1:13-14 that we have redemption through *His beloved Son*, a few verses later, Paul wrote, *For by Him all things were created, both in the heavens and on earth* (Colossians 1:16). However, in the JWs' translation of the Bible, the NWT, in order to deny the deity of Christ, they deceitfully insert a single word that changes the meaning of the text. Their version of Colossians 1:16 reads this way: "Because by means of him *all other things* were created." By adding the word *other*, it gives the impression Jesus Christ was a created being, which is blatant heresy.

Finally, let's touch on the many false prophecies and the date-setting the Watchtower Society has been guilty of numerous times. It has been reported that Charles T. Russell studied oriental religions and pyrami-dology, and he believed the Great Pyramid contained signs and mysteries directly from God. If JWs have a recurring theme they live by, it would be "the end is near." They have predicted the end of the world to occur in 1914, 1925, and 1975.

Jehovah's Witnesses are taught Jesus actually took up His throne and began ruling from heaven in 1914. Apparently, the outbreak of World War I proved Satan had been kicked out of heaven. They interpreted World War I to be the Tribulation and also believed that the World War I generation would live to see Armageddon. Naturally, then, it follows that in 1920, Joseph F. Rutherford's book was published based on a message he first gave in 1918: *Millions Now Living Will Never Die*, and on page 89 he stated, "Therefore, we may confidently expect that 1925 will mark the return of Abraham, Isaac, Jacob and the faithful prophets of old, particularly those named by the apostle in Hebrews 11, to the condition of human perfection."

In the *Watchtower* on April 1, 1923, the Society stated on page 106: "Our thought is, that 1925 is definitely settled by the Scriptures. As to

Noah, the Christian now has much more upon which to base his faith than Noah had upon which to base his faith in a coming deluge."

But in *Awake*, October 8, 1968, the following sheepish admission went out to all JWs: "True, there have been those in times past who predicted an 'end to the world,' even announcing a specific date. Yet nothing happened. The 'end' did not come. They were guilty of false prophesying. Why? What was missing? . . . Missing from such people were God's truths and evidence that he was using and guiding them."

As if you need further evidence, in *Awake* magazine on May 22, 1969, the Watchtower falsely addressed young people, saying, "you will never grow old in this present system of things" because the current "corrupt system is due to end in a few years."

Only a false prophet will set wrong dates and make erroneous predictions. The New Testament is extremely clear on this subject. This is not even an exhaustive list of doctrines, facts, and practices of Jehovah's Witnesses, but you would think that with this kind of history, fewer people would join its ranks. But tragically, the Watchtower Bible and Tract Society keeps gaining new converts so it is up to those of us who are informed and who are concerned about their souls to share the truth. It is sad that there may not be a religious organization more committed to publishing its message, and they are some of the nicest people who are sincerely deceived by doctrines of man.

Evangelical writer, pastor, and Anglican clergyman J. C. Ryle was a rare champion for truth in the Church of England during the nineteenth century. He welcomed controversy, believing it was difficult yet necessary to clarify doctrine and make the church stronger, and he stated there was one thing worse than controversy: "that is false doctrine tolerated, allowed, and permitted without protest."

"Three things there are which men never ought to trifle
with – a little poison, a little false doctrine, and a little sin."
– J. C. Ryle

Chapter 15

What About Mormonism and Roman Catholicism?

Elijah came near to all the people and said, "How long will you hesitate between two opinions? If the LORD is God, follow Him; but if Baal, follow him." But the people did not answer him a word (1 Kings 18:21); *For many will come in My name, saying, 'I am the Christ,' and will mislead many* (Matthew 24:4-5).

Jesus Christ is the truth and His name is above every name. He is the one being attacked, and almost every one of us knows someone who is or who was once deceived by some religious system, false teaching, or even apostasy within the Christian church today. God willing, these four chapters will help open the eyes of some who are in bondage to darkness or still lost.

The great problem of mankind is sin. The great problem of religion is that doing good deeds does not lead to salvation. Due to man's pride, opinions begin to water down or even replace the Scriptures with traditions or more palatable doctrines such as good works, often elevating man's ideas over a holy God and His Word. Let's examine two more major religions.

MORMONISM, THE CHURCH OF JESUS CHRIST OF LATTER-DAY SAINTS (LDS)

Born in Vermont, fourteen-year-old Joe Smith struggled with organized religion and the fact that each denomination claimed to be the true church. As the story goes, Joe was seeking God for wisdom on what church to join. According to Smith, while he was praying in a secluded area near his home in northwestern New York, darkness surrounded him and he saw a light descend from heaven. Claiming that God and Jesus, the Son, stood before him separately, the Son told him that all religious creeds and denominations were an abomination.

Smith then reportedly lived a rebellious lifestyle for three years and sought another revelation. An angel named Moroni appeared to him and told young Joe he would receive the fullness of the everlasting gospel, and the angel directed him to a buried book of golden plates inscribed with a Judeo-Christian history of ancient civilization. He soon published the *Book of Mormon* and within the next decade, he attracted tens of thousands of followers and had created a religion. Established less than two hundred years ago, there are approximately 15 million Mormons worldwide and a reported 84,000 missionaries spreading their religion on six continents.

Conveniently, after the *Book of Mormon* was published, the angel took away the golden plates, leaving no evidence. The Mormons teach that the true church ceased to exist at one point and thanks to Joseph Smith (1805 – 1844), it was restored on April 6, 1830. Smith organized the Church of Christ in Palmyra, New York, calling it a restoration of the early church, and the next year Smith and his followers moved west and planned to build their own communal society. Joseph Smith became their "seer, a translator, a prophet, an apostle of Jesus Christ."

One man's creation, new revelation, another gospel, no proof, no witnesses, and another religion claiming to be the only way. Has truth again been redefined? Part of the LDS theology can be summed up this way: "As man is, God once was; As God is man may become." Mormons are taught that there are many gods occupying different sections of the universe and their heavenly Father, called "Elohim," was once a man created by another god.

Briefly settling in Kirtland, Ohio, Mormon missionaries were sent out, revelations were published, and a temple was built. In 1838, Smith announced the church would be renamed the Church of Jesus Christ of Latter Day Saints, or LDS. They established another community in Independence, Missouri, and according to a prophecy by Smith, a valley near there is the original location of the garden of Eden. Two of the early doctrines of Joseph Smith were polygamy (plural marriages) and baptisms for the dead. Smith also taught that matter was eternal and God had developed through time and space. God only assembled the earth from preexisting materials and then had drawn on "a cohort of spirits from the pool of eternal intelligences."

Opposition and persecution grew in these areas due to heretical Mormon teachings and the Mormons were reportedly forced out of the area. Joseph Smith was arrested for treason in Carthage, Missouri, and while Smith was in the town jail, Brigham Young led the congregation across the Mississippi River to establish the city of Nauvoo, Illinois. Smith escaped and added to his resumé military leader (he created a militia) and politician as he became mayor of the small town near the Missouri and Iowa borders. In January 1844, Smith decided to run for president of the United States.

A brand-new newspaper at the time, the *Nauvoo Expositor*, published its first and only edition on June 7, 1844, containing affidavits testifying that Joseph Smith read a new revelation giving men the privilege of marrying ten virgins. The paper also criticized Smith's power and attacked his plan to "Christianize a world by political schemes and intrigue," and denounced some false doctrines including teachings of many gods, and that God was once a mortal man.[137]

As mayor, Smith declared the paper a public nuisance and ordered the city marshal to destroy it, and so the printing press and all remaining newspapers were dragged into the street and burned. Publisher of another (*Warsaw Signal*) paper, Thomas C. Sharp, incited a citizen call to action against Smith declaring it wrong "to rob men of their property and rights." Joseph Smith and his brother, Hyrum, were shot and killed by a mob at the Carthage city jailhouse on June 27, 1844.

137 Wikipedia, "Life of Joseph Smith from 1839 to 1844," *en.wikipedia.org/wiki/Life_of_Joseph_Smith_from_1839_to_1844.*

After Smith's death, a dispute arose over who would be the new leader, which led to several sects of Mormonism including the Reorganized Church of Jesus Christ of Latter Day Saints, which was under the authority of Smith's eldest son, Joseph Smith III, who was eleven years old at the time of his father's death. A few other sects under prominent leaders moved to different parts of the country. The main denomination migrated to the Utah Territory under Brigham Young, and pioneers eventually built the Salt Lake Temple and much of the city.

Later, another split occurred over the doctrine supporting plural marriages. Along with this, Smith had taught another major departure from fundamental Christian teaching about God:

> We have imagined and supposed that God was God from all eternity. I will refute that idea, and take away the veil, so that you may see. These are incomprehensible ideas to some, but they are simple. *It is the first principle of the Gospel to know for a certainty the Character of God, and to know that we may converse with him as one man converses with another, and that he was once a man like us; yea, that God the Father of us all, dwelt on an earth, the same as Jesus Christ himself did, and I will show it from the Bible* (*Teachings of the Prophet Joseph Smith*, pp. 345-346).

Notice Smith claims God the Father was a man who lived on the earth. Where do LDS get their guidance and teachings from? Mormons emphasize the importance of new revelation and use four different books to compile their beliefs: *The Book of Mormon, Doctrine and Covenants* (revelations from Joseph Smith), *The Pearl of Great Price* (sayings attributed to Moses and Abraham), and the Bible.

To LDS, all Christian churches are abominations, since in the first vision Joseph Smith had, he was told at the time only false churches existed on earth. It was up to Smith to restore the true gospel. Mormons claim the God of the Bible is their authority, but they skirt around the answer if you ask them why they do not believe Jesus is the truth and the only way to the Father. If they trusted the Bible, they would believe *all* of what Jesus taught.

In fact, they have modified the Bible, expanding some teachings and contradicting others. They can claim to be part of Christianity – they call the *Book of Mormon* "Another Testament of Jesus Christ" – but their doctrines are far out in left field of biblical orthodoxy. There has been a recent push to promote common ground and minimize the distinctions between the two faiths, but from LDS beliefs about who God is and what happens after we die, the majority of Mormon doctrines are completely inconsistent with the Word of God.

Here are some fascinating facts about the teachings of Mormonism:

- Mormons can become gods and goddesses.

- Goddesses will spend eternity in full submission to their god-husband.

- Mormon women will give birth "forever and ever" to spirit-babies.

- Mormon men can have multiple wives in heaven – eternal polygamy.

- Heavenly Father is an exalted man who lives with his goddess wife, Heavenly Mother, on a planet near the great star Kolob.

- American Indians are descendants of the wicked Lamanites, who were Israelites that God cursed with dark skin.

- God the Father had sex with Mary to conceive Jesus, who is the half-brother of Lucifer. (*Journal of Discourses*, vol. 8, p. 115; Mormon Doctrine, p. 547)

- Mormons need four secret handshakes to get into the Celestial heaven.[138]

Joseph Smith once said there are men living on the moon who dress like Quakers and live to be nearly one thousand years old. Since he was wrong about life on the moon as well as other prophecies, is it safe to trust him about the way to heaven? (*The Young Woman's Journal*, vol. 3, pp. 263-264.)

---

138 Jill Martin Rische, Top 10 Amazing Facts of Mormonism, *www.waltermartin.com/pdfs/Top_10_Amazing_Facts_of_Mormonism.pdf*.

As far as authority goes, LDS believe all revelations given to their president and elders as well as to past Mormon leaders, who have changed certain church teachings to accommodate new situations in the culture or government.

Author Roger Patterson states that ultimate authority for the modern Mormon is vested in the president of the church because he is the "prophet, seer, and revelator" of the current dispensation. This doctrine of continuing revelation denies Christian teachings of inerrancy, sufficiency, and absolute truth as well as ultimate authority of the Bible. Patterson quotes Mormon elder Merrill C. Oaks whom the LDS website calls "The Living Prophet" and "Our Source of Pure Doctrine," as Oaks makes the case for obedience to modern prophets:

> Just over two years before his death, the prophet Joseph Smith published the Articles of Faith. The ninth article of faith states, "We believe all that God has revealed, all that He does now reveal, and we believe that He will yet reveal many great and important things pertaining to the Kingdom of God." I will speak concerning the final sentence.

> This principle of continuing revelation is an essential part of the kingdom of God. In the fourth and fifth verses of the *Doctrine and Covenants* section 21, the Lord declared to the church their obligation to heed the guidance of His prophet: "Wherefore, meaning the church, thou shalt give heed unto all his words and commandments which he shall give unto you as he receiveth them, walking in all holiness before me; For his word ye shall receive, as if from mine own mouth, in all patience and faith."

Another point of emphasis is that the Mormon godhead is three divine persons united in purpose, *not* in being. Their first Article of Faith states, "We believe in God, the Eternal Father, *and* in His Son, Jesus Christ, *and* in the Holy Ghost." Christians however, believe in three Persons in one God. Moreover, if God was a physical man who had a physical

Son and was exalted to godhood as Smith and Mormon prophets teach, how can the Father exist as an "eternal" being?

Jesus is believed to be the firstborn spirit child of Heavenly Father and Mother in a period known as the preexistence. Brigham Young and others in the LDS church have taught there are multiple mothers (celestial marriages), but this is not official Mormon doctrine today. President Orson Pratt stated, "the Father and Mother of Jesus, according to the flesh, must have been associated together in the capacity of Husband and Wife." Apparently, the Virgin Mary was temporarily "the lawful wife of God the Father" ("Celestial Marriage," Orson Pratt, *The Seer,* 1853, p. 158).

The year Joseph Smith died, he gave what is known as "The King Follett Sermon," in which he clearly stated God was once an exalted man, Jesus is the eldest spirit brother, and Lucifer was the second-born among billions of spirit beings. Please understand this teaching is apostasy, a departure from the essential truth of Scripture. In the account of creation the Bible states, *In the beginning God created the heavens and the earth* (Genesis 1:1). And also, *All things came into being through Him [Jesus], and apart from Him nothing came into being that has come into being* (John 1:3).

We had better get creation and the deity of Jesus Christ correct. How can we have assurance of salvation if parts of the Bible are in question? The fact is the book of Genesis is actual history, and we must treat it as such because God, in Scripture, does just that. It is foundational.

The great evangelical Christian theologian, author, and pastor Francis Schaeffer stated, "The Christian message begins with the existence of God forever, and then with creation. It does not begin with salvation. We must be thankful for salvation, but the Christian message is more than that. Man has value because he is made in the image of God."

Mormons believe Jesus (working with a counsel of spirits) is the *organizer* of the earth from existing matter while Christians believe Jesus is Creator of the universe from nothing. These are two pivotal distinctions. There is even controversy within the LDS church about the creation of Adam and Eve, since some early Mormon prophets taught that Adam was Elohim, which is known as the Adam-God Doctrine.

Most Mormons today reject their own prophets' *inspired* teachings as they were commanded by recent prophets such as President Spencer W. Kimball in a General Conference address in 1976. What do Mormons do when there are contradictions in their doctrines? Similar to Islam and the concept of abrogation, Mormons believe the latter or most recent prophecy overrules and replaces the former, earlier doctrine. Convenient, wouldn't you say?

Speaking of Adam and Eve, the fall of man is considered a blessing in Mormon theology because without it, the spirits could not be tested and progress toward godhood (2 Nephi 2, *Book of Mormon*). Their Articles of Faith 1:2 states, "We believe that men will be punished for their own sins, and not for Adam's transgression." Latter Day Saints believe in "free agency" and a view of salvation resulting from what we do in this "probationary" period of life on earth.

> "For we labor diligently to write, to persuade our children,
> and also our brethren, to believe in Christ, and to be recon-
> ciled to God; for we know that it is by grace we are saved,
> **after all we can do**" (2 Nephi 25:23, emphasis added).

In addition, in Moroni 10:32, it states, "and **if ye shall** deny yourselves of all ungodliness, and love God… **then is his grace sufficient** for you" (emphasis added). Though it is clear from their teachings, most LDS still may reject the fact that Mormonism promotes a form of righteousness by works as a basis for salvation.

Beginning at age twelve, young Mormons begin participating in baptisms for the dead, and families can have sealing ceremonies so they can be "forever families" in the afterlife. Large earthly families are encouraged to take part in this in order to provide physical bodies for spirit children who are still waiting to enter their probation. Also, in order to complete the work of proxy baptism and other temple ordinances, Mormons are devoted to studying genealogies because they need to know names of family members in order to seal them "for time and all eternity." They also believe in continued communication with those who have died.

Only those who acknowledge Joseph Smith are able to enter the celestial kingdom. In the Mormon *Journal of Discourses*, volume 7:45,

Brigham Young taught that "no man or woman in this dispensation will ever enter into the celestial kingdom of God without the consent of Joseph Smith. . . . He holds the keys of that kingdom for the last dispensation – the keys to rule in the spirit-world. . . . He reigns there as supreme being in his sphere, capacity, and calling as God does in heaven."

Both Joseph Smith and Brigham Young were reportedly involved in Freemasonry, which is why you see the influence of its rituals and symbolism in Mormon temple construction and secret rituals. Smith's father was a Master Freemason enrolled in a lodge in New York, and his older brother was a mason as well. The oaths, handshakes, and ritual dress of the LDS temple ceremonies are strikingly similar to those of the Freemasons and their progression from one level to the next. The square and compass markings on early Mormon temple garments are clearly borrowed from the symbol of Freemasonry.[139]

Some have questioned the Mormon Church's non-profit status. There are about 160 LDS temples worldwide with more under construction, and entrance is generally restricted to church members in good standing only. Annual revenues for the LDS organization were estimated to be $5 billion, with total assets between $25 to $30 billion dollars. The church has done quite well financially.

We cannot conclude this section without at least mentioning the practice of polygamy and some of the findings related to Mormon prophets. Joseph Smith had approximately forty wives, either married to him or sealed in temple ceremonies to be his wives in eternity, and at least fourteen of those wives were married to other men. Plural marriage has been a public relations nightmare for many in the Mormon Church, and they've been addressing the issue more frequently since 2013.

Reportedly, Smith prayed to God asking why He allowed men to have many wives in the Old Testament. But to suggest God commanded or initiated the patriarch to practice plural marriage is not supported by Scripture. (Sarah convinced Abram to have a child with Hagar.) In an article for the Christian Research Institute, Eric Johnson pointed out specific prohibitions from Leviticus 18, including having:

---

139   Bodie Hodge and Roger Patterson, *World Religions and Cults Volume 1* (Green Forest, AR: Master Books, 2015), 267.

(Verse 17) Sexual relations with a woman and her daughter (yet Smith married Patty Bartlett Sessions and her daughter, Sylvia Sessions);

(Verse 18) Sisters as wives (yet Smith married three pairs of sisters – the Johnsons, the Lawrences, and the Partridges); and

(Verse 20) Relations with a neighbor's wife (yet ten of Smith's wives were already married to men he knew quite well).

It is said that Joseph Smith's original wife, Emma, never publicly testified to him having multiple wives, even though it was "an excruciating ordeal" to live with, and she threatened to divorce him many times. While Joseph directed that his personal letters to other wives be destroyed, not all of them were. One historian claimed that by September 1843, "most of Emma's friends had either married Joseph or had given their daughters to him," so we can have sympathy for her, knowing Smith actively sought out and secretly married other women.[140]

Smith coerced young women and girls, promising unimaginable blessings for them if they married him, and he often retold a story about an angel appearing to him "three times between 1834 and 1842, commanding him to proceed with plural marriage." The angel finally convinced Smith during the third and final appearance when he appeared with a drawn sword, "threatening Joseph with destruction unless he went forward and obeyed." For Smith, plural marriage represented the pinnacle of his theology of exaltation: the husband as king and priest, surrounded by queens and priestesses eternally procreating spirit children.

The benefits could even extend to the girl's earthly family. For instance, Helen Mar Kimball, Smith's twenty-fifth wife, claimed that Smith promised her that "if you will take this step, it will ensure your eternal salvation [and] exaltation, and that of your father's household [and] all of your kindred." Her response? "This promise was so great that I gave myself to purchase so glorious a reward." Some may argue

---

140 Eric Johnson, "Plural Marriage and Joseph Smith: A PR Nightmare in Mormonism," *CHRISTIAN RESEARCH JOURNAL*, volume 38, number 05 (2015). *www.equip.org/article/plural-marriage-joseph-smith-pr-nightmare-mormonism/*.

that even though there is evidence for Smith having many wives, it does not mean he slept with any or all of them.

But Mormon historian Richard Lyman Bushman writes, "Nothing indicates that sexual relations were left out of plural marriages." Author Todd M. Compton adds that Smith had seventeen wives under the age of twenty-eight, including ten teenage girls. Three years after Joseph Smith died, Emma remarried a non-Mormon, Lewis C. Bidamon, in 1847, and rather than join Brigham Young and move to Utah, Emma Smith stayed in Illinois.

Let's wrap up with a few major LDS doctrines. While hell is known as outer darkness, they believe most everyone will be saved and enter into one of these levels or kingdoms in the afterlife: the celestial kingdom, the terrestrial kingdom, the telestial kingdom, and outer darkness (Mormon Doctrine, p. 348). Mentioned earlier, leaders have taught Jesus's incarnation was the result of a physical relationship between God the Father and Mary. Mormons also believe Jesus is a god, but any human can also become a god (*Doctrine and Covenants* 132:20; Teachings of the Prophet Joseph Smith, pp. 345 – 354).[141]

Mormonism contains contradictions and internal inconsistencies and it cannot provide a coherent framework for a worldview. If multiple gods are omniscient and omnipotent, how can people be sure they are worshipping the right one? Is it possible Mormon prophets have spoken from their own minds and desires and not on behalf of Jesus Christ?

The truth is there is only one true God (Deuteronomy 6:4; Isaiah 43:10; 44:6-8), and He has always existed and always will (Deuteronomy 33:27; Psalm 90:2; 1 Timothy 1:17). God was not created – He is the Creator (Genesis 1; Psalm 24:1; Isaiah 37:16), He is perfect and no one else is His equal (Psalm 86:8; Isaiah 40:25). God the Father is not, nor was He ever, a man (Numbers 23:19; 1 Samuel 15:29; Hosea 11:9); He is Spirit (John 4:24), and not made of flesh and bone (Luke 24:39). Jesus defined marriage: one man, one woman (Matthew 19:5-6).

So many more Scriptures support the fact that Mormon teachings are in contrast with Christian teachings, as these hold two different gospels. Latter Day Saints have hijacked the name and glory of the Lord

---

141 Got Questions, "What is Mormonism? What do Mormons believe?" *www.gotquestions. org/Mormons.html.*

Jesus to sell their religion to those who are less informed, searching, or spiritually needy. Abundant resources are available with information on the teachings of the Church of Jesus Christ of Latter Day Saints for those wanting to do more research.

> *But even if we, or an angel from heaven, should preach to you a gospel contrary to what we have preached to you, he is to be accursed!* (Galatians 1:8)

ROMAN CATHOLICISM

Through the centuries, many have confessed Christ or have taken a stand for truth even when it was dangerous to do so. On April 18, 1521, a monk seeking the approval of God, Martin Luther, stood before the emperor Charles V and powerful church and state leaders of the imperial court in Germany. They demanded Luther renounce his doctrines challenging the Roman Catholic Church to repent and reform its corrupt traditions and teachings. Martin Luther answered, "My conscience is captive to the Word of God. I cannot and will not recant anything, for to go against conscience is neither right nor safe. God help me. Amen."

There are some wonderful Christians wrestling with the decision to stay or leave the Catholic Church. Regarding the central, essential teachings of the Christian faith, I agree with many of the Catholics I know. When it comes to the doctrine and traditions of the Roman Catholic Church, I disagree on many issues. However, lest you think this section is intended to bash Catholics and prove they're wrong, please know I've written extensively in my previous books on heresies within Protestant and evangelical churches ("Counterfeit Christianity" and "Emerging into Confusion") including the redefined social justice apostasy.

No church or denomination is immune to deception. Sincere believers are sharply divided on doctrine, morality, social issues, traditions, and politics. I have learned not to judge those who are Catholic or those who are young in the Christian faith. Some say being Catholic is the same as being Christian, while others firmly state, "I am a Catholic, not a Christian!" I would ask both, what do you mean by that? The primary concern is what is true according to God's Word and how we live that out.

Most of us know professing Christians, Catholics, Mormons, Muslims, Buddhists, and others who do not exactly agree with or follow their own church's or religion's teachings. To the best of our ability, we must discern what is biblical and what is not. I do not claim to be right about everything, and I understand God will hold me accountable for my assessments and commentary, but I believe the following information is from reputable sources, including former Catholics, which I hope will be encouraging, challenging, and helpful to you in your pursuit of truth.

About 1.3 billion Roman Catholics live in the world, with the largest numbers in Brazil, Mexico, and the Philippines. Given the number of practitioners of Catholicism and the church's influence, it is critical we compare its teachings and application to what is found in Scripture. The Roman Catholic Church (hereafter, "RCC") is the only religion that has its own political territory as an independent state (Vatican City, a walled enclave of 110 acres) with its own central bank, as well as diplomatic relations with other countries.

Power in the church belongs to the pope or "Supreme Pontiff," also said to be the "Vicar of Christ" on earth. *Vicar* literally means "one serving as an agent or substitute." The Bible teaches *there is one God, and one mediator also between God and men, the man Christ Jesus* (1 Timothy 2:5), moreover, the pope is often referred to as "Holy Father," a title reserved for God alone.

As successor to Peter (we'll address this later), the pope exercises authority over more than 3,200 bishops in the church which are themselves viewed as successors of the apostles of Jesus. According to the Second Vatican Council, bishops "have by divine institution taken the place of the apostles as pastors of the Church, in such wise that whoever listens to them is listening to Christ, and whoever despises them despises Christ and him who sent Christ."[142]

The RCC claims to be the only church on earth that has Jesus Christ as its founder, and the pope as its earthly head. Though there is both a Western (majority of Catholics) and Eastern liturgy, there is complete unity and submission to the pope, who serves for life or until he resigns. Headquartered at the Vatican in Rome, under the pope there

---

142 Libreria Editrice Vaticana, *Catechism of the Catholic Church* (New York: Doubleday, 1994), 249, 254.

is the College of Cardinals who elect and assist him in governing the church. (Most Cardinals are archbishops.) Three degrees within the college are bishops, priests, and deacons.

The hierarchy continues with archbishops who preside over Catholic churches in major cities and populated areas. Next in line are the bishops, who head up each diocese and supervise all the church's teachings and activities in their parishes, assuring faithfulness to Catholic doctrine. Each local parish is led by a priest who oversees and carries out masses, ministers to members, and offers instruction. Then there are hundreds of religious orders of nuns, monks, and missionaries including the Society of Jesus whose members are known as Jesuits. They control most Catholic educational institutions of higher learning.

As for origins of the RCC, the belief is Jesus ordained Peter as the head of the worldwide church (essentially, the first bishop of Rome) and its successors (popes) now have headship over the church. One Scripture used by Catholics to support the claim Peter was given supreme authority is in Matthew 16:18-19 when Jesus said to Peter, *I will give you the keys of the kingdom of heaven* and, *upon this rock I will build My church; and the gates of Hades will not overpower it*. Catholics believe Peter, the rock, was the church's foundation, but Christians believe Jesus's apostles were unique and had no successors.

The Bible cannot contradict itself, and yet, Paul wrote to the Ephesian church that Jesus Christ is the cornerstone of God's household, *having been built on the foundation of the apostles and prophets, Christ Jesus Himself being the corner stone* (Ephesians 2:20). Peter certainly was one of the main apostles, but to clarify, another Scripture states, *For no other foundation can anyone lay than that which is laid, which is Jesus Christ* (1 Corinthians 3:11 NKJV). The New Testament further teaches there were two offices in the early Christian church: elders and deacons.

Catholic doctrine takes another bold step claiming infallibility of the pope's teachings. They believe when the pope speaks from the chair (*ex cathedra*) on issues pertaining to faith, morals, and practice, he is teaching as Christ's representative and the Holy Spirit guarantees the pope cannot lead the church into error. When he is not speaking *ex cathedra*, it is then possible the pope could be fallible in something he says.

Author Ron Rhodes, president of Reasoning from the Scriptures Ministries, adds:

> "Not only is the pope infallible when speaking *ex cathedra* on matters of faith and practice, the bishops too are infallible when they speak 'with one voice' – that is, when all the bishops agree on a doctrine. They are assured freedom from error "provided they are in union with the Bishop of Rome and their teaching is subject to his authority."
>
> Such a view is understandable in light of the Catholic teaching on *apostolic succession*. This refers to the "uninterrupted handing on" of episcopal power and authority from the apostles to contemporary bishops. . . . The teaching Magisterium (from the Latin word for "master") . . . functions as the authoritative teaching body of the church that safeguards doctrines.[143]

Is there a need for a Magisterium? Believers are filled with the Holy Spirit, our teacher. Scripture is our guide: *Thy word is a lamp unto my feet and a light unto my path* (Psalm 119:105 KJV). Individual Christians are encouraged to study the Scriptures (2 Timothy 2:15) and test all things for themselves (1 Thessalonians 5:21; 1 John 4:1) like the "noble-minded" Bereans in the book of Acts. When the apostle Paul preached to them in the synagogue, the Bereans *received the word with great eagerness, examining the Scriptures daily* (Acts 17:11) to confirm Paul's teachings.

Catholics also believe St. Peter's Basilica in Vatican City was built above Peter's tomb and Peter lived there, but this claim is problematic as there is no biblical or historical evidence Peter ever went to Rome. Tradition does hold that Peter was crucified upside down in Rome, but he ministered mostly to the Jews in Jerusalem, Judea, Samaria, Galilee, and Antioch. Moreover, if Peter was in Rome, why didn't Paul, the apostle God sent to the Gentiles, mention him in his letter to the Roman Christians when he mentioned twenty-seven other believers (Romans 16) to conclude his letter?

Scripture does not indicate any apostle attaining a supreme position

---

143   Ron Rhodes, *The 10 Most Important Things You Can Say to a Catholic* (Eugene, OR: Harvest House Publishers, 2002), 44-45.

in New Testament times. Paul even affirmed he was at least on the same level as the others: *for in no respect was I inferior to the most eminent apostles, even though I am a nobody* (2 Corinthians 12:11). If there is any claim that Peter was infallible, too many Scriptures indicate the opposite. Paul corrected Peter in Antioch over his hypocrisy (Galatians 2:11-14), and James seemed to have more authority at the Council of Jerusalem (Acts 15:1-35). Peter refers to himself as a "fellow elder" and tells others to *shepherd the flock of God* (1 Peter 5:1-4). The disciples even argued about which one of them was the greatest.

Another primary issue to consider is the authority of Scripture. We do have common beliefs including being created in the image of God, the trinity, the virgin birth, the full deity and humanity of Jesus, the definition of marriage and the value of every human life, Jesus's resurrection, and eternal punishment. A big distinction between Catholics and Christians is how we view the Bible as a whole. Most Catholics view the Bible as inspired, *and* as having equal authority with the RCC and tradition. Christians view the Bible as the supreme, final authority for faith and practice.

Christians often refer to the *canon* of Scripture when mentioning the select books within the Holy Bible that were evaluated for their consistency and inspiration. *Canon* comes from a Greek word meaning "measuring stick," so when the *canon of Scripture* is mentioned, we are referring to all the books that constitute God's perfect Word.

The Bible warns against anyone adding to God's Word, so since the Catholic Bible is much bigger, why the difference and which one is inspired? Protestants and Catholics agree about the inspiration of the entire New Testament, but they differ over some works of literature in the Old Testament. These pieces are commonly referred to as the *Apocrypha*, which means "hidden" or "doubtful," and were written in the time between the Old and New Testaments when God sent no prophets.

The Apocrypha refers to disputed books rejected by Protestants, but Catholics and Orthodox groups accept and believe they belong in the canon. Those who claim these documents as inspired prefer to call them "deuterocanonical" or "books of the second canon." The Roman

Catholic Council of Trent stated, "The Synod . . . receives and venerates . . . all the books."

According to Got Questions:

> The nation of Israel treated the Apocrypha/
> Deuterocanonical books with respect, but never accepted
> them as true books of the Hebrew Bible. The early
> Christian church debated the status of the Apocrypha/
> Deuterocanonicals, but few early Christians believed they
> belonged in the canon of Scripture. The New Testament
> quotes from the Old Testament hundreds of times, but
> *nowhere* quotes or alludes to any of the Apocryphal/
> Deuterocanonical books. Further, there are many
> proven errors and contradictions in the Apocrypha/
> Deuterocanonicals.[144]

The RCC decided these books belonged in the Bible, and the Catholic Council of Trent (1545 – 1563) canonized these books about fifteen hundred years after they were written. Some councils such as Hippo (AD 393) were influenced by Augustine who felt the Apocrypha should be canonized because of their mention of "extreme and wonderful suffering of certain martyrs," and because the books were contained in the Septuagint of his day. However, evidence seems to suggest the original Septuagint did not contain the Apocrypha.

Five primary tests were used to discern and decide which books belonged in the canon: 1) Was the book written or backed by a man of God such as a prophet or apostle? 2) Is the book authoritative, meaning, does it have a sense of "thus saith the Lord"? 3) Does the book tell the truth about God and doctrine as it has been revealed by previous revelation? 4) Does the book give evidence of having the power of God? 5) Was the book accepted by the people of God? From these tests, the answer to each question is "no," so the Apocrypha does not belong in the canon.

God does not contradict Himself, and there are writings in those books that contradict doctrines in the Old and New Testaments. Church

---

144   Got Questions, "What are the Apocrypha/Deuterocanonical books?" *www.gotquestions. org/apocrypha-deuterocanonical.html.*

fathers disagreed on the Apocrypha even though some apparently used them for devotional purposes. Even if someone quoted from the Apocrypha does not mean the books are God breathed. Not only are there historical errors, but the books also do not display the power and authority of God, nor were they widely accepted until the mid-1500s after the Council of Trent.

Some of what the Apocrypha teaches is true and correct, but due to historical and theological errors, it is necessary to view the books as fallible religious documents of man, and not as the inspired, authoritative Word of God. The Apocrypha/books of the second canon support some beliefs and practices of the RCC which are not in agreement with the Bible, such as praying for the dead, petitioning "saints" in heaven for their prayers, worshipping angels, and "alms-giving" atoning for sins.

EARLIER HISTORY

Peering back at early church history, the first three centuries were filled with severe persecution throughout the Roman Empire. During this time, the Christian churches also had to deal with false teachings and heresy within, about which the New Testament often warns believers. Talk of a universal (*catholic*) church began in the middle of the second century (this did not mean Roman Catholic), and the role of bishop evolved as being superior to deacons, elders, and pastors (also called priests). By the fourth century, bishops in major cities such as Rome gained preeminence.

Because the apostles Paul and Peter were martyred in Rome, the capital of the empire, and the church there was one of the largest and wealthiest in the world, the idea of apostolic succession became a doctrine and the bishop of Rome was seen as the "first among equals" in authority.

According to historian, theologian, and researcher Dr. Terry Mortenson:

> Also during this time, a separation between clergy and
> laity developed, with the bishop being regarded as a dis-
> penser of grace, and some began to view the Lord's Supper
> (communion) as a sacrifice to God. Whereas in the New

Testament baptism was administered to a person after he believed, in the second and third centuries some bishops began to practice infant baptism as an initiation into the Christian faith.

Things changed dramatically in AD 313 when after almost three centuries of persecution against Christians, the Roman emperor Constantine fully legalized Christianity. He restored confiscated property to the church, made Sunday a day of worship and rest, and transformed Byzantium (modern-day Istanbul) by renaming it Constantinople and making it his eastern capital. He also ordered the building of the Church of the Holy Sepulchre near the supposed tomb of Jesus in Jerusalem.[145]

Some suggest the date of Constantine's alleged conversion was AD 312, but nonetheless, the changes he made ultimately led to the RCC. When the doctrinal dispute over the deity and humanity of Christ arose, Constantine presided over the Council of Nicaea in AD 325, even though he held no official authority in the churches. It is said he was not baptized until on his deathbed in AD 337, but by that time, Christianity was practically the official "state" religion of the Roman Empire. So began a history of increasing spiritual and moral corruption of the church as the state ruled the church and then later, through the popes, the church controlled the state.

The term *Roman Catholic* was defined by Emperor Theodosius I in AD 380, in a document called the Theodosian Code. Giving the church power over the empire, he referred to those who hold to the "religion which was delivered to the Romans by the divine apostle Peter" as "Roman Catholic Christians." During the fourth through sixth centuries, monasticism (withdrawing from society for religious reasons) and asceticism (practicing rigorous self-denial regarding life's comforts) grew due to the worldliness of the institutional church.

Other emperors convened councils of bishops to iron out disputes over authority, doctrine, and church structure. As a result, not only

---

145   Terry Mortenson, *World Religions and Cults Volume 1* (Green Forest, AR: Master Books, 2015), 78.

did Roman emperors gain some authority within the church, but these councils also strengthened the office of the bishop. The first Roman Catholic pope is said to have been Leo I, as he took the episcopal throne in AD 440 and, apparently backed by the emperor at the time, began to assert supremacy over the other bishops. He did not use the title "pope," but he established the doctrinal foundation of the papacy. *Pope* comes from the Latin word *papa*.

To be fair, there were many churches in the first four centuries that did stay true to the authority of Scripture and traced their lineage back to the apostles, *not* to the Church of Rome. In the New Testament, terminology for spiritual leaders of a church such as elder, pastor, and bishop were used interchangeably. Some historians suggest the fall of the Roman Empire in AD 476 and the rise of the Catholic Church are two parts of the same history because power was transferred from one entity to the other.

As historical side notes, during the seventh and eighth centuries the Eastern church dealt with the threat of Islam while the Western church sought to evangelize northern and western Europe. In the tenth and eleventh centuries, needed reforms were made dealing with wealth and corruption in the monasteries.

Regarding Islam, it must be noted that Catholic priests and Christians have been persecuted throughout history. Today they are persecuted and/or executed by radical Muslims and ISIS for not believing in Allah and Muhammad. Regarding the church's relationship with Muslims, however, the Catechism (841) states, "The plan of salvation also includes those who acknowledge the Creator, *in the first place* amongst whom are the Muslims; these *profess* to hold the faith of Abraham, and *together* with us they adore the one, merciful God, mankind's judge on the last day" [330] (emphasis added).

According to the Bible, it is the Jews who are His chosen people "in the first place," and though Muslims acknowledge *a* creator they do not believe in *the* Creator, nor do they believe Jesus is God. You may also recall that the line of descendants from Isaac is not the same as from Ishmael, so do Muslims truly hold the faith of Abraham? With two different deities and scriptural authorities, can Catholics be united with

Muslims in worship? Is this taught because Mary is the only woman mentioned in the Quran? By proclaiming salvation for unbelievers here, the Catechism seems to teach a different gospel suggesting that faith in Jesus Christ is not required.

Gregory I "the Great" became bishop in AD 590 and exercised the power of the office, increased the wealth of the church, and established it as a formidable power in politics. From that time on, the church and state were fully intertwined as the Holy Roman Empire, and the pope exercised authority over kings and emperors. Gregory the Great believed in the inspiration of Scripture, but he also regarded church tradition as an equal authority. He carried on the idea of purgatory and considered the celebration of the Eucharist to be a sacrifice of Christ's body and blood.

This teaching claims that by divine miracle, the bread and wine of the Eucharist are converted into the literal body and blood of Christ but without changing appearance (*transubstantiation* – from the Latin term *transsubstantiato*, meaning "change of substance").

> *But Christ came as High Priest of the good things to come,*
> *with the greater and more perfect tabernacle not made with*
> *hands, that is, not of this creation. Not with the blood of*
> *goats and calves, but with His own blood* **He entered the**
> **Most Holy Place once for all, having obtained eternal**
> **redemption**. (Hebrews 9:11-12 NKJV, emphasis added)

The Eucharist (or Mass) is the most important of the Roman Catholic sacraments, but it appears to involve a re-sacrificing or re-presenting the offering of Jesus Christ over and over in every church, every day. The Old Testament concept of offerings and sacrifices were to appease a holy God (soothe His wrath and cover the people's sins). The New Testament teaches Jesus fulfilled the Law, including His priestly work, tore the massive veil in the high priest's temple from top to bottom, proclaimed it "finished," and sat down at the right hand of the Father in heaven. A priest never sat down until he completed his required duties. But the Catholic Council of Trent stated, "This sacrifice [of the Mass] is truly propitiatory. . . For by this obligation the Lord is appeased."

When Jesus had the Last Supper with His disciples, He held the bread in His hands and said, *This is my body which is given for you; do this in remembrance of Me.* Then He stated, *This cup is the new covenant in My blood,* as He held the chalice, so it was obviously a symbolic act as He was there with them in person (Luke 22:17-20). Christians believe Jesus meant for His words to be symbolic in this context. Two of the many Scriptures taken figuratively include *Taste and see that the LORD is good* (Psalm 34:8), and *desire the pure milk of the word, that you may grow thereby, if indeed you have tasted that the Lord is gracious* (1 Peter 2:2-3).

Some historians suggest that during the earlier centuries, forced mass conversions took place and many pagans came into the church. To help these converts feel comfortable in the church, priests and bishops introduced the use of images into the liturgy and the veneration of angels, saints (martyrs from earlier centuries), relics, pictures, and statues.

Dr. Terry Mortenson further explains:

> More "holy days," including Christmas, were officially added to the church calendar. In addition to the sacraments of baptism and the Lord's Supper, the prominent theologian Augustine and other church leaders added new sacraments: marriage, penance, confirmation, and extreme unction. Augustine also helped to develop the doctrine of purgatory (a spiritual state of final purification after death and before entering heaven).
>
> The veneration of Mary, the mother of Jesus, developed rapidly during this time. Belief in her perpetual virginity (introduced in the middle of the second century) and in her sinlessness placed her at the head of the list of "saints," and festivals in her honor sprang up. People began to believe that she had intercessory powers to influence Jesus on behalf of believers. Veneration of other saints included the selling of relics from their bodies.[146]

The Great Schism of 1054 was the first of two major divisions in the RCC. An orthodox patriarch named Cerularius of Constantinople was excommunicated for not recognizing the authority of the pope,

---

146 Mortenson, *World Religions and Cults Volume 1,* 80.

and Cerularius excommunicated the pope of Rome in a dispute about the use of unleavened bread in the Eucharist. This was the formal distinction between the Catholic and the Eastern Orthodox Church. Five years later, Pope Nicholas II removed the ability of the people to elect the pope and gave this power to the College of Cardinals.

At least seven major crusades took place between about 1095 and 1290 intended to resist the advancement of Islam in Europe and kill heretics as well as anyone who resisted the supremacy of the pope. The inquisitions were first instituted by Pope Innocent III (1198 – 1216) whose crusading armies tortured and killed thousands of godly Christians the church had condemned as heretics in southern France and northern Italy. It is estimated that over the next six hundred years, seventy-five popes ordered or approved of brutal methods of torture and murder in efforts to force Christians, Jews, and Muslims to abandon their faith and follow the RCC, the "Holy Mother Church." In attempts to rule over church and society, some reports suggest millions suffered and died in these inquisitions.

Two priests who were forerunners to Martin Luther and inspired him were John Wycliffe and Jan Hus. Wycliffe (1330 – 1384) was a priest who painstakingly translated the Bible into English so the common man could read the truth and see the errors in RCC doctrine. He died of a disease, but in 1428, his body was exhumed and burned as a heretic by church authorities. Jan Hus, considered the first church reformer, was a Czechoslovakian priest who adopted the mission of Wycliffe, but he was burned at the stake for his efforts in 1415.

Martin Luther initially viewed the RCC as the true expression of Christianity which had been corrupted by false doctrines and unbiblical practices over time. This year is the five hundredth anniversary (1517) of Luther's famous Ninety-Five Theses he nailed to the door of the church in Wittenberg, Germany, exposing doctrinal and practical errors in the Catholic Church. One major practice Luther opposed was the selling of indulgences, which was declared a dogma by Pope Clement VI in 1343. A person paid money to the church to obtain forgiveness, and to free himself from the temporal penalty of sin. Money could also be paid to shorten a loved one's time in purgatory. Luther and others condemned these practices and other unbiblical doctrines.

In 1542, Pope Paul III set up the Roman Inquisition, punishing Protestants through the confiscation of property and imprisonment. He also called the Council of Trent (1545 – 1563 in Trento and Bologna, Italy) to respond to Protestant teaching and the Reformation, and in that Council, affirmed the Apocrypha and church traditions as equal in authority with the Bible. The Council of Trent also affirmed the doctrines of transubstantiation and purgatory as well as Jesus's mother, Mary, being sinless (Session VI, Canon 23, Catechism 493). Since that Council, other controversial doctrines were officially added including papal infallibility and exalting Mary.

TEACHINGS ABOUT THE VIRGIN MARY

It is nearly impossible to compare the Mary of Roman Catholicism with the one briefly described in the pages of Scripture. She was blessed and shown favor from God, and to her credit she obeyed the Lord, referring to herself as "the servant (handmaid, bondservant) of the Lord" essentially saying, "may Your will be done." The Virgin Mary is a true example of faith. She is to be recognized for her important role in world history and for the grief she must have experienced as Jesus was crucified. However, referring to Deuteronomy 6:13, Jesus makes it clear, saying, *You shall worship the Lord your God and serve Him only* (Luke 4:8).

> *While Jesus was saying these things, one of the women in the crowd raised her voice and said to Him, "Blessed is the womb that bore You and the breasts at which You nursed." But He said, "On the contrary, blessed are those who hear the word of God and observe it." (Luke 11:27-28)*

Doctrines having no Scriptural support include that the Virgin Mary was born without the effects of original sin (the *Immaculate Conception* added in 1854, Pope Pius IX), meaning she did not have a sin nature derived from Adam, and that she also remained a virgin throughout her life. Presently, Mary is the "spiritual mother" to everyone whom Jesus came to save. As humanity's spiritual mother, Mary intercedes by bringing the gifts of salvation. "Therefore the Blessed Virgin is invoked in the Church under the titles of Advocate, Helper, Benefactress, and Mediatrix" (*Co-Redeemer*).

According to Matt Slick at Christian Apologetics and Research Ministry, Roman Catholicism teaches Mary is "the all-holy ever-virgin Mother of God" (Catechism of the Catholic Church 721, hereafter referred to as "CCC"), the "Queen over all things" (CCC 966), who is "full of grace" (CCC 722), the "Mother of God and our mother" (CCC 2677), the "new Eve" (CCC 726), and the "seat of wisdom" (CCC 721). She had no original sin (CCC 508), and never committed sin (CCC 493). She is "second only to her Son" (Vatican II, Dogmatic Constitution on the Church, par. 66) and sits "on the right hand of the majesty on high" (Pope Pius X, Ad Diem Illum Laetissimum, 14). In fact, "no man goeth to Christ but by His Mother" (Pope Leo 13th, Octobri Mense). It was Mary who "crushed the poisonous head of the most-cruel serpent and brought salvation to the world" (Pope Pius IX, Ineffabilis Deus).

It is she who "delivers our souls from death" (CCC 966), and "continues to bring us the gifts of eternal salvation" (CCC 969). "Mary, by her spiritual entering into the sacrifice of her divine son for men, made atonement for the sins of man" (*Fundamentals of Catholic Dogma* 4, Ott, page 213). Therefore, we can "entrust all our cares and petitions to her" (CCC 2677), "give ourselves over to her now" (CCC 2677), "pray to her" (CCC 2679), and have devotion to her (CCC 971). She was "taken up body and soul into the glory of heaven" (CCC 974). When speaking of the Church, "we can find no better way to conclude than by looking to Mary" (CCC 972). In her, the church is holy (CCC 867). "Mary is the Church's model of faith and charity" (CCC 967). Finally, in paradise the church gathers "around Jesus and Mary" (CCC 1053).[147]

I wonder how many Catholics are unaware of these teachings. One doctrine to expound on is the Catholic Church's official dogma of the Assumption of Mary. Declared by Pope Pius XII in 1950, Mary did not die and suffer decay as all other human beings have and will, but was miraculously taken body and soul to heaven. Pius stated it was "forbidden" to reject this and warned that anyone who changed, countered, or opposed this new doctrine would "incur the wrath of Almighty God."

---

147 Matt Slick, "Summary of Catholic teachings about Mary," CARM, *carm.org/ catholic-mary-summary*.

"By the authority of our Lord Jesus Christ, of Blessed
Apostles Peter and Paul, *and by our own authority, we
pronounce*, declare, and define it to be a divinely revealed
dogma: that the Immaculate Mother of God, the ever
Virgin Mary, having completed the course of her earthly
life, was assumed body and soul into heavenly glory"
(emphasis added).

The concern and need for caution here is that not only are men claiming authority, but also the exaltation of Mary robs Jesus of all worship,
honor, trust, and glory deserving of Him alone.

For faithful Catholics loyal to their church, in order to obey their
popes, bishops, and priests, one logical practice and tradition that has
developed through the years due to these fantastical teachings is praying the Rosary. This practice increased after what are claimed to be
appearances or *apparitions* of Mary, saints, or angels in places such as
Guadalupe, Mexico (1531), Lourdes, France (1858), Fatima, Portugal
(1917), and Medjugorje, Bosnia and Herzegovina (1981). While I do not
pretend to know exactly what was seen, healthy skepticism is encouraged. Could any of these have been perpetrated by "deceitful workers"
of the Enemy? The apostle Paul warned that *even Satan disguises himself
as an angel of light* (2 Corinthians 11:13-14).

Promoted within the Catholic Church as a means of strengthening
one's faith, resisting evil, growing spiritually, and generally benefiting
society, the first problem is that much of the Rosary prayer is directed
to Mary, not Jesus. While the first portion of the Hail Mary quotes
part of Luke 1:28, there is no scriptural basis for (1) praying to Mary,
(2) addressing her as *holy*, or (3) calling her *our life* and *our hope*. The
whole second half of the Hail Mary and portions of the Hail, Holy
Queen are not biblical.

Writing for Eternal Word Television Network (EWTN), Father
William Saunders wrote about the history of the Rosary and stated, "The
rosary is one of the most cherished prayers" of the Catholic Church.
Though he admitted the origins of the Rosary are sketchy at best, he
said, "Tradition does hold that St. Dominic (d. 1221) devised the rosary
as we know it." Saunders added:

The use of "prayer beads" and the repeated recitation of prayers to aid in meditation stem from the earliest days of the Church and has roots in pre-Christian times.

In 1571, Pope Pius V organized a fleet under the command of Don Juan of Austria the half-brother of King Philip II of Spain. While preparations were underway, the Holy Father asked all of the faithful to say the rosary and implore our Blessed Mother's prayers, . . . that our Lord would grant victory . . . Pope St. Pius V established the Feast of the Holy Rosary on October 7, where the faithful would not only remember this victory, but also give thanks to the Lord for all of His benefits and remember the powerful intercession of our Blessed Mother.[148]

Not only did Jesus teach us to not use meaningless or *vain repetitions* when we pray (Matthew 6:7), He never referred to Himself as the "Son of Mary" although some Catholics refer to Him as such. Apart from Acts 1:14 and a handful of verses in the Gospels, Mary is not mentioned in the Bible. Considering the Holy Spirit-inspired New Testament was written by several authors addressing spiritual doctrines and providing guidance for the Christian church, none gave Mary the level of devotion or place of supreme importance the RCC gives her.

SAVED BY GRACE THROUGH FAITH

Finally, perhaps one of the most important subjects we could discuss in any context is salvation and justification by grace through faith alone. Naturally, many people think of Martin Luther when this topic comes up. Justification is an act of God toward the person who believes in the finished work of Jesus Christ. Christians are justified or declared righteous by faith, based solely on His sacrifice whereby God credits to our account the obedience and righteousness of Christ.

Where the Bible teaches we are eternally and irrevocably justified through the Lord Jesus, the Catholic Church teaches salvation from the coming judgment of God is a lifelong process, not a one-time event or

---

148 Father William Saunders, "History of the Rosary," *www.ewtn.com/library/answers/rosa-ryhs.htm.*

profession of faith. They believe the sacrament of baptism is "the door which gives access to the other sacraments." The church believes baptism causes the new birth, makes the person a child of God, and gives him the grace of initial justification.

This teaching, along with the necessity of sacraments is confusing as it mixes scriptural truth with man-made requirements accumulated over centuries and thus introduces errors and muddies up the process of sanctification. Even though the Bible teaches *faith without works is useless* (James 2:26), works, actions, or obligations have nothing to do with salvation. One disturbing aspect of Roman Catholic theology is the teaching that the grace of justification can be gained and lost and gained and lost, that it is conditional justification.

The apostle Paul wrote to the Ephesians that after having heard the true gospel of our salvation and having believed, we are sealed in Christ *with the Holy Spirit of promise*, which is referred to as a deposit, *pledge*, or even a "guarantee" *of our inheritance* (Ephesians 1:13-14). This transaction does not seem like something we can add to.

To the Christians in Rome, Paul wrote, *by the works of the Law no flesh will be justified in His sight* (Romans 3:20), and *we maintain that a man is justified by faith apart from works of the Law* (Romans 3:28), and also:

> But now apart from the Law the righteousness of God
> has been manifested, being witnessed by the Law and the
> Prophets, even the righteousness of God through faith in
> Jesus Christ for all those who believe; for there is no distinc-
> tion; for all have sinned and fall short of the glory of God,
> being justified as a gift by His grace through the redemption
> which is in Christ Jesus; whom God displayed publicly as a
> propitiation in His blood through faith. This was to demon-
> strate His righteousness, because in the forbearance of God
> He passed over the sins previously committed; for the dem-
> onstration, I say, of His righteousness at the present time, so
> that He would be just and the justifier of the one who has
> faith in Jesus. (Romans 3:21-26)

When it comes to salvation and justification, some Catholics may mention Christ, His death, burial, and resurrection, as well as our need for grace and faith, but they will "add a life of meritorious works" and required participation in the rituals and sacraments of the RCC. While Catholics do acknowledge the *necessity* of grace, they do not acknowledge the *exclusivity* of grace. Dr. Ron Rhodes states:

> Catholics believe that the salvation process starts out with "first actual grace." This grace is "first" in the sense that it is God who initially reaches out to a person and gives him the grace that will enable him to seek God, have faith, and prepare his soul for baptism and justification. It is "actual" in the sense that good acts are the goal.

> This grace does not have an automatic influence. A person must respond to it – *yield to its influence* – for it to become effectual. . . . If he rejects this grace and ends up dying, he is lost. Catholics believe that following initial justification, there is a second aspect of justification that occurs throughout life as the person continues to cooperate with God's grace and progress in good works, thereby meriting the further grace necessary for him or her to enter eternal life.[149]

Let's be clear: merely claiming to have faith is insufficient. Genuine faith will always result in good works because of the fruit of the Holy Spirit in a saved person's life. Admittedly, we could use a much greater emphasis on sanctification in the Christian church as a whole these days, but the process of sanctification, regeneration, and doing good works has nothing to do with justification by faith. So then, works are a *result* of justification, not a *condition* for it.

Quickly, five truths according to the Bible regarding justification:

1. It is not gradual, but instantaneous;

2. The sinner is not made righteous through holy living, but is declared righteous in the sight of God;

3. Righteousness is imputed or reckoned;

---

149 Ron Rhodes, *The 10 Most Important Things You Can Say to a Catholic* (Eugene, OR: Harvest House Publishers, 2002), 65-66.

4. We are justified by faith alone in Christ's saving work alone, not by Christ plus what we do; and

5. Justification is once for all.

Jesus said, *He who believes in the Son has eternal life* (John 3:36). Our salvation is a gift of God, *not as a result of works, so that no one may boast* (Ephesians 2:8-9).

Sadly, some Catholics (as well as some Christians) I know do not have a proper understanding of the gospel and the biblical Christian worldview, and they become defensive when questioned about their church's doctrine or about the authority of the pope. Roman Catholic Church history has left a black eye on biblical Christianity in many ways, three of which include persecution through past military crusades, massive corruption, and the countless shameful years of both homosexual and heterosexual debauchery by too many clergy.

To be fair, in both the Catholic and Protestant church there are too many believers in name only, living just like the world, going along with the doctrines of men. Some Catholics however, misrepresent the church's teachings by practicing a superstitious form of religion while attending mass to attract good luck or avoid feeling guilty.

What is critical here is our pursuit of the integrity of Scripture, *the* source of truth, and that our conscience is captive to God's Word. There are plenty of Roman Catholics who have a true saving faith in the Lord Jesus, and to be completely honest, I know some who live godlier, more compassionate lives and serve others better than many Christians – including myself at times. It is just confusing why they choose to remain within that doctrinal system.

Thank God, we are all works in progress, His workmanship (Ephesians 2:10). A good rule of thumb is that we seek and know the truth, and abide in faith, hope, and love, because *the greatest of these is love* (1 Corinthians 13:13). And if we love others with the love of God, we will tell them the truth no matter the cost.

CONCLUSION

Sayyid Ali Muhammad, Mirza Husayn-Ali Nuri (Baha'i), Siddhartha

Gautama (Buddhism), the Dalai Lama, Muhammad (Islam), Charles Taze Russell, Joseph Franklin Rutherford (JWs), Joseph Smith, Brigham Young (Mormons), Alice Baily, Mary Baker Eddy (Christian Science), Charles and Myrtle Fillmore (Unity), Theophilus Lindsey, the popes (RCC), Anton LaVey, Helena Blavatsky, L. Ron Hubbard (Scientology), Maharishi Mahesh Yogi (TM), Gerald Gardner (Wicca), Aleister Crowley, Deepak Chopra, and followers after them have attempted to redefine the truth and create a god in their own image.

Pray for more watchmen and more discernment in the church today. Pray for strong pastors and leaders, men of God who are unashamed of the gospel and who preach the truth without compromise. The more things change the more they remain the same. The priests during the time of Malachi were guilty of apostasy and many were led astray because of them. They departed from the standard of teaching held by Aaron, the first in the Levitical priesthood. They claimed the privileges of the covenant but rejected the conditions of it.

God warned and disciplined the priests at that time and followed up by sending a curse for not honoring the name of the Lord (Malachi 2:1-2). But He commended Aaron for speaking the truth *and* turning sinners back to God, a responsibility lacking in churches today (James 5:20). Regarding Levi's obedience compared to false teachers, Malachi states:

> *True instruction was in his mouth and unrighteousness*
> *was not found on his lips; he walked with Me in peace and*
> *uprightness, and he turned many back from iniquity. For the*
> *lips of a priest should preserve knowledge, and men should*
> *seek instruction from his mouth; for he is the messenger of*
> *the LORD of hosts. But as for you, you have turned aside from*
> *the way; you have caused many to stumble by the instruction;*
> *you have corrupted the covenant of Levi," says the LORD of*
> *hosts. "So I also have made you despised and abased before*
> *all the people, just as you are not keeping My ways but are*
> *showing partiality in the instruction.* (Malachi 2:6-9)

A true religion or teaching does not contradict itself, and either something is of God or it is of the devil. What we have seen in these four chapters is deception, depravity, corruption, lust for power, traditions of man, and doctrinal contradictions leading to much confusion about what is true. One way we might sum up these religious teachings is fallible man trying to replace God, and with the exception of atheism, claiming divinity or godhood. Sadly, countless millions of souls have been deceived.

Chapter 16

That's a Wrap! (It All Comes Down to Jesus)

You are of your father the devil, and you want to do the desires of your father. He was a murderer from the beginning, and does not stand in the truth because there is no truth in him. Whenever he speaks a lie, he speaks from his own nature, for he is a liar and the father of lies. But because I speak the truth, you do not believe Me. Which one of you convicts Me of sin? If I speak truth, why do you not believe Me? He who is of God hears the words of God; for this reason you do not hear them, because you are not of God. (John 8:44-47)

"Christianity, if false, is of no importance. If true, is of infinite importance. The only thing it cannot be is moderately important." – C. S. Lewis

In nearly every false religion, philosophy, and belief system, you can find an aspect of verisimilitude, teachings that have an appearance of truth, at least on the surface. Most people wouldn't fall for these doctrines if they were blatantly and obviously false. Then again, plenty of religious teachings are, quite frankly, bizarre, and people are still deceived. This is why it is so important to know the truth and be able to recognize counterfeits.

The stark reality is, man can redefine truth to his heart's desire, but that will not change the truth. Nothing can change God's eternal Word.

To the consternation of many who have defiantly and willfully denied Jesus Christ, every knee will bow to His majesty one day, and every tongue will confess that He is Lord (Philippians 2:10-11).

In the 1994 book by John MacArthur, *Reckless Faith* (no longer in print), he tells about visiting a couple in the South during a trip. The woman made and sold quilts and as he was at their home waiting for her to bring quilts out, he noticed the husband half-watching a religious broadcast on television and half-reading a religious magazine. A few resources from solid evangelical publishers and piles of various religious books and literature were scattered around the room.

MacArthur asked the man if he was a believer and he curiously responded, "A believer in what?" Being more specific, he asked the man if he was a Christian; he held up the magazine he was reading and said, "Well, sure." It was a publication of a well-known cult. MacArthur noticed a few evangelical best sellers along with materials from radio and TV ministries and even a few decent Bible study aids. At that moment, the man jotted down information for free literature offered by the TV preacher.

MacArthur scanned the mixture of literature. Among it were stacks of *The Watchtower* magazine, a copy of *Dianetics*, a Book of Mormon, *Science and Health*, some literature from the Franciscan brothers, and an incredible array of stuff from nearly every conceivable cult and "ism." Observing the smorgasbord of material, MacArthur said, "These all represent different beliefs. Do you accept any one of them?"

The man said, "I find there's good in all of it. I read it all and just look for the good."

Just then, his wife came back with a stack of quilts she had made, and though MacArthur eventually bought a solid-colored one with a very nice pattern, the first quilt she showed him was an ugly patchwork of different sizes, colors, and prints of fabric. It was a perfect metaphor for her husband's religion, featuring bits and pieces from many belief systems. In putting together a patchwork faith, he thought it was good and beautiful, but in God's eyes it was an abomination.[150]

Lots of folks today have that same philosophy and think they are

---

150   John MacArthur, *The Truth War* (Nashville, TN: Thomas Nelson, 2007), 187-188.

hanging on to the good without committing to a single belief system. It is a false "Coexist" religion and it makes you want to say, just pick one. But you know as well as I do there is only one path to truth and eternal salvation and it is through Jesus Christ alone, by grace alone through faith alone.

Tragically, with all the noise of today's social media, instant news, and distracting technology in a volatile culture including the new religion of extreme tolerance, this generation is constantly exposed to more information than any other in history. Few take the necessary time to thoroughly examine religious claims and teachings even though many profess to have the truth. As a result, well-meaning people are confounded by the variety of choices.

It really is all about Jesus who thankfully made the exclusive claim, "I am the Truth." Hopefully, after reading this book, even seekers will acknowledge it is impossible to redefine the real Jesus. It starts and finishes with Him.

No religious system goes back to the beginning the way Christianity does. We need to go back to the fall of mankind and the first spoken prophecy in Scripture, and understand from the Genesis 3:15 curse that God had everything prepared. Satan would cause Christ to suffer on the cross (bruise his heel) while Jesus would destroy Satan with a fatal blow (crush his head). This prophecy is paramount to understanding the story of redemption and this battle of good versus evil, Christ the author of truth versus Satan the father of lies.

When the perfect religious, cultural, and political conditions were in place, Jesus Christ left the Father's presence in eternity and entered the atmosphere of our world and completed the work the Father sent Him to do. According to God's will and master plan, Jesus will return again when everything is in alignment after a predetermined portion of history is played out.

Christ, the soon-coming King, will fulfill the promises of God including the completion of our salvation (relief), and will deal out judgment on those who denied Him (retribution). His feet will stand on the Mount of Olives to the east of Jerusalem once again, the Lord will be king over all the earth, and one religion will be left standing as the name of Jesus will be the only one (Zechariah 14:4, 9).

> *For after all it is only just for God to repay with afflic-*
> *tion those who afflict you, and to give relief to you who*
> *are afflicted and to us as well when the Lord Jesus will be*
> *revealed from heaven with His mighty angels in flaming fire,*
> *dealing out retribution to those who do not know God and*
> *to those who do not obey the gospel of our Lord Jesus. These*
> *will pay the penalty of eternal destruction, away from the*
> *presence of the Lord and from the glory of His power, when*
> *He comes to be glorified in His saints on that day, and to be*
> *marveled at among all who have believed—for our testimony*
> *to you was believed.* (2 Thessalonians 1:6-10)

That's the truth. We will marvel at our glorified Lord and Savior. Mockers and scoffers will continue, but as Peter encouraged believers, *the day of the Lord will come like a thief,* suddenly and unexpectedly. He also encouraged great patience because *with the Lord one day is like a thousand years, and a thousand years like one day* (2 Peter 3:8-10). We plan our day around the twenty-four-hour clock, but God has already written this day as well as all of human history – past, present, and future. We are restricted by time; He is limitless.

Skeptics keep rejecting the gospel and biblical morality, but they'd have to be in denial to ignore or deny the historical accuracy of Scripture we touched on earlier. Consider archaeological finds demonstrating that people, places, and events mentioned in the Bible are real and quite accurately described. No other religious work can make this boast. Archaeologists have often depended on the Scriptures to lead them to locations of astounding historical discoveries. Honest researchers and workers in this profession affirm that their findings often support key portions of Bible stories.

CHRIST

But what about those who claim the Bible is a biased source? We have incredible documentation of renowned secular historians such as Josephus who wrote about how Jews and Gentiles were both drawn to

Jesus, "a wise man [if it be lawful to call him a man]." Josephus even testified that just as the prophets had foretold, "he appeared to them alive again" after Pilate had condemned Him to the cross. This would be considered extra-biblical testimony.

Other secular sources contain a surprising amount of information about the Messiah. First-century Roman Cornelius Tacitus, considered one of the more accurate historians of the ancient world, mentioned superstitious "Christians," named after Christus (Latin for *Christ*), who was executed by Pontius Pilate during the reign of Tiberius.

Suetonius, chief secretary to Emperor Hadrian, wrote of a man named Chrestus (Christ) who lived during the first century (Roman Annals 15.44). And Julius Africanus, writing around AD 221, tried to explain away the darkness occurring at Jesus's crucifixion: "On the whole world, there pressed a most fearful darkness; and the rocks were rent by an earthquake, and many places in Judea and other districts were thrown down. This darkness Thallus, in the third book of his History, calls, as appears to me without reason, an eclipse of the sun" (Julius Africanus, Chronography, 18:1).

There are some things we can conclude from this account: Jesus lived, He was crucified, and there was an earthquake and darkness (at the point of His crucifixion).

According to Richard M. Fales, "Writings confirming His birth, ministry, death, and resurrection include Flavius Josephus (A.D. 93), the Babylonian Talmud (A.D. 70 – 200), Pliny the Younger's letter to the Emperor Trajan (approx. A.D. 100), the Annals of Tacitus (A.D. 115 – 117), Mara Bar Serapion (sometime after A.D. 73), and Suetonius' Life of Claudius and Life of Nero (A.D. 120)."[151]

The apostle John (AD 6 – 100) was the youngest of Jesus's disciples and witnessed His life, miracles, death, and resurrection. He was the son of Zebedee and Salome, and the brother of James. John wrote a primary gospel, the important book of Revelation, and three letters in the New Testament. Outside of the apostles and Jesus's inner circle that knew Him, the earliest mentions in historical documents describe Jesus as divine.

151 The Evidence Bible, "Jesus never even existed," 5/9/2017, *dailyevidence.wordpress.com/2017/05/09/jesus-never-even-existed/*.

Each of the twelve disciples of Jesus, including those among the 120, probably taught and discipled many other believers. The apostle John personally taught Polycarp, Papias, and Ignatius. One example (among perhaps thousands), is Ignatius (AD 35 – 117), who also called himself Theophorus (which means "God Bearer"). Polycarp was converted to Christianity by the apostles themselves, eventually became the Bishop of Smyrna (modern-day Turkey), and wrote a letter to the Philippian church referencing at least fourteen New Testament books!

Moreover, church tradition describes Ignatius as one of the children Jesus blessed in the gospel accounts. Ignatius was a student of John the apostle and eventually became bishop at Antioch (Turkey), following the apostle Peter. He wrote important letters to the early church and seven of them survive to this day. Why are these letters important? Because they prove the New Testament documents were already written (establishing early testimony) and familiar to the early Christians. In his letters, Ignatius quoted or alluded to many New Testament books.[152]

Finally, here's a quote from around AD 207 by the theologian known as Tertullian, full name being Quintus Septimius Florens Tertullianus (155 – 220), a bold Christian witness in Carthage, North Africa: "We who believe that God really lived on earth, and took upon him the low estate of human form, for the purpose of man's salvation, are very far from thinking as those do who refuse to believe that God cares for anything. . . . Fortunately, however, it is a part of the creed of Christians even to believe that God did die, and yet that He is alive forevermore."

Sadly, there are some who actually think Jesus is not a real person, let alone God. I heard one young woman suggest Jesus was a myth made up by religious people wanting to control society. Moreover, there are those who are either disingenuous or who flat out refuse to acknowledge the truth. Even CNN reran its original series, *Finding Jesus*, in March, and according to the *Daily Wire*, the headline on the CNN website read: "Evidence Against Jesus' Existence." (Presumably to attract more skeptics?) It was later changed to "Decoding Jesus: Separating man from myth."

Much of that article on CNN's website argued that Jesus was probably

---

152   J. Warner Wallace, "Testing the Gospels from John to Hippolytus," 12/26/2013, *coldcase-christianity.com/2013/ testing-the-gospels-from-john-to-hippolytus/*.

a myth, even refuting the secular historians I just mentioned. Know your Bible, friends, and pray for the Holy Spirit to lead you in every conversation with unbelievers. The lies out there are mountainous.

Some even deny or ignore the massive prophetic evidence that Jesus Christ fulfilled over three hundred messianic prophecies about His ancestry, birth, life, ministry, death, resurrection, and ascension, and many of them fulfilled to the slightest specific detail. Just one true fulfilled prophecy should be sufficient to establish the Bible's supernatural origin. Professor and author Peter Stoner calculated the scientific probability that any one person could fulfill just *eight* prophecies from Scripture. The odds are an astounding one in ten to the seventeenth power (100,000,000,000,000,000).

According to Gleason Archer, a scholar of the Old Testament:

> "As I have dealt with one apparent discrepancy after another and have studied the alleged contradictions between the biblical record and the evidence of linguistics, archaeology, or science, my confidence in the trustworthiness of Scripture has been repeatedly verified and strengthened by the discovery that almost every problem in Scripture that has ever been discovered by man, from ancient times until now, has been dealt with in a completely satisfactory manner by the biblical text itself – or else by objective archaeological information."[153]

God is loving, and He certainly does not get a kick out of people going to hell as some have argued. Through the brutal, heart-wrenching offering of His Son Jesus Christ, it sounds more like God has done everything possible to provide a way out while not interfering with the free will of those He created. In this respect, He certainly is a "pro-choice" God. We are free to love, accept, and obey Him, or to hate, reject, and rebel against His Word.

The choice is ours: truth or consequences.

CULTURE

With public debates over identity and what bathroom a person should

---

153   Archer Gleason, *Encyclopedia of Bible Difficulties* (Grand Rapids, MI: Zondervan, 1982), 11-12.

use, it is easy to see consequences of our past silence about the truth of God and creation, and the lack of opposition to rampant immorality. Kids growing up today have more pressures, propaganda, and perversions coming at them than we can expect them to handle on their own.

Research shows young people make up their minds extremely early in life about crucial moral and spiritual issues, often well before parents realize it. And if those children attend public schools, they are often presented with so much controversial and questionable information that many parents find themselves answering questions about sexuality, pop culture, or politics years before they would have discussed these issues with their kids at home.

The more we understand about how the Enemy advances and how he seeks to distort the truth and destroy all that is godly, holy, righteous, and pure, the better prepared for battle we will be. Satan is out to pervert or obliterate what God has designed, especially the family unit, which is defined by Him and begins with the union of one man and one woman encouraged to procreate.

One way the Enemy and his minions are working overtime to confuse the masses and discredit the Bible is by blurring or even removing the lines between gender and sexuality. This means God no longer "assigns" or designates a person as male or female. One of the terms they use is *gender reassignment* surgery. Another man-made description of a person wanting to look more like the opposite sex is *gender transition*, which in reality does not exist.

According to many medical experts, even though in extremely rare cases slight physical mutations occur (because we live in a fallen world due to sin) where partial or both sexual organs are present, a person's gender is still binary. Not only is this determined by God, it is also a result of chromosomes, DNA, and genetic markings of the individual. But children today are being raised in a society that considers gender to be fluid or changeable, which is why many young people are confused about sexuality.

We must not confuse sex with gender. Anyone can act out their sexual desires and feelings, but behavior has nothing to do with God-given gender. If LGBTQ activists, atheists, humanists, leftists, and secularists get their way and can convince enough people that gender is fluid, then they muddy and discredit the foundational truths of Scripture such as creation. Without God it would be a meaningless, existence based on the theory of evolution or a big bang which supports the idea of a random, purposeless life where individuals have little or no value.

We have strayed so far as a society from God's common-sense purpose for life, marriage, and healthy sexual intercourse. It used to be that sex was acknowledged as biblically being reserved for marriage, and children were an expected result. But one consequence of the sexual revolution, the hippie rebellion, and the feminist movement was the "need" for contraception. Until that time, the greatest restraint to having sex outside of marriage was the possibility of an unplanned pregnancy leading to a baby. But people demanded they be free to have sex without producing children. So the birth control movement took off, and they made abortion part of the immoral progression so people could have unbridled sex with no consequences.

Therefore, even if someone used birth control and still happened to get pregnant, you could then take it a step further and eliminate that life in a mother's womb. This "convenience" (abortion) became popular to the point that people didn't worry about contraception anymore. It became commonplace to just kill a baby if a woman became pregnant, and worse, a woman could decide at any point through nine months whether or not to let the baby live. Even animals know better and protect their young.

If you think supervening God's sovereignty is playing with fire, you're right. The more life, marriage, and family were devalued and minimized, the more adultery, divorce, pornography, homosexuality, and rape accelerated. Then came the "need" for same-sex couples to "manufacture" a baby because they couldn't do so naturally. Human beings are not created that way, but with modern scientific advances, the will of men (or women) rules. You can now have children without sexual intercourse. This is a perversion of the purpose for marriage and sex – a counterfeit, no longer within God's framework.

The result? Erosion of the family, the only sovereign unit that exists as a barrier to the outside world. But now you don't need a husband or a wife or even a family in order to have a baby. Satan is working to destroy what God beautifully designed. Jesus meant it when he said, *What God has joined together, let not man separate* (Mark 10:9).

This overt trashing of ethics and biblical morality has meant nothing but trouble for a nation no longer united and no longer under God who once blessed it. When we consider the efforts that necessarily go into protecting our religious freedoms, we must now ask ourselves if we deserve to maintain those freedoms when we have so easily turned our backs on God. But He is forgiving, longsuffering, and merciful, and because of those freedoms, the gospel of repentance can be preached and more people can be saved, that is, if Christians are obedient to His call.

This is where you and I come in. We must repent of our own apathy, recognize the unbiblical aspects of American Christianity, and live for the Lord Jesus rather than for ourselves. I don't know about you, but I need to take Bible study, discipleship, and prayer more seriously and change some habits. I am not talking about legalism, but rather spiritual discipline and basic time management. Generally, our churches are weak and of little consequence while our culture is nearly beyond remedy.

Around us are reachable individuals who need to hear about the love Jesus Christ has for them, and you and I are here for this purpose. We serve a mighty God and an everlasting Savior, a God of the miraculous, and with Him, nothing is impossible. As we face the realities written about in this book, the task is admittedly sobering and daunting, and recent church trends are problematic, but Jesus is still our victorious and risen Lord, His love endures forever, and His truth is marching on.

We are messengers of this truth. We are Christians because we find our identity, our life, and our purpose in Christ. As long as our identity is in Him and not in things of this world, we can do the work He leads us to do, and we'll succeed in the purposes for which He created us.

CONCLUSION

Truth will always be under assault. Jesus Christ will always be a dividing line between two sides of eternity. As we exalt the name above every name in our churches, do we care that Jesus's name is being profaned throughout our culture? Do we understand the high priority and level of prominence God places on the Holy Scriptures and on His name?

> *I will worship toward Your holy temple, And praise*
> *Your name For Your lovingkindness and Your truth; For*
> *You have magnified Your word above all Your name.*
> (Psalm 138:2 NKJV)

The Bible will continue overcoming and withstanding the tests of time. With or without us, God's Word will prosper in the purposes for which He sent it (Isaiah 55:11). But if you finish this book, put it down, and don't take any action to defend and declare the truth, then even though you have gained facts and knowledge, it didn't really penetrate your heart – and others will not benefit.

We must encourage and challenge one another in part by asking, how are we using the precious time God has allotted us? Are we spending most of it on earthly comforts, leisure, entertainment, and our own plans and pleasures – or are we cultivating an eternal perspective and investing in the kingdom and people of God as we strive to live counter culture for Christ?

Henry Ward Beecher stated, "Living is death; dying is life. On this side of the grave we are exiles, on that, citizens; on this side, orphans, on that, children; on this side, captives; on that, freemen; on this side, disguised, unknown; on that, disclosed and proclaimed as the sons of God."

God sent Jesus so whoever believes in Him could have eternal life in His presence. If you have never received God's free, perfect gift, why wait any longer? We are not guaranteed tomorrow, and yet, you can have the assurance of salvation right now, and the Holy Spirit will guide you in the truth. And if you're a believer but have not been living fully for Christ, why not pivot and rededicate your life?

> *I have chosen the way of truth; Your judgments I*
> *have laid before me. I cling to Your testimonies.*
> (Psalm 119:30-31a NKJV)

Stay in the Word of Life, my friend! We see only this very brief portion of human history in which we live, but God sees the end from the beginning. Keep believing in Jesus Christ for salvation and keep standing on biblical truth. Press on in Christ! Victory is guaranteed. Never turn back. Never quit praying, never stop speaking the truth, and never grow weary of doing good, *for in due season we will reap, if we do not give up* (Galatians 6:9 ESV).

This race set before us is not a quick sprint, but one for which we need godly training and endurance. It is like a marathon relay in which those who have gone before us ran their race, handed us the baton, and either we will see Christ return (the finish line!) or you and I will hand off the baton to believers who come after us. Pray for wisdom that we might hear, "Well done."

> *I was very glad to find some of your children walking in truth, just as we have received commandment to do from the Father.* (2 John 4)

Father in heaven, *teach us to number our days* (Psalm 90:12)! May Your will be done. Guard our hearts and minds, increase our faith, steady our feet, strengthen our arms for battle, and help us walk in Your truth – until that day – in Jesus's name, Amen.

Meet the Author

D avid Fiorazo is an author, public speaker, content contributor, and co-host of the daily radio talk show *Stand Up for the Truth*. He has been involved in Christian ministry for over twenty-five years and the broadcasting industry for over thirty years. He loves the living Word of the only true God and seeks to defend and proclaim Christ without apology or compromise. David has spoken at church groups, political groups, men's retreats, festivals, and education conferences. He also fills the pulpit, sharing from God's Word at Sunday services on occasion and is open to speaking opportunities. He and his wife, Rosanna, live near Green Bay, Wisconsin.

Connect with David Fiorazo

www.davidfiorazo.com

www.facebook.com/DavidFiorazo

www.twitter.com/fiorazo

www.youtube.com/user/DFiorazo

www.linkedin.com/in/davidfiorazo

The Cost of Our Silence, by David Fiorazo

There are consequences when God's people take the path of least resistance and back out of culture. One only needs to look at our society to see we are living with those consequences today.

- Why do you think so many Christians pursue comfort over commitment to Christ?

- Do you sometimes feel overwhelmed by the darkness and moral decline in society today and wonder what happened to the salt and light?

- How have we reached a point where Christians who do preach the gospel and speak up about sin are called hateful, intolerant, or judgmental?

Christian in name only, America has become an epicenter for the culture war as too many of us keep ducking the issue of sin. Due to decades of Christians being silent, failing to preach the gospel and speak the truth in love, we've reached a tipping point in which political correctness refuses to coexist with religious freedom. Why do you think Christians who defend God's Word are often called hateful, intolerant, or judgmental? There are consequences in this life and for eternity, when Christians take the path of least resistance. We cannot reverse the moral decline, but we can choose to stand for righteousness as we pray for revival and be the salt and light Jesus called us to be while we're still here.

Available where books are sold.

ERADICATE, by David Fiorazo

Eradicate identifies two major problems causing the spiritual and moral decline in our country: the secular agenda to blot out God, and the apathy of Christians. This book will expose the anti-Christian movements in America and give you a thorough understanding of the foundational battle for truth. With 78% of Americans claiming to be Christians, how did it get to the point where Christianity is having less of an influence on our culture than culture is having on Christianity? Too many believers have conformed to our culture and we're now suffering the consequences as a nation.

The Bible contains much prophecy concerning end times, warning us to not be ignorant so we can be bold and fight the good fight of faith. As Christians, we'll predictably face more hostility and possibly increased persecution in America as we draw closer to Jesus Christ's return. It is now more pivotal than ever that we prepare ourselves, know the truth of Scripture, and understand the direction our country has taken.

God is being blotted out of America. Christians are being silenced by accusations of hate and intolerance. The government, media, Hollywood, the abortion industry, and academia are not going to defend Christian values – it's up to you and me...We saw the vitriol of those who oppose Christian values when Chick-fil-A president Dan Cathy took a stand for traditional marriage and was attacked by leftists and homosexual activists. The choice is ours: we can face the reality of what is happening in America and take action, or we can look the other way. This republic under God continues to be a successful, glorious alternative to atheism, communism, socialism, and tyranny in the world, but today, our very freedoms are being threatened.

Available where books are sold.